ELIHU BURRITT LIBRARY
C.C.S.U.
NEW BRITAIN, CONNECTICUT

REFERENCE

STATISTICS ON
WeApoNs & VIoLEnce

STATISTICS ON
Weapons & Violence

A Selection of Statistical Charts, Graphs and Tables About Weapons and Violence
From a Variety of Published Sources with Explanatory Comments

Timothy L. Gall and
Daniel M. Lucas, *Editors*

Peter C. Kratcoski, Ph.D.
Professor of Criminal Justice Studies and Sociology
Kent State University
and
Lucille Dunn Kratcoski, M.A.
Research Associate,
Contributing Editors

Gale Research
An ITP Infromation/Reference Group Company

ITP
Changing the Way the World Learns

NEW YORK • LONDON • BONN • BOSTON • DETROIT
MADRID • MELBOURNE • MEXICO CITY • PARIS
SINGAPORE • TOKYO • TORONTO • WASHINGTON
ALBANY NY • BELMONT CA • CINCINNATI OH

Eastword Publications Development Inc. Staff
Timothy L. Gall and Daniel M. Lucas, *Editors*

Gale Research Inc. Staff
Donna Wood, *Coordinating Editor*

Mary Beth Trimper, *Production Manager*
Shanna Heilveil, *Production Assistant*
Cynthia D. Baldwin, *Product Design Manager*
Michelle DiMercurio, *Art Director*

While every effort has been made to ensure the reliability of the information presented in this publication, Gale Research Inc. does not guarantee the accuracy of the data contained herein. Gale accepts no payment for listing; and inclusion in the publication of any organization, agency, institution, publication, service, or individual does not imply endorsement of the editors or publisher. Errors brought to the attention of the publisher and verified to the satisfaction of the publisher will be corrected in future editions.

∞™ The paper used in this publication meets the minimum requirements of American National Standard for Information Sciences-Permanence Paper for Printed Library Materials, ANSI Z39.48-1984.

This publication is a creative work fully protected by all applicable copyright laws, as well as by misappropriation, trade secret, unfair competition, and other applicable laws. The authors and editors of this work have added value to the underlying factual material herein through one or more of the following: unique and original selection, coordination, expression, arrangement, and classification of the information.

All rights to this publication will be vigorously defended.

Copyright © 1996
Gale Research Inc.
835 Penobscot Bldg.
Detroit, MI 48226-4094

Printed in the United States of America

```
Library of Congress Cataloging-in-Publication Data

Statistics on weapons & violence : a selection of statistical charts,
  graphs, and tables about weapons and violence from a variety of
  published sources with explanatory comments / Timothy L. Gall and
  Daniel M. Lucas, editors ; Peter C. Kratcoski and Lucille Dunn
  Kratcoski, contributing editors.
       p.   cm.
    Includes bibliographical references and index.
    ISBN 0-7876-0527-1 (alk. paper)
   1. Violence--United States--Statistics.  2. Weapons--United
 States--Statistics.  3. Crime--United States--Statistics.  4. United
 States--Social conditions--1980-  --Statistics.  I. Gall, Timothy L.
 II. Lucas, Daniel M.  III. Kratcoski, Peter C.,   1936-
 IV. Kratcoski, Lucille Dunn, 1937-
   HN90.V5S834 1995
   303.6'0973'021--dc20                                        95-44897
                                                                    CIP
```

ITP™ Gale Research Inc., an International Thomson Publishing Company
ITP logo is a trademark under license.

10 9 8 7 6 5 4 3 2 1

How to use this book

This book presents statistics on weapons and violence in the United States. Each of the statistical presentations appears on a two-page spread. The table or graphic containing the statistics is presented on a left-hand page and the explanatory text, the source citation, and contact information appears on the facing right-hand page. Also included in this volume is a general introduction to the problems concerning weapons and violence and a glossary of related terminology. Finally, a thorough index facilitates ease of use.

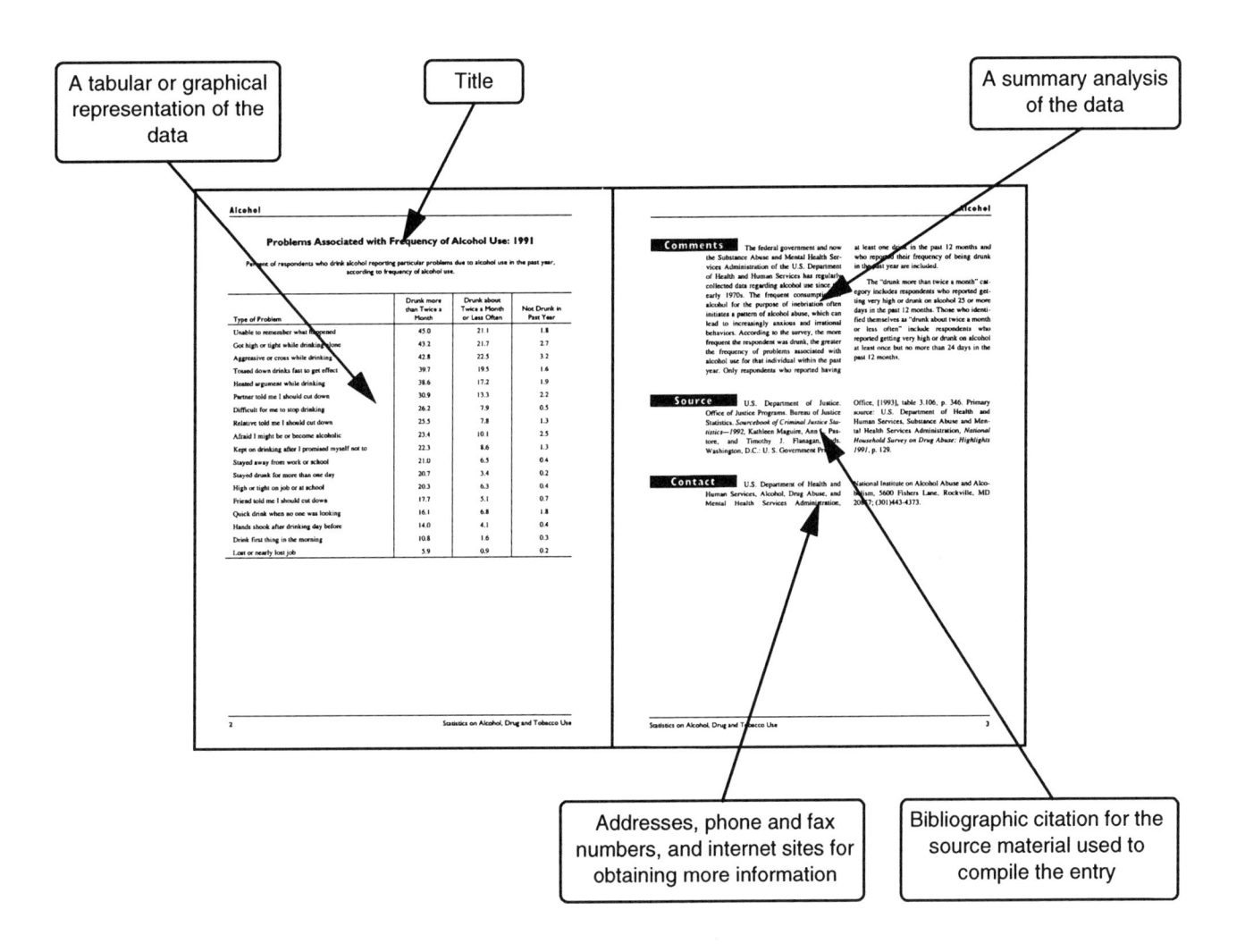

- A tabular or graphical representation of the data
- Title
- A summary analysis of the data
- Addresses, phone and fax numbers, and internet sites for obtaining more information
- Bibliographic citation for the source material used to compile the entry

Statistics on Weapons & Violence

Advisory Board

Judith H. Higgins
Director of LRC, Valhalla High School Library, Valhalla, New York

Connie Lawson
Librarian, Maple Heights Regional Library, Cuyahoga County Public Library, Maple Heights, Ohio

Deborah Lee
Librarian, Los Angeles County Public Library, Rowland Heights, California

John Ranahan
Teacher, Lake Ridge Academy, Oberlin, Ohio

Linda Taft
Librarian, Morgantown High School, Morgantown, West Virginia

Lynda C. Tirhi
Librarian, Nimitz High School Library, Irving, Texas

Table of Contents

How to Use this Book v
Advisory Board vi
Introduction xi
Acknowledgments, Sources and Contacts xix

WEAPONS

Historical Perspective
Firearms Available for Sale in the United States, 1946–93 2
Guns Available for Sale 4
Who Keeps a Gun at Home? 6
What Weapons Have Murderers Used Most Often? 8

Weapons and Defense
What Happens in a Confrontation with an Armed Robber? 10
Civilian Justifiable Homicides, by Weapon, 1989–93 12
Self-Protective Measures Employed by Victims 14
Self-Defense with Firearms, 1987–92 16

Weapons and Crime
What Kinds of Weapons Do Robbers Like to Use? 18
Robberies by State and Type of Weapon Used in 1993 20
What Kinds of Weapons Are Used in Aggravated Assaults? 22
Aggravated Assaults by State and Type of Weapon Used, 1993 24
Weapons Violation Arrests in 1992 & 1993 by Age Group 26
Thefts of Firearms, 1987–92 28
The Role of Firearms in Federal Sentences 30
Which Weapons Do Criminals Use Most Often? 32
How Likely Is It that Someone Will Be Shot and Killed or Injured During a Crime? 34
Who Is the Victim of a Handgun Crime? 36
If a Gun is Present During a Violent Crime, How Often Is a Shot Fired? 38
Inmates' Gun Usage in Crimes 40
Murders, Robberies, and Aggravated Assaults in Which Firearms Were Used 42

Weapon Use in Homicides and Suicides
Murder Victims, by Specific Type of Weapon Used, 1989–93 44
Deaths Due to Firearms and Nonfirearms by Manner of Death
   for Persons 1–34 Years of Age in the United States, 1985–90 46
Murder Circumstances by Weapon in 1993 48
Murder in the States by Weapon, 1992 & 1993 50

Firearm Injuries
Firearm Accident Fatality Rates, 1903–93 52
Deaths from Firearm Accidents, 1993 & 1994 54

Table of Contents

    Deaths Caused by Firearms Injuries, 1993 56
    Firearm Accident Fatalities by Type of Gun Involved, 1979–91 58

Youth and Guns
    Percentage of High School Students in 1993 Who Carried a Weapon or a Gun 60
    Gun Possession Among Juvenile Inmates and Students in 1991 62
    Where Juveniles Obtain Guns 64
    Reasons Juveniles Obtain Guns 66

VIOLENCE

Historical Perspective
    Suicide and Homicide Rates, 1900–93 70
    Violent Crime Index Rate in the United States, 1960–93 72
    Violent Crime Is Increasing 74
    How Much Does Violent Crime Change from One Year to the Next? 76
    How Do Violent Crime Rates Compare with the Rates of Other Life Events? 78

Violent Criminals
    Number of State Prisoners in Custody for Violent Offenses, 1979–92 80
    Percent of State Prisoners in Custody for Violent Offenses, 1979–92 82
    Does Locking Up Violent Criminals Help Reduce Violent Crime? 84
    Convictions and Sentences for Violent Crimes, Compared to the Number of Arrests in 1992 86
    Released Violent Offenders in 1992 by Type of Offense and Average Time Served 88
    Gang-Related Violent Crimes Prosecuted in 1991 90
    How Long Are Violent Criminals Staying in Prison? 92
    Where Do Violent Crimes Occur? 94
    Where Does Violence Occur When Committed by a Stranger, Friend, Relative, or Acquaintance? 96

Victims of Violent Crime
    Who Are the Victims of Violent Crime? 98
    Reasons Given for Reporting or Failing to Report Violent Crimes 100
    How Many Crime Victims Are Violent Crime Victims? 102
    Victimization Rates for Violent Crimes, 1973–92 104
    Percent of Victimizations from Crimes of Violence Reported to the Police, 1973–92 ... 106
    What Kind of Violent Crime Is Most Frequent? 108
    How Often Does a Violent Crime Involve More Than One Victim? 110
    Amount of Economic Loss from Violent Crimes, 1992 112
    Total Economic Loss to Victims of Crime, 1992 114
    How Old Are Victims of Violent Crime? 116
    Where Do the Injured Victims of Violent Crime Go for Help? 118

Violent Crime—Murder, Rape, Robbery, Assault
    How Old Are Murderers and the People They Kill? 120
    Murder Circumstances in 1993 by Relationship of Victim to the Offender 122
    Why a Murder? 124
    Murders and Murder Rates by State/Territory, 1993 126
    Number and Rate of Reported Forcible Rapes, 1993 128
    When Is a Rape Reported to the Police? 130
    How Often Does a Rape Victim Know the Offender? 132

Table of Contents

Number and Rate of Reported Robberies, 1993 134
When Is a Robbery Reported to the Police? 136
Where Are Robberies Happening? 138
Aggravated and Simple Assault Rate in 1993 140
Aggravated Assaults in the States Ranked by Number and by Rate, 1993 142
When Is an Assault Reported to the Police? 144

Domestic Violence—Family Violence, Spousal Abuse, Child Abuse

Violent Crime within the Family 146
Murders within the Family 148
Victim and Defendant Characteristics for Murder within the Family 150
Violent Victimizations among Intimates, 1987–92 152
Homicide Committed among Intimate Partners, 1977–92 154
Trends in Reporting Child Abuse, 1976–93 156
Sources of Child Maltreatment Reports, 1993 158
Number of Child Abuse Victims by Type of Maltreatment, 1993 160
How Old Are Abused Children? 162
Relationship of Perpetrator to Child Abuse Victim, 1993 164

Youth Violence—Violence at Schools, Gang Violence, Juvenile Violence

How Much of the Crime Problem Is at School? 166
Students in 6th–12th Grade Reporting a Violent Victimization at School 168
Fights at High Schools, 1993 170
A State-by-State Look at Fighting among High School Students 172
Violence at Schools 174
Campus Violence 176
Percentage of Students Reporting Victimization and Fear of Attack, by Gang Presence at School 178
Types of Gangs and Their Crimes 180
Gang-Related Crime by Gender 182
How Much Violence Is Involved in Juvenile Delinquency? 184

Violence in the Workplace—Homicides, Nonfatal Assaults and Violent Acts

Who Is Most Likely to be Murdered at Work? 186
Homicides at Work in the Ten Largest Metropolitan Areas, 1992 188
Circumstances of Workplace Homicides, 1992 and 1993 190
Which Industries Have the Most Workplace Homicides? 192
How Much of All Violent Crime Occurs at Work? 194
Average Annual Number of Victimizations at Work, 1987–92 196
How Much Time Does a Victim of Violent Crime Lose from Work? 198
Violent Acts at the Workplace Resulting in Injuries 200
Which Industries Are Most Affected by Violent Assaults at the Workplace? 202

Glossary 205

Index 213

Introduction

by
Peter C. Kratcoski, Ph.D., Chairperson
Department of Criminal Justice Studies
Kent State University, Kent, Ohio
and
Lucille Dunn Kratcoski, M.A.
Research Associate

Statistics on Weapons & Violence contains very up-to-date, important information on the availability, ownership, and use of weapons in the United States; the presence of weapons in crime incidents, either as threatening devices in the hands of offenders or self-protection instruments used by potential victims; the frequency and number of firearm-related accidents; and possession and use of guns by youths. Data related to the many forms of violence that occur in American society, the number of violent criminals, their offense histories, their length of incarceration for violent crimes, and the number and characteristics of victims of violent crime are also presented. This information, gathered from government reports and summaries of victimization surveys, is provided through tables and graphs, with discussions and explanations added to help interpret them. Sources of additional information are also given with each table.

Although weapons may include firearms, knives or other objects, or parts of the human body (hands, fists, feet), firearms are overwhelmingly the weapons used in crimes or confrontations. Handguns are the most frequently employed firearms.

Private ownership and use of firearms have always been part of the American life-style. In colonial times, they were used to protect the settlers from hostile Indians, or from other invaders. The early history of America is one of frontier skirmishes, battles with the French or British for territory, and the need for protection in newly settled areas where law and order had not yet been established.

The 1800s saw slave-owner vs. abolitionist tensions and civil war. The intimidation of minorities or immigrants, labor disputes, underworld battles between organized crime syndicates, and assassinations of important political figures have marked America's recent history.

Firearms have played a prominent role in all of these activities. In addition, when the United States began as a primarily agrarian country, an enduring pattern of hunting and recreational use of guns was established. Today, the United States has more firearms in the hands of private citizens than any other nation in the world. Since 1899, more than 200 million firearms have been available for sale in the United States, and nearly half of all households possess one or more firearms.

Before World War II, rifles and shotguns, sometimes termed "long guns," far outnumbered handguns. In the late 1940s, handguns represented less than 20% of the firearms available. However, the proportion of handguns increased tremendously in succeeding years. In 1993, 50% of all firearms for sale in the United States were handguns. The decrease in the use of long guns and increase in the demand for handguns parallel the steady urbanization of the American population. As people moved to cities and left rural areas, the need for long guns for hunting or other uses declined, and handguns became popular as security equipment for those crowding into congested urban areas or adjoining suburbs. Unfortunately, they also became the weapons of choice for those engaged in violent crime. Surveys of gun ownership have revealed that those who possess them are predominantly males. Whites are more likely than blacks to own guns, but the racial differences are smaller for ownership of handguns than for guns in general. Ownership is higher among middle-aged persons than for those in other age groups. Persons in rural areas use their weapons for hunting, recreational shooting, and protection, while those in urban areas view them chiefly as means of protection.

The use of firearms in violent crimes has been constantly escalating. Of the murders committed in 1993, 82% involved firearms, and 70% of those firearms were

Introduction

handguns. Firearm use in other violent crimes, such as aggravated assault and robbery, has also increased. The rise in firearm-related juvenile violent crime, particularly "drive-by" shootings and gang violence, has intensified public concern about the easy availability of firearms.

In the 1990s, debate over gun control reached fever pitch. Advocates of control maintained that there is a high correlation between the availability of firearms and the commission of violent crimes. They argued that the time had come for strong intervention. Suggested gun-control laws included waiting periods and background checks before allowing the purchase of firearms, and the registration of all weapons, both those currently possessed and new acquisitions. Limits on the number of guns that could be purchased and the length of time between purchases were also suggested. Removal of firearms from the hands of private citizens was viewed as a way of reducing gun-related violence. In some cities programs were instituted for individuals to turn in their guns to authorities in exchange for money, food vouchers, or other incentives.

Opponents of gun control, led by the National Rifle Association (NRA), maintained that limiting the availability of firearms would not reduce violent crime and, in fact, might lead to increases. They argued that the Second Amendment to the U.S. Constitution guarantees citizens the right to "keep and bear arms." They also pointed out that regulation of the private ownership or sale of guns would not deter criminals from securing them, since they would obtain them outside legitimate channels by purchasing them from unauthorized dealers or stealing them. The end result would be that citizens who wished to purchase guns for legitimate reasons would be deterred from doing so by bureaucratic regulations, while criminals' access to firearms would continue unabated. Proponents of control countered these arguments by stating that the Second Amendment reference to "the right of the people to keep and bear arms," in fact alludes to the rights of states to maintain their own militias rather than to private gun ownership. Also, since many guns are acquired by criminals in burglaries, restrictions on the availability of guns would reduce the number held privately that could be stolen for future use in crimes.

The debate culminated in the passage of the Brady Bill in November 1993, named for James Brady, former president Ronald Reagan's press secretary who was shot and wounded during an attempted assassination of the president. The Brady Bill established a national five-day waiting period and a background check for the purchase of a handgun. Although this procedure has demonstrated some slight deterrent effect in keeping guns out of the hands of persons who might use them for violent crimes, it does not address the issue of acquisition of guns through unlawful channels or reduce the tremendous number of firearms already in circulation. It is clear that the question of how the availability of firearms relates to the occurrence of violent crimes is one that will continue to be an important consideration in American criminal justice.

Is American Society Becoming More Violent?

We noted earlier that America's history is one of violent confrontations, with weapons often used to settle disputes or to frighten or dissuade persons from certain courses of action. The fact that America has always been a violent society is underlined by the high suicide rates in this country. Suicide is the ultimate act of violence, since it is directed against oneself. Suicide rates during the twentieth century peaked in 1932 and have declined since that time, but they are still higher than homicide rates.

In the late 1980s and the 1990s, it seems that American life has been saturated with violence. Revelations of the extent of domestic violence and child physical and sexual abuse in this country, concealed or underreported for years, have shocked many. The amount of violence presented in the media has escalated until it is difficult to find any film or television program that does not contain some violence. Violent crime captures the headlines daily, and record-setting murder rates, gang violence on the streets and in the schools, car-jackings, or violent incidents in the workplace have increased citizens' fears.

What Causes Violent Behavior?

It is important to realize that aggression and violence are interrelated. Although aggression and violence are present in every society, the amount varies

Introduction

tremendously. Aggression, an effort to forcefully dominate or injure another, can take forms other than violent behavior, including threats, spreading malicious rumors, or stalking. Hostile aggression, which involves angry reactions to the behavior of others, frequently results in violent acts. Such violent crimes as homicide, manslaughter, rape, or assault can be forms of hostile aggression. Instrumental aggression, in contrast, is goal-oriented, undertaken to obtain possessions that someone else may have. Instrumental aggression may occur as violent crime, such as robbery, or nonviolent crime, such as burglary.

Explanations of aggression include the hypothesis that humans, like other animals, are aggressive and violent by nature and will manifest this trait when there is a threat to their well-being or territory. Aggression may also occur as a result of being frustrated, threatened, or blocked from achieving one's goals. When this happens, the aggression may not be directed toward the person or group causing the frustration but toward a weaker, more vulnerable target. This may explain some domestic violence or offer insights into why members of racial minorities are often targets of violent acts during periods of economic depression. Aggressive violence may also be directed toward oneself. Unable to find a suitable relief outlet for his or her need to behave aggressively, a person may commit suicide.

Although some aggression may be instinctive or due to psychological factors, social learning is believed to be a more likely cause of aggressive and violent behavior. The learning process begins at birth, and those in constant daily interaction with children have the greatest effect on them. If a child witnesses or experiences a considerable amount of violence and aggression in the home, the probability that this child will grow up to be violent and aggressive increases. As the range of associates of the child extends beyond the immediate family into the school and the neighborhood, the influence of the family continues but others also begin to shape a youth's behavior. In some cases, aggression and violence become the major themes of interactions both in the home and outside it, and young people become socialized in what has been termed a "culture of violence." From childhood, they observe and are part of life-styles that use violence as a response to frustrations or difficulties. Everyday situations such as neighborhood noise or what are perceived as spoken or implied insults may be responded to with aggressive violence. This is true in acquaintance-to-acquaintance interactions, and also in relating to strangers. At sporting events or when driving on highways, persons who are angry or frustrated with what is occurring may erupt in violent activity. When handguns were not so widely owned, these situations might have resulted in fist fights or assaults with other weapons that caused minor injuries. Now they may end in death.

In fact, violence has always been present in America, but in most instances it was confined to inner-city neighborhoods. This is no longer true. Victimization by strangers is becoming more common, and violence is occurring in areas that were considered safe in the past. An ever-increasing amount of this violence is committed by young, minority, inner-city youths, sometimes characterized as the "underclass." They live in economically disadvantaged areas and are often the offspring of young, unmarried women with little experience in disciplining or caring for children. Constantly exposed to the culture of violence, they grow up without positive role models, observing that drug dealers and other criminals in their neighborhoods are the financially successful persons. Lack of resources for or interest in education in their home environments makes them likely to fail in school and drop out. This in turn leaves them poorly prepared for employment and more inclined to view criminal activity as the most practical way to obtain the things they need for day-to-day survival.

Statistics on Weapons & Violence

The statistics presented in this volume provide opportunities for us to examine the matter of weapons and violence from various perspectives. We can review the history of firearm ownership in the United States and determine if violence escalated or abated with trends toward increased or reduced firearm purchase. We can look at the question of whether victims of violent crimes who had firearms available to protect themselves were less seriously victimized than those who did not. The direct effect of the presence of firearms in a residence, in terms of their possible use in family violence situations, suicides, or accidental injuries to family members can also be considered. In addition, the use of guns by high school students (who have no legal right to own them), either for personal protection or to

Introduction

commit crimes, can be evaluated. Statistics on the use of weapons other than firearms in the commission of violent crimes are also provided. Violence in America can be analyzed by studying the violent crime trends and their year-by-year fluctuations. Information on the types of violent crimes for which persons have been imprisoned, the length of their sentences, and the actual time they spent in prison is given. Profiles of the victims of violent crimes, gathered through victimization surveys, are available. Data on domestic violence, violence in the schools, gang violence, and violence in the workplace are also presented.

Interpretation of Statistics on Weapons & Violence

The information in this book is given in the form of statistics and graphic illustrations of trends identified in the statistical material. In order to correctly interpret the numbers, it is necessary to understand how the data were collected and exactly how the findings are shown in the charts.

Statistics are masses of numerical data. Persons who are trying to discredit or downplay statistical findings may use the expression, "Statistics lie." Although the numbers themselves do not lie, it is possible for those who interpret, analyze, or present them to lie, or at least to manipulate the manner in which the findings are interpreted. Thus, efforts to discredit statistics should focus on the errors or distortions by those who interpret them, not on the statistics themselves. Even when analysts are making sincere efforts to present a true interpretation of statistical findings, they may err because they do not realize the true meaning and/or limitations of the data.

Careful interpretation is especially important in trying to understand the various reports, charts, and figures that pertain to weapons and violence. Information on issues involving weapons and violence is used by law enforcement administrators and personnel, school officials, employers, social agencies, and local, state, and federal government officials as the basis for planning, preventive intervention, or deterrent action. It is essential that the material on which such actions are based is interpreted correctly.

Methods of Obtaining Information

Many of the statistics presented in this book are taken from the *Uniform Crime Report (Crime in the United States)*, compiled each year by the Federal Bureau of Investigation (FBI). Other major references for material in this volume are the *Sourcebook of Criminal Justice Statistics*, compiled by the U.S. Bureau of Justice Statistics; and summaries of services rendered or surveys taken by government agencies, including the Centers for Disease Control, the National Center on Child Abuse and Neglect, the National Institute of Justice, the Office of Juvenile Justice and Delinquency Prevention, and the Bureau of Labor Statistics. These reports, either for a particular year or as summaries of longer periods, show number totals or illustrate trends through graphs. The information relates to gun ownership, victimization of children through abuse or neglect, domestic violence, violence in the schools or the workplace, delinquent or criminal behavior, fear of crime, and actions taken to reduce the chances of being victimized.

Another major source of data is the National Crime Victimization Survey *(Criminal Victimization in the United States)* conducted each year by the Bureau of Justice Statistics. In this research, more than 100,000 U.S. residents complete a questionnaire about their experiences or lack of experience with crime during a particular year to measure the levels of criminal victimization and the circumstances surrounding the event. The incidents reported in the survey may or may not have been reported to the police.

Although all of the researchers involved in gathering the data presented in this book tried to obtain accurate information, the methods they used to obtain it differed. For example, the FBI's *Uniform Crime Report* contains information gathered by asking each local, state, and federal law enforcement agency to compile yearly crime statistics. All types of crime known to the police are reported in the tables, but the *Uniform Crime Report* places special emphasis on "index crimes." These are the most serious offenses, subdivided into violent and property crimes. The number of offenses reported to the police and those cleared by arrest in each category are included. Trends in criminal behavior are also identified through tables that make five- and ten-year comparisons of criminal activity. Although the *Uniform Crime Report* is the most widely quoted and authoritative source of crime statistics, it has limitations that need to be recognized. The information may not be complete, since not all police jurisdictions submit their statistics. Also, crimes that are never reported to the police are not included in the tabulations. The reports from other agencies have similar limitations. Only those incidents that were brought to the attention of an agency are part of the statistical tabulations. For example, it is certain that the actual number of incidents of domestic violence and child abuse and neglect far exceeds that reported.

The National Crime Victimization Survey, in contrast, gathers its data by asking members of certain households a series of questions pertaining to victimizations they may have experienced. Information obtained through such surveys may not be present in arrests statistics. For example, if an intended victim was able to threaten or ward off an assailant, so that no reportable crime occurred, this comes to light and is recorded in a victimization survey. Also, persons do not always report crimes to the police. For example, a rape victim may not report the assault because she is too traumatized. Victims of robberies or burglaries may not report the incidents because there is little hope of recovering the stolen property. Those chosen for the National Crime Victimization Survey are part of what is termed a "representative sample." The persons surveyed are chosen in such a way that the findings from questioning them can be regarded with a high degree of certainty as representative of the entire U.S. population because of the scientific way in which the households were selected.

There are other ways of obtaining data about weapons and violence. Although government agencies have the resources and the expertise to complete nationwide surveys, private researchers can also gather valuable information. Government agencies, such as the National Institute of Justice, or private groups like the Mott or Carnegie Foundations, contract with universities or private research agencies to fund research. For example, a Carnegie-supported study of youth violence in the schools not only attempted to ascertain the amount of violent behavior occurring there, but also related this to such factors as absenteeism, poor academic performance, and actual physical harm to students. Such surveys, like the National Crime Victimization Survey, rely on information provided by the respondents rather than on official records from law enforcement or other government agencies. In self-report studies, the possibilities of under- or over-reporting exist. A person who has been victimized may forget to mention the incident or feel it is not relevant to the questions being asked. A person who has committed a crime or act of violence may choose not to report it. There is often no way to confirm the accuracy of data collected in this way. For example, in self-report surveys where high school students are given a list of acts that are law violations and asked to report how many times they performed them, the anonymity guaranteed to the youths prevents the researchers from comparing the reported behavior to school or juvenile court records.

Forms in Which Statistics Are Presented

In examining statistical information, it is crucial to know the form in which the figures are presented. The most common presentation is the total number (persons arrested, homes burglarized) in a specific time period. Generally, a percentage figure will also be given. If you wish to know the number of homicides committed in a given year, the total number is the point of reference. However, if you are interested in finding out what part of the total number of crimes committed in a given year were homicides, percentages would be more important. To compare the total number of homicides reported in a given year with the total number of homicides for which arrests were made in that year, both the number and the percentage of the total would be needed.

The mere presentation of numbers may be misleading and can lead to erroneous interpretations. One way to avoid this is to make use of rates. If you compare the number of homicides reported in 1983 with the number reported in 1993, the number in 1993 is considerably higher. Does this mean that the homicide *rate* has increased significantly, or is it simply that the population has increased during the ten-year period so that the *number* of homicides has gone up while the *percentage* of the total number of persons in the United States who were homicide victims in both years has stayed the same? To determine the homicide rate, the number of offenses would be compared to the number of persons in the population, using a dividing point such as 100,000 persons. For example, if there were 200,000,000 people in the United States in 1983 and 300,000,000 in 1993, but the number of homicides

Introduction

committed in the two years was the same, the rate per 100,000 persons would have decreased. It is important, then, when looking at the tables in this book, to determine whether total numbers, rates, percentages, or combinations of all three are presented or compared, and to interpret the data accordingly.

In summary, before using or quoting statistics in reports or using them to support a position, it is necessary to:

- identify the source of the statistics and determine if it is reliable;

- discover the method used to obtain the information;

- ascertain the scope of the statistical application (can the findings be applied only to a limited group of persons or to the general population?);

- mention the limitations, if any, of the manner in which the statistics can be applied; and

- understand the form in which the statistics are presented (total numbers, percentages, rates).

Weapon Use and Violent Crime

Violent crime, as statistically recorded by the FBI in its *Uniform Crime Reports*, is divided into four categories: murder and non-negligent manslaughter, forcible rape, robbery, and aggravated assault. All violent crimes include force or threat of force. Murder and non-negligent manslaughter involve the willful killing of one human being by another; forcible rape is the carnal knowledge of a female forcibly and against her will, including sexual assaults or attempts to commit rape by force or threat; robbery is taking or attempting to take anything of value from a person or persons by force or threat of force or violence; and aggravated assault is an unlawful attack by one person upon another for the purpose of inflicting severe bodily injury, usually by use of a weapon or means likely to produce death or great bodily harm. Attempted aggravated assault is also included in this category.

The weapons used to commit violent crimes may include firearms; knives or other cutting or stabbing instruments; blunt objects, such as clubs or hammers; personal weapons (hands, feet, or fists); and other objects that might be used to inflict bodily harm. The prevalence of use of a particular weapon tends to vary with the violent crime:

- According to the FBI, firearms are the preferred weapons of murderers, with 82% of the murders in 1993 committed with firearms. Handguns made up 70% of the firearms used. Knives or cutting instruments ranked second, used in 13% of the murders. This hierarchy of weapon-use held true for the 30 years from 1964-93, with firearms used in more than half of the murders every year, and knives and other cutting or stabbing instruments ranking second. Firearms were used most often when the murder was the result of an argument. In murders that resulted when offenders were trying to commit other crimes, 72% were committed with firearms.

- According to the National Crime Victimization Survey, rapists are less likely to use firearms than other weapons. In 1992, 26% of the forcible rape incidents involved use of firearms, while weapons other than knives or blunt objects were used in 37% of the incidents, blunt objects were used in 20%, and knives in 17%.

- According to the FBI, firearms were the most commonly used weapons in robberies during the 1970s and early 1980s, but in the late 1980s use of strong-arm tactics (punching, beating, shoving) became more frequent. In the 1990s, use of firearms and strong-arm tactics was about equal (40%), while knives or other weapons were used in the remaining 20%.

- The number of aggravated assaults has grown tremendously, increasing more than 500% from 1964 to 1993, according to the FBI. Firearm use in these assaults has shown a pattern of increase, and in 1990 was 25%. Personal weapons (hands, feet, or fists) were used in 26% of the aggravated assaults that year, and the remainder were carried out with blunt objects (31%) or knives or cutting instruments (18%).

- When the FBI compared the rates of firearm use from 1980 to 1992, their use in violent crimes increased 27%. Although the rate of use in murders showed no increase, the rate of use in aggravated assaults grew 57%, and use in robberies increased 8%.

Introduction

- A survey of state prison inmates by the Bureau of Justice Statistics found that 30% of them had carried a handgun during commission of the violent crime for which they were incarcerated, and 16% had fired it. Sentences for offenses involving firearms tend to be more severe. Ninety-three percent of the federal offenders who used firearms were sentenced to prison, compared to 72% of those who did not use them in their crimes.

- The National Crime Victimization Survey found that, over a twelve-year period, 15% of the victims of violent crimes in which handguns were used by the offenders were injured, and 16% of these were injured from a shooting. However, 98% of the victims survived the criminal incidents. A five-year comparison (1987–92) revealed that blacks were almost three times as likely as whites to have been the victims of crimes committed with handguns. The majority of the victims were young black males (ages 16–35). Self-protective measures by victims included threatening or attacking the offender with a weapon in only about 2% of the incidents. In most cases, the victims ran away, resisted or appeased the offender, or got help from others without using a weapon. However, since an intended victim's use of a firearm for defense may prevent the criminal event from happening, such use may be greatly underreported. The survey tabulated 80,000 incidents in a five-year period (1987–92) in which victims with guns defended themselves. Two-thirds used the guns to threaten, and one-third attacked the offenders with guns. Nineteen percent of the victims in these incidents sustained injuries.

- The FBI reports of justifiable homicides (incidents in which private citizens killed serious offenders during the criminal events) increased from 273 in 1989 to 356 in 1993. However, other such incidents may have been reported in the statistics as self-defense homicides. Some criminologists estimate that the actual number of homicides related to victim self-defense in 1993 was between 1,700 and 3,200.

- A survey by the Bureau of Justice Statistics, conducted each year over a twenty-year period, revealed that victims of robberies who defended themselves were less likely to lose property than those who did not. However, those who defended themselves were also more likely to be injured.

- According to the National Safety Council, rates of fatal accidental injuries by firearms have gradually decreased throughout the twentieth century. In 1993, about 9% of the accidental shootings were of children under fifteen who found the firearms involved in the accidents in their own homes.

- A survey by the Centers for Disease Control and Prevention revealed that in 1993 more than 22% of the high school students in the United States had carried a weapon of some type during the 30 days preceding the survey, and 8% of these had carried a gun. A survey by the National Institute of Justice of male inmates in juvenile correctional facilities and male students in ten inner-city public high schools near the institutions found that 83% of the inmates had owned guns prior to their confinement, and 22% of the students owned guns at the time of the survey. Both groups listed protection as the main motive for acquiring firearms.

Violent Crime Trends

Since the 1960s, violent crime has significantly increased, although the amount has fluctuated from year to year. Today, it makes up a much larger portion of total crime than it did in the past. The most significant trend in violence is the increase in crime rates for younger offenders. It is projected that, if present trends continue, juvenile arrests for violent crime, which rose nearly 50% in the five years from 1988 to 1992, will double by the year 2010. Other trends in violence have also been noted:

- The number of prisoners sentenced for violent offenses is constantly rising, but their proportion in the total prison population has actually declined, largely because of the enormous increase in the number of persons sentenced to these facilities for drug offenses. Changes in many state criminal codes have resulted in determinate (fixed amount of time) sentences for many offenses, with specifications that additional time be added if a firearm was involved in the incident. A mandatory minimum amount of time served before release is also

Introduction

set. Most violent offenders are released before completion of their sentences, after serving about 60% of their time. The effect of longer sentences or time served in reducing violent crime is impossible to determine. Obviously, violent criminals cannot commit additional offenses in the community while they are incarcerated. In addition, if an offender is held in prison during the high violent-crime-potential years (up to age 35), this may be a preventive measure.

- The number of victims of violent crime far exceeds that reported. Although homicide victimization reported may be close to the actual number, it is estimated that rapes may occur five to ten times more often than the recorded number, and only a fraction of assaults are reported. A violent crime may not be made known to the police if the perpetrator is a friend or relative; because of fear of retaliation by the offender; due to embarrassment or fear of the investigative process; because the victim is involved in some type of criminal activity related to the offense; or on account of feelings that the police or others will do nothing about it.

- Rates of reported violence among family members have reached all-time highs. Females are most often the victims of domestic violence, and children age seven or younger are the most frequent targets of abuse. Neglect, physical abuse, and sexual abuse are the most common forms of child mistreatment, and parents or relatives are the offenders in nearly 90% of the cases.

- Violence in schools is a matter of great national concern. A 1991 study by the Centers for Disease Control and Prevention found that 1 in 25 high school students carries a gun. A national survey of school violence in 1993 (the Metropolitan Life Survey of the American Teacher) found that 25% of the students and 10% of the teachers had been victims of violence in or near their public schools in that year. On college and university campuses, violent crimes are less frequent than property crimes. The most common violent crimes committed there are aggravated assaults, according to the FBI.

- Gang violence also occurs in the schools, often related to drug dealing or inter-gang rivalries. Through busing, members of rival gangs from various neighborhoods may be brought together in a common school location, resulting in violence. In schools, gang members may seek to intimidate teachers and other students, extort money from students, vandalize facilities, and create general classroom disruption.

- Violence also occurs in the workplace. Most homicides here are related to robberies, and more than 80% of these are shootings. Persons employed in retail jobs, such as restaurants, grocery stores, or gas stations, are most at risk. Workplace homicides occur more often in urban than in rural areas. Other than homicides, assaults are the violent crimes most frequently committed in the workplace.

Summary

The statistics on weapons and violence contained in this volume paint an alarming picture. Our American society is becoming more violent, and the chances of being a victim of violent crime are increasing. Violent crime occurs in family life, schools, and in the workplace. Areas that are common meeting places, including downtown areas of cities, malls, retail establishments, and streets and highways, can be sites of victimization. Fear that violent incidents will occur has caused many persons to restrict their activities, change the routes they travel, and not venture out alone, particularly at night. Although the greatest increases in violence have occurred in urban areas, suburban and rural residents are also becoming more fearful and cautious. Private citizens continue to purchase firearms, particularly handguns, to protect themselves, even though the presence of the weapons in their homes may put them at risk for accidental injury. Youth violence is projected to increase at an unprecedented rate in the coming years.

Proposed solutions to these problems include efforts to control the behavior of violent offenders by imprisoning them for longer periods of time or by limiting their access to firearms, the most frequently used weapons in violent crimes. However, these measures may have little effect in the long run. More long-range action is needed, and this involves attacking the sources of the lifestyles and cultural norms that have caused poor, economically, socially, and educationally deprived youths to turn to violent crime as a way of life.

Acknowledgments, Sources and Contacts

ACKNOWLEDGMENTS

The following persons offered advice and support during the research and compilation of this volume. Their expertise contributed significantly to this compilation of data on weapons and violence in the United States.

Edgar A. Suter, M.D., Chair of Doctors for Integrity in Research & Public Policy (San Ramon, California).

Micki C. Fox, Business Manager, Tennessee Law Revue Association, Inc. (Knoxville, Tennessee).

Guy Toscano, Economist, Office of Safety, Health and Working Conditions, Bureau of Labor Statistics (Washington, DC).

National Safety Council (Itasca, Illinois).

Les Stanford, Information Programs Branch, Bureau of Alcohol, Tobacco and Firearms (Washington, DC).

MAJOR DATA GATHERING PROGRAMS

In compiling data for *Statistics on Weapons & Violence* the editors drew upon a well established body of statistical information. Many of the sources cited in this volume come from a number of national survey programs. Presented in this section is a brief overview of these programs.

The Census of Fatal Occupational Injuries

The U.S. Department of Labor's Bureau of Labor Statistics administers the Census of Fatal Occupational Injuries (CFOI). The CFOI, begun in 1992, covers about twenty different aspects regarding workers who died on the job. The CFOI includes information on demographics of the fatally injured worker and on the circumstances surrounding the event. This volume uses information from the CFOI regarding homicides and assaults at the workplace.

The CFOI draws upon multiple sources of information to ensure accuracy. These sources include numerous types of administrative documents from federal and state agencies, such as: death certificates, medical examiner records, workers' compensation reports, and regulatory agency reports. The CFOI also utilizes news reports and follow-up questionnaires to business establishments.

Correctional Populations in the U.S.

Correctional Populations in the U.S. (CPUS) presents a tabulation of persons under some form of correctional supervision. The U.S. Department of Justice, Office of Justice Programs maintains the CPUS program. Since 1926, the Bureau of the Census has compiled detailed prisoner statistics. The CPUS series has detailed information on admissions, releases, sentences and time served, inmates under sentence of death, recidivism, and crowding. The CPUS information used in this volume deals with offenders sentenced for violent crimes.

Current Mortality Sample

The National Center for Health Statistics (NCHS) conducts the Current Mortality Sample (CMS). The NCHS is a branch of the Centers for Disease Control and Prevention, which in turn is part of the U.S. Department of Health and Human Services' Public Health Service. The CMS systematically samples 10% of all death certificates picked randomly each month after the state offices have counted the certificates. The CMS gathers information on deaths and death rates in the U.S. by age, race, sex, and cause. This information is then used to estimate national proportions.

This volume incorporates information from the NCHS primarily for recent homicide and suicide numbers and rates, and for firearm deaths. Estimates of deaths and death rates are based on a sample of death certificates and are subject to sampling variability. The preliminary sample information for cause-of-death is adjusted to match the provisional counts of deaths. This means that information presented in the final report supersedes information in an initial report.

Acknowledgments, Sources and Contacts

Juvenile Court Statistics

The Office of Juvenile Justice and Delinquency Prevention (OJJDP), a branch of the U.S. Department of Justice, annually gathers statistics regarding juvenile delinquency cases. The National Center for Juvenile Justice prepares this information for the OJJDP through the Juvenile Court Statistics (JCS) annual series.

The JCS series measures juvenile delinquency using "disposed" cases. A disposed case is one in which a definite action took place or is currently underway. It does not necessarily mean that the case is closed. Violent offenses are measured as "person offenses" and include: criminal homicide, forcible rape, robbery, aggravated assault, simple assault, other violent sex offenses, and other person offenses.

The National Child Abuse and Neglect Data System

The National Center on Child Abuse and Neglect (NCCAN), working with state governments, carries out the administration of the National Child Abuse and Neglect Data System (NCANDS). The NCCAN is a branch of the U.S. Department of Health and Human Services' Administration on Children and Families. The NCANDS consists of two components. The first part consists of aggregated data submitted by the states, and the second part collects automated case-level data from participating states. The aggregated information focuses on four main areas, including numbers of reports, investigations, victims, and perpetrators.

The National Crime Victimization Survey

The National Crime Victimization Survey (NCVS) is sponsored by the U.S. Department of Justice's Bureau of Justice Statistics. The NCVS measures aspects of crime at the national level. Over 100,000 randomly selected persons age twelve and older from about 49,000 households are given questionnaires that ask about personal and household experiences with crime. Households stay in the sample for three years and interviews occur at six-month intervals. New households rotate into the sample on an ongoing basis. The NCVS has used this stable data collection method since 1973, making it possible to estimate national proportions of crime.

The NCVS is especially useful in measuring unreported crimes. This is accomplished through asking about information on crimes suffered by individuals and households, regardless of whether or not an incident was ever reported to the police. Since the NCVS measures both reported and unreported crime, any changes in the hesitance to report crime or in technological improvements in keeping records do not affect the results.

The NCVS collects detailed information about victims of crime. Characteristics of victims in the NCVS include: demographic description, relationship with the offender, whether or not the crime was part of a series of crimes over a six-month period, self-protective measures used and assessment of their effectiveness, and what the victim was doing when victimized. The NCVS occasionally includes special supplements about particular topics such as school crime or violence against women.

The NCVS also is useful because it collects information that is not available or unknown in the initial police report. This follow-up information includes contacts the victim has made with the criminal justice system after the crime, extent and costs of medical treatment, and recovery of property.

The NCVS, however, does not measure homicides because it is impossible to survey murder victims. It also does not measure any crimes that happen to children under twelve years of age, since they are omitted from the survey.

The Uniform Crime Reports

The Federal Bureau of Investigation (FBI) maintains the Uniform Crime Reports (UCR) program. The UCR program, which began in 1929, measures police workload and activity. Local police departments, which represent about 95% of the U.S. population, voluntarily report information to the FBI. The information includes details on the following crimes reported to police: homicide, forcible rape, robbery, aggravated assault, burglary, larceny-theft, motor vehicle theft, and arson.

The UCR data consist of monthly law enforcement reports made directly to the FBI or to centralized state agencies that then report to the FBI. Each report submitted to the UCR program is examined thoroughly for

Acknowledgments, Sources and Contacts

reasonableness, accuracy, and deviations that may indicate errors. Large variations in crime levels may indicate a change in record-keeping procedures, incomplete reporting, or changes in a jurisdiction's boundaries. Monthly reports are compared with previous submissions and with those of similar agencies to identify any unusual changes in an agency's crime counts.

The UCR, unlike the NCVS, can provide local data about states, counties, cities, and towns. It also measures crimes affecting children under twelve years of age. Experts agree that the NCVS can not provide reliable information about this segment of the population. The UCR program also counts the number of arrests and details on arrested persons. The UCR also collects information on the number of homicides (murders and nonnegligent manslaughters). These crimes must go uncounted in a survey that interviews victims. The UCR also gathers data on the circumstances surrounding homicide and the characteristics of homicide victims.

The UCR program, unlike the NCVS, relies on reported information and cannot address the hidden problem of unreported crimes. The UCR also utilizes information from initial police reports, even though the information on such reports often changes later. Inconsistency in reporting among the thousands of law enforcement agencies that submit reports also affects the UCR program.

The Youth Risk Behavior Surveillance System

The Youth Risk Behavior Surveillance System (YRBSS) is a survey sponsored by the Centers for Disease Control and Prevention (CDC). The CDC is a branch of the U.S. Department of Health and Human Services' Public Health Service. The YRBSS is used to monitor six categories of priority health risk behaviors among young people. These behaviors include: actions that contribute to unintentional and intentional injuries, tobacco use, alcohol and other drug use, sexual behaviors, dietary behaviors, and physical activity.

The YRBSS includes national, state, and local school-based surveys of high school students. National surveys took place in 1990, 1991, and 1993. Comparable state and local surveys were also conducted in those years. The 1993 YRBSS report summarizes the results of 16,296 respondents from the national survey, 24 state surveys, and 9 local surveys. Health and education officials nationwide routinely use information from the YRBSS to design school health policies and programs that reduce risks associated with the leading causes of disease and death.

PRIMARY SOURCES

The following sources are cited in this volume as sources of statistical data on weapons and violence.

Kates, Don B., et al. "Guns and Public Health: Epidemic of Violence or Pandemic of Propaganda?" 62 *Tennessee Law Review* 513 (1995) (forthcoming, August 1995). Used by permission of the Tennessee Law Review Association, Inc., College of Law—Dunford Hall, 915 Volunteer Blvd., Knoxville, TN 37996.

Kleck, Gary. *Point Blank: Guns and Violence in America* (New York: Aldine De Gruyter, 1991).

National Safety Council. *Accident Facts 1994*.

U.S. Department of Health and Human Services, Public Health Service, Centers for Disease Control and Prevention, National Center for Health Statistics, *Monthly Vital Statistics Report*.

U.S. Department of Health and Human Services, Public Health Service, Centers for Disease Control and Prevention, *Morbidity and Mortality Weekly Report*.

U.S. Department of Health and Human Services, National Center on Child Abuse and Neglect, *Child Maltreatment 1993: Reports From the States to the National Center on Child Abuse and Neglect* (Washington, DC: U.S. Government Printing Office, 1995).

U.S. Department of Health and Human Services, Public Health Service, Centers for Disease Control and Prevention, National Institute for Occupational Safety and Health, *Preventing Homicide in the Workplace* (Cincinnati, Ohio: National Institute for Occupational Safety and Health, 1993).

U.S. Department of Justice, Bureau of Justice Statistics. *Correctional Populations in the United States, 1992*

Acknowledgments, Sources and Contacts

(Washington, DC: U.S. Government Printing Office, 1995).

U.S. Department of Justice, Bureau of Justice Statistics. *Criminal Victimization in the United States, 1992* (Washington, DC: U.S. Government Printing Office, 1994).

U.S. Department of Justice, Bureau of Justice Statistics, "Criminal Victimization 1993" (Washington, DC: U.S. Government Printing Office, May 1995).

U.S. Department of Justice, Bureau of Justice Statistics, "Child Rape Victims, 1992" (Washington, DC: U.S. Government Printing Office, June 1994).

U.S. Department of Justice, Bureau of Justice Statistics, "The Costs of Crime to Victims" (Washington, DC: U.S. Government Printing Office, February 1994).

U.S. Department of Justice, Bureau of Justice Statistics, "Federal Firearms-Related Offenses" (Washington, DC: U.S. Government Printing Office, June 1995).

U.S. Department of Justice, Bureau of Justice Statistics, "Felony Sentences in State Courts, 1992" (Washington, DC: U.S. Government Printing Office, January 1995).

U.S. Department of Justice, Bureau of Justice Statistics, "Firearms and Crimes of Violence: Selected Findings" (Washington, DC: U.S. Government Printing Office, February 1994).

U.S. Department of Justice, Bureau of Justice Statistics, "Guns and Crime" (Washington, DC: U.S. Government Printing Office, April 1994).

U.S. Department of Justice, Bureau of Justice Statistics. *Highlights from 20 Years of Surveying Crime Victims* (Washington, DC: U.S. Government Printing Office, 1993).

U.S. Department of Justice, Bureau of Justice Statistics, "Murder in Families" (Washington, DC: U.S. Government Printing Office, July 1995).

U.S. Department of Justice, Bureau of Justice Statistics, "Prison Sentences and Time Served for Violence" (Washington, DC: U.S. Government Printing Office, April 1995).

U.S. Department of Justice, Bureau of Justice Statistics, *School Crime: A National Crime Victimization Survey Report* (Washington, DC: U.S. Government Printing Office, 1991).

U.S. Department of Justice, Bureau of Justice Statistics, *Sourcebook of Criminal Justice Statistics—1992* (Washington, DC: U.S. Government Printing Office, 1993).

U.S. Department of Justice, Bureau of Justice Statistics, *Survey of State Prison Inmates, 1991* (Washington, DC: U.S. Government Printing Office, 1993).

U.S. Department of Justice, Bureau of Justice Statistics, "Violence and Theft in the Workplace" (Washington, DC: U.S. Government Printing Office, July 1994).

U.S. Department of Justice, Bureau of Justice Statistics, "Violence between Intimates" (Washington, DC: U.S. Government Printing Office, November 1994).

U.S. Department of Justice, Bureau of Justice Statistics, "Violent Crime" (Washington, DC: U.S. Government Printing Office, April 1994).

U.S. Department of Justice, Federal Bureau of Investigation, *Crime in the United States, 1993* (Washington, DC: U.S. Government Printing Office, 1994).

U.S. Department of Justice, National Institute of Justice, Office of Justice Programs, "Gang Crime and Law Enforcement Recordkeeping" (Washington, DC: U.S. Government Printing Office, August 1995).

U.S. Department of Justice, National Institute of Justice, Office of Justice Programs, "Prosecuting Gangs: A National Assessment" (Washington, DC: U.S. Government Printing Office, February 1995).

U.S. Department of Justice, National Institute of Justice, Office of Juvenile Justice and Delinquency Prevention, "Gun Acquisition and Possession in Selected Juvenile Samples" (Washington, DC: U.S. Government Printing Office, December 1993).

U.S. Department of Justice, Office of Juvenile Justice and Delinquency Programs, *Juvenile Court Statistics, 1991* (Washington, DC: U.S. Government Printing Office, 1994).

Acknowledgments, Sources and Contacts

U.S. Department of Justice, Office of Juvenile Justice and Delinquency Prevention, "Offenders in Juvenile Court, 1992" (Washington, DC: U.S. Government Printing Office, October 1994).

U.S. Department of Labor, Bureau of Labor Statistics, Office of Safety, Health and Working Conditions, *Census of Fatal Occupational Injuries, 1993* (Washington, DC: U.S. Government Printing Office, 1994).

U.S. Department of Labor, Bureau of Labor Statistics, *Annual Survey, 1993* (Washington, DC: U.S. Government Printing Office, 1994).

Other Sources Consulted

Kopel, David B. *The Samurai, the Mountie, and the Cowboy: Should America Adopt the Gun Controls of Other Democracies?* Buffalo, N.Y.: Prometheus Books, 1992.

Lang, Susan S. *Teen Violence*. New York: Franklin Watts, 1994.

Moore, Jack B. *Skinheads Shaved for Battle*. Bowling Green, Ohio: Bowling Green State University Popular Press, 1993.

Oliver, Marilyn Tower. *Gangs: Trouble in the Streets*. Springfield, N.J.: Enslow Publishers, Inc., 1995.

CONTACTS

The following organizations can be contacted for additional information of the subject of weapons and violence.

Children's Defense Fund, 25 E St. NW, Washington, DC 20001. (202) 628-8787.

The Children's Safety Network at the National Center for Education in Maternal and Child Health, 2000 15th St. N., Suite 701, Arlington, VA 22201. (703) 524-7802.

Coalition to Stop Gun Violence, 100 Maryland Ave., Washington, DC 20002. (202) 544-7190.

Gun Owners of America, 8001 Forbes Place, Suite 102, Springfield, VA 22151. (703) 321-8585.

Handgun Control Inc., 1225 I St. NW, Suite 1100, Washington, DC 20005. (202) 898-0792.

The Heritage Foundation, 214 Massachusetts Ave. NE, Washington, DC 20002. (202) 546-4400.

Jews for the Preservation of Firearms Ownership Inc., 2872 S. Wentworth Ave., Milwaukee, WI 53207. (414) 769-0760.

National Clearinghouse for the Defense of Battered Women, 125 S. 9th St. Suite 302, Philadelphia, PA 19107. (215) 351-0100.

National Clearinghouse on Child Abuse and Neglect Information, P.O. Box 1182, Washington, DC 20013-1182. (800) 394-3366.

National Coalition Against Domestic Violence, P.O. Box 18749, Denver, CO 80218-0749. (303) 839-1852.

National Maternal and Child Health Clearinghouse, 8201 Greensboro Dr. Suite 600, McLean, VA 22102. (703) 821-8955, ext. 254/255.

National Resource Center on Domestic Violence, 6400 Flank Dr. Suite 1300, Harrisburg, PA 17112-2778. (800) 537-2238.

National Rifle Association, 1600 Rhode Island Ave. NW, Washington, DC 20036. (800) 672-3888.

National Safety Council, 1121 Spring Lake Dr., Itasca, IL 60143. (708) 285-1121.

National Victim Center, 2111 Wilson Blvd., Suite 300, Arlington, VA 22201. (703) 276-2880.

U.S. Department of Health and Human Services, Public Health Service, Centers for Disease Control and Prevention, National Center for Health Statistics, 6525 Belcrest Rd., Hyattsville, MD 20782. Data dissemination: (301) 436-8500.

U.S. Department of Health and Human Services, Public Health Service, Centers for Disease Control and Prevention, 1600 Clifton Rd. NE, Atlanta, GA 30333. (404) 332-4555. The CDC also maintains a World-Wide Web server at http://www.cdc.gov/.

U.S. Department of Health and Human Services, Public Health Service, Centers for Disease Control and

Acknowledgments, Sources and Contacts

Prevention, National Institute for Occupational Safety and Health, 4676 Columbia Parkway, Cincinnati, OH 45226. (800) 356-4674.

U.S. Department of Justice, Bureau of Justice Statistics Clearinghouse, Box 6000, Rockville, MD 20850. (800) 732-3277.

U.S. Department of Justice, Federal Bureau of Investigation, Uniform Crime Reports, Criminal Justice Information Services Division, Washington, DC 20535. Information Dissemination: (202) 324-5015.

U.S. Department of Justice, Juvenile Justice Clearinghouse, P.O. Box 6000, Rockville, MD 20849. (800) 638-8736.

U.S. Department of Justice, National Institute of Justice, National Criminal Justice Reference Service, Box 6000, Rockville, MD 20849. (800) 851-3420. Inquiries can also be sent by e-mail to askncjrs@aspensys.com.

U.S. Department of Labor, Bureau of Labor Statistics, Office of Safety, Health and Working Conditions, 2 Massachusetts Ave., NE, Washington, DC 20212-0001. Census of Fatal Occupational Injuries office: (202) 606-6175.

U.S. Department of the Treasury, Bureau of Alcohol, Tobacco, and Firearms, Washington, DC 20226. (202) 927-8500.

WeAPoNs

Weapons

Firearms Available for Sale in the United States, 1946–93*

Estimated number of firearms (in thousands) for sale in the U.S., 1946–93*

Year	Handguns	Rifles	Shotguns	Total
1946	119	693	598	1,410
1947	186	904	843	1,933
1948	346	1,113	991	2,450
1949	181	816	1,032	2,029
1950	186	804	1,309	2,299
1951	274	646	1,008	1,928
1952	386	505	920	1,811
1953	347	511	993	1,851
1954	322	414	760	1,496
1955	367	532	796	1,695
1956	466	549	886	1,901
1957	475	605	766	1,846
1958	467	572	597	1,636
1959	587	747	707	2,041
1960	546	836	660	2,042
1961	505	757	654	1,916
1962	540	723	678	1,941
1963	613	759	726	2,098
1964	671	849	847	2,367
1965	924	980	1,027	2,931
1966	1,118	1,082	1,119	3,319
1967	1,565	1,080	1,210	3,855
1968	2,367	1,281	1,368	5,016
1969	1,523	1,408	1,334	4,265
1970	1,533	1,326	1,428	4,287
1971	1,640	1,431	1,632	4,703
1972	2,071	1,747	1,465	5,283
1973	1,887	1,902	1,633	5,422
1974	2,023	2,133	2,243	6,399
1975	2,163	2,147	1,807	6,117
1976	1,976	2,104	1,638	5,718
1977	1,925	1,921	1,387	5,233
1978	1,903	1,904	1,553	5,360
1979	2,171	1,965	1,555	5,691
1980	2,449	1,947	1,485	5,881
1981	2,591	1,722	1,164	5,477
1982	2,708	1,711	931	5,350

[Continued]

Firearms Available for Sale in the United States, 1946–93*

[Continued]

Year	Handguns	Rifles	Shotguns	Total
1983	2,219	1,283	1,080	4,582
1984	1,905	1,271	1,236	4,412
1985	1,684	1,368	922	3,974
1986	1,538	1,203	783	3,524
1987	1,842	1,378	1,125	4,345
1988	2,236	1,374	1,231	4,841
1989	2,353	1,627	1,142	4,334
1990	2,109	1,288	937	5,122
1991	1,904	988	584	3,486
1992	2,361	2,034	1,162	5,557
1993	3,881	2,659	1,220	7,760

* Firearms for sale = [domestic production + imports] − exports

Comments The Bureau of Alcohol, Tobacco, and Firearms (ATF), a branch of the Department of the Treasury, is responsible for the regulatory, taxation, and law enforcement aspects regarding firearms. The ATF annually tallies the number of guns available for sale in the U.S. for activities such as hunting, target shooting, and security.

According to the ATF, the total number of firearms available for sale in the U.S. during 1899–1993 amounted to 222,974,000. The ATF calculated the total by summing together domestic firearm production and imports for those years, then subtracting firearm exports for the same period. These statistics only count the number of guns that were available for sale (beginning with 1946), and do not distinguish between guns sold and dealer inventory. Also, the statistics do not measure the number of firearms in circulation among the civilian population, or include guns stocked by U.S. armed forces.

These ATF statistics also do not account for guns destroyed or rendered unfit for use. Also excluded are souvenir guns brought into the country after conflicts involving U.S. armed forces, guns smuggled into or out of the U.S., and guns manufactured illegally. The ATF is prohibited from compiling a national registry of firearm possession and does not collect firearm sales data. The ATF estimated in 1994 that licensed firearm dealers in the U.S. sell about 7.5 million guns per year, including about 3.5 million handguns.

Source Federal Bureau of Investigation, Criminal Justice Information Services Division, Programs Support Section.

Contact Federal Bureau of Investigation, Uniform Crime Reports, Criminal Justice Information Services Division, Washington, DC 20535. Information Dissemination: (202) 324-5015.

Weapons

Guns Available for Sale

Percent of firearms available for sale* in the U.S. by gun type, 1946–93.

Year	Handguns	Rifles	Shotguns
1946	9%	49%	42%
1947	10%	47%	43%
1948	14%	46%	40%
1949	9%	40%	51%
1950	8%	35%	57%
1951	14%	34%	52%
1952	21%	28%	51%
1953	19%	28%	53%
1954	21%	28%	51%
1955	22%	31%	47%
1956	24%	29%	47%
1957	26%	33%	41%
1958	29%	35%	36%
1959	29%	36%	35%
1960	27%	41%	32%
1961	26%	40%	34%
1962	28%	37%	35%
1963	29%	36%	35%
1964	28%	36%	36%
1965	32%	33%	35%
1966	34%	32%	34%
1967	41%	28%	31%
1968	47%	26%	27%
1969	36%	33%	31%
1970	36%	31%	33%
1971	35%	30%	35%
1972	39%	33%	28%
1973	35%	35%	30%
1974	32%	33%	35%
1975	35%	35%	30%
1976	34%	37%	29%
1977	37%	37%	26%
1978	35%	36%	29%
1979	38%	35%	27%
1980	42%	33%	25%
1981	47%	32%	21%
1982	51%	32%	17%
1983	48%	28%	24%

[Continued]

Guns Available for Sale

[Continued]

Year	Handguns	Rifles	Shotguns
1984	43%	29%	28%
1985	42%	35%	23%
1986	44%	34%	22%
1987	42%	32%	26%
1988	46%	28%	26%
1989	54%	38%	26%
1990	46%	25%	19%
1991	55%	28%	17%
1992	42%	37%	21%
1993	50%	34%	16%

* Firearms for sale = [domestic production + imports] – exports

Comments Firearms available for sale in the United States have risen from 1,410,000 in 1946 to 7,760,000 in 1993, a 540.0% increase. However, available handguns are up 3,100.6%, according to the federal Bureau of Alcohol, Tobacco, and Firearms (ATF). There were 3,881,000 handguns available for sale in 1993, versus 119,000 in 1946.

During the same period, availability of rifles rose 283.7%; shotguns available were up 104.0%. Between 1946 and 1993, handguns as a percentage of total firearms available rose from 8.4% to 50.5%.

ATF is responsible for the regulation, taxation, and enforcement of laws regarding firearms. It annually tallies the number of guns available for sale in the United States for activities such as hunting, target shooting, and security.

These statistics only count the number of guns that were available for sale (beginning with 1946) and do not distinguish between guns sold and dealer inventory. Also, the statistics do not measure the number of firearms in circulation among civilians or include guns stocked by U.S. armed forces.

These ATF statistics also do not account for guns destroyed or made unfit for use. Also excluded are souvenir guns brought into the country after conflicts involving U.S. armed forces, guns smuggled into or out of the United States, and guns manufactured illegally.

The ATF is prohibited from compiling a national registry of firearms possession and does not collect firearms sales data. The ATF estimated in 1994 that licensed firearms dealers in the U.S. sell about 7.5 million guns per year, including about 3.5 million handguns.

Source Bureau of Alcohol, Tobacco, and Firearms, "ATF Facts," November 1994.

Contact The Department of the Treasury, Bureau of Alcohol, Tobacco, and Firearms, Washington, DC 20026. Public Affairs Branch: (202) 927-8500.

Weapons

Who Keeps a Gun at Home?

Respondents reporting a firearm in their home (percent), U.S., 1973–91.

Respondent	1973	1974	1976	1977	1980	1982	1984	1985	1987	1988	1989	1990	1991
National	47	46	47	51	48	45	45	44	46	40	46	43	40
Sex													
Male	53	51	52	55	56	54	53	54	51	50	55	53	50
Female	43	42	43	47	41	39	40	36	43	33	39	34	32
Age													
18–20 yrs.	50	34	38	54	48	51	44	39	43	33	35	40	22
21–29 yrs.	43	48	45	45	48	41	37	40	35	34	33	34	36
30–49 yrs.	51	49	52	55	50	51	48	48	51	42	48	46	40
50+ yrs.	46	44	44	49	46	44	49	44	47	42	50	42	42
Race													
White	49	48	58	53	50	48	48	46	49	43	50	45	42
Black & others	38	32	37	34	29	30	30	29	33	28	23	29	29
Region													
Northeast	22	27	29	32	27	32	32	28	31	25	32	30	28
Midwest	51	49	48	53	52	48	44	48	46	41	46	44	42
South	62	59	60	62	59	52	52	53	55	47	53	52	50
West	47	42	44	46	44	47	49	40	47	42	48	39	32
Occupation													
Professional/business	48	45	46	48	45	42	42	40	45	39	46	38	35
Clerical	42	43	40	49	45	39	41	40	45	37	37	38	35
Manual	48	48	48	52	48	49	48	48	46	41	52	50	47
Farmer	83	79	62	66	81	77	84	78	75	82	87	83	56

Weapons

Comments

Almost every demographic group in a survey on firearms possession showed a drop in gun ownership between 1973 and 1991, an opinion survey found. Only in the Northeast did ownership rise, from 22% of households in 1973 to 28% in 1991.

The information comes from the National Opinion Research Center and the Roper Center for Public Opinion Research.

The federal government does not have the authority to require national registration of gun owners, and so no accurate national count of the number of guns in circulation exists. Information from this annual survey, however, helps give an indication as to how common gun ownership is among different sectors of the American population.

The survey poses the question: "Do you happen to have in your home or garage any guns or revolvers?" If the survey's sample represents all households in the nation, it is possible to estimate how common gun ownership is.

For instance, the U.S. Bureau of the Census counted 95,669,000 households in 1990. If 43% of those households each had just one firearm that year, then there would have been over 41 million guns in circulation. Such an estimate, however, is likely to be inaccurate since it assumes the selected sample group is perfectly representative of the nation. The estimate also fails to account for the ownership or condition of the firearms and has no way of counting multiple guns in the same household.

Although national gun ownership registration is prohibited, some people have accused federal agents of defying federal laws by computerizing lists of firearms buyers from dealer records. Such violations reportedly have no penalties and allow individuals no chance of seeking justice through the legal system.

Source

The National Opinion Research Center and the Roper Center for Public Opinion Research, as cited by the U.S. Department of Justice, Bureau of Justice Statistics, *Sourcebook of Criminal Justice Statistics—1992*, (Washington, DC: U.S. Government Printing Office, 1993), p. 209.

Contact

U.S. Department of Justice, Bureau of Justice Statistics Clearinghouse, Box 6000, Rockville, MD 20850. (800) 732-3277.

Weapons

What Weapons Have Murderers Used Most Often?

Percent distribution* of murders and nonnegligent manslaughters in the U.S. known to police, 1964–93.
(A nonnegligent manslaughter is another type of willful killing and excludes accidents).

Year	Total Number of Murders and Nonnegligent Manslaughters	Firearm	Cutting or Stabbing Instrument	Blunt Object	Personal Weapons†	Other‡	Unknown or Not Stated
1964	7,990	55	24	5	10	3	2
1965	8,773	57	23	6	10	3	1
1966	9,552	59	22	5	9	2	1
1967	11,114	63	20	5	9	2	1
1968	12,503	65	18	6	8	2	1
1969	13,575	65	19	4	8	3	1
1970	13,649	66	18	4	8	3	1
1971	16,183	66	19	4	8	2	1
1972	15,832	66	19	4	8	2	1
1973	17,123	66	17	5	8	2	2
1974	18,632	67	17	5	8	1	1
1975	18,642	65	17	5	9	2	2
1976	16,605	64	18	5	8	2	3
1977	18,033	62	19	5	8	2	3
1978	18,714	64	19	5	8	2	3
1979	20,591	63	19	5	8	2	3
1980	21,860	62	19	5	8	2	4
1981	20,053	62	19	5	7	2	3
1982	19,485	60	21	5	8	2	3
1983	18,673	58	22	6	9	2	3
1984	16,689	59	21	6	8	3	4
1985	17,545	59	21	6	8	3	4
1986	19,257	59	20	6	8	2	4
1987	17,859	59	20	6	8	2	4
1988	18,269	61	19	6	8	2	4
1989	18,954	62	18	6	7	2	4
1990	20,273	64	17	5	9	2	4
1991	21,676	66	16	5	7	2	4
1992	22,716	68	15	5	6	2	5
1993	23,271	70	13	4	6	2	5

* Percents may not add to 100% because of rounding.
† Includes beatings, strangulations, and pushing someone to their death.
‡ Includes arson, poison, explosives, narcotics, asphyxiation, and drowning.

Weapons

Comments Use of firearms in U.S. homicides rose from 55% of cases in 1964 to 70% in 1993, according to the Federal Bureau of Investigation.

The FBI's Uniform Crime Reporting (UCR) program said total homicides rose from 7,990 in 1964 to 23,271 in 1993. There were drops in every other category of weapon defined (cutting or stabbing instruments, blunt objects, personal weapons, and other). The only other rise was in the category for weapons unknown; here there was a rise from 2% to 5%.

UCR requests that detailed information be transmitted to the FBI whenever a murder is committed. The number of agencies reporting and the populations represented vary from year to year. Also, the actual number of offenses shown may differ from other tables that reflect only the initial reports on the offenses.

Source U.S. Department of Justice, Federal Bureau of Investigation, *Crime in the United States* (various years) as cited by Bureau of Justice Statistics, *Sourcebook of Criminal Justice Statistics—1992*, (Washington, DC: U.S. Government Printing Office, 1993), p. 381. U.S. Department of Justice, Federal Bureau of Investigation, *Crime in the United States, 1993*, p. 18.

Contact U.S. Department of Justice, Federal Bureau of Investigation, Uniform Crime Reports, Criminal Justice Information Services Division, Washington, DC 20535. Information Dissemination: (202) 324-5015.

Weapons

What Happens in a Confrontation with an Armed Robber?

The effects of self-protective measures on the outcome of robberies in the U.S. during 1973–92. Percent of confrontational robberies that resulted in property loss, injury, and serious injury, by weapon offender used.

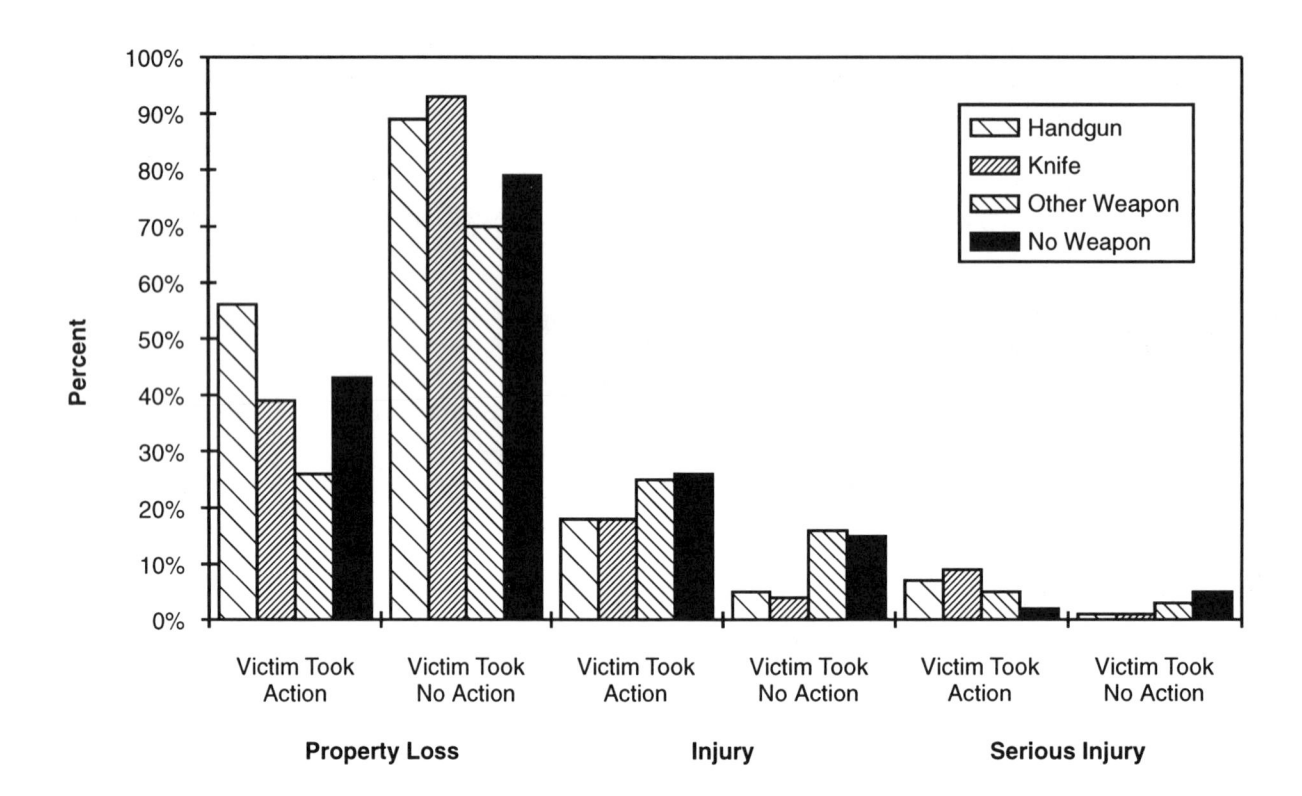

Robbery Outcome	Handgun	Knife	Other Weapon	No Weapon
Property Loss				
Victim took action	56	39	26	43
Victim took no action	89	93	70	79
Injury				
Victim took action	18	18	25	26
Victim took no action	5	4	16	15
Serious Injury				
Victim took action	7	9	5	2
Victim took no action	1	1	3	5

Comments

Fighting back against a robber may reduce the chances for property loss but increases the likelihood that the victim will be injured.

A Bureau of Justice Statistics (BJS) survey of robberies between 1973 and 1992 shows that property losses were lower in every category when the victim fought back. The study was broken down according to crimes committed with handguns, knives, other weapons, or no weapons. When the robber had a gun, property losses were greatest, whether the victim fought back or not. A victim who did not fight back stood far less risk of injury in all categories. All of the injuries listed in the study were nonfatal.

The effectiveness of a victim's defensive response depended on what type of weapon the offender had. For example, whenever the victim took defensive action, property loss occurred most frequently when the robber used a handgun. Injuries occurred most frequently to victims who took action when the offenders used no weapons or weapons other than handguns or knives (including rifles and shotguns). Serious injury (requiring two or more days of hospitalization) occurred most often when the victim took action against an offender armed with a knife.

Source

U.S. Department of Justice, Bureau of Justice Statistics. *Highlights from 20 Years of Surveying Crime Victims* (Washington, DC: U.S. Government Printing Office, 1993), p. 30.

Contact

U.S. Department of Justice, Bureau of Justice Statistics Clearinghouse, Box 6000, Rockville, MD 20850. (800) 732-3277.

Weapons

Civilian Justifiable Homicides, by Weapon, 1989–93

Reported number of criminals killed by private citizens in the U.S. during the commission of a felony.

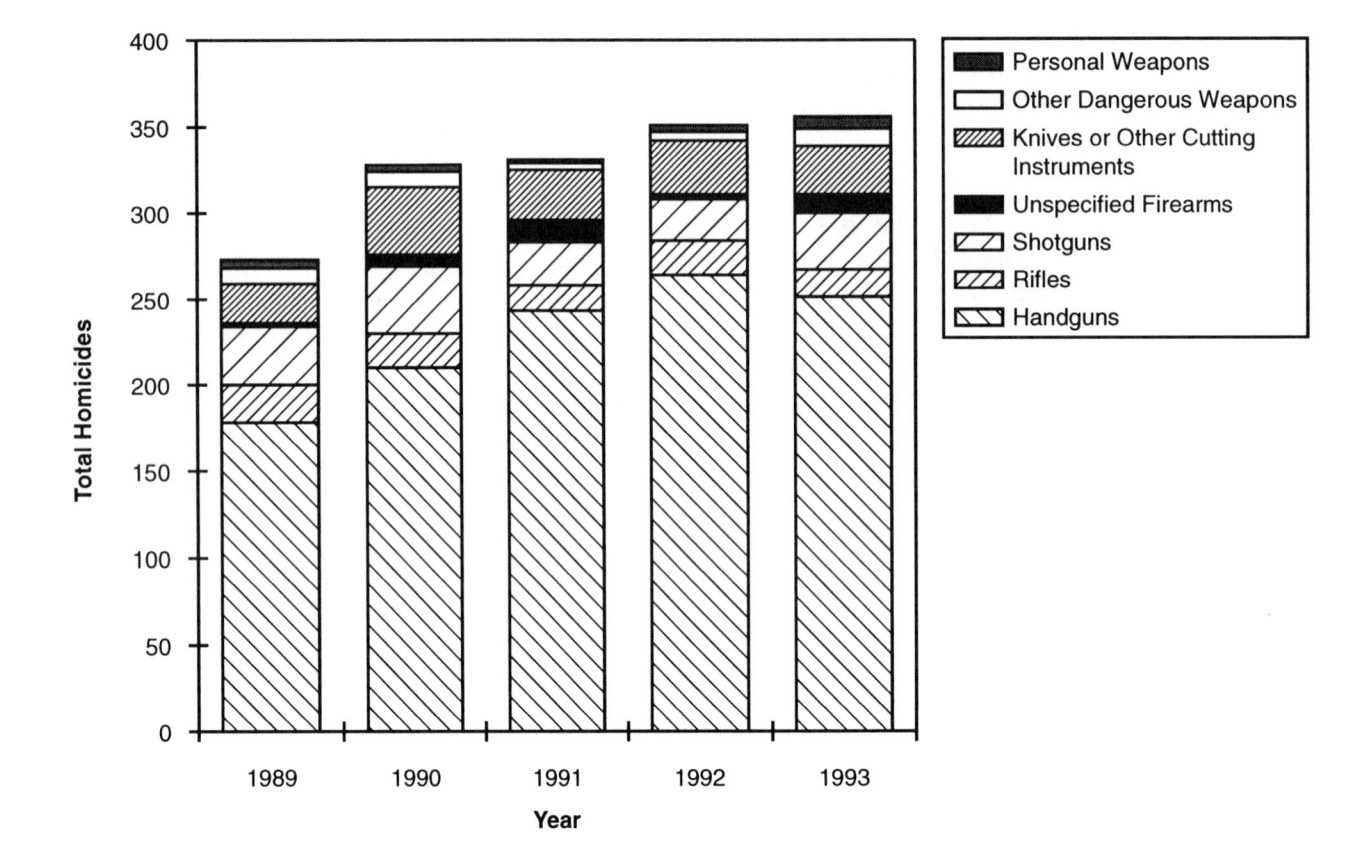

Type of Weapon	1989	1990	1991	1992	1993
All firearms	236	276	296	311	311
Handguns	178	210	243	264	251
Rifles	22	20	15	20	16
Shotguns	34	39	25	24	33
Unspecified firearms	2	7	13	3	11
Knives or other cutting instruments	23	39	29	31	28
Other dangerous weapons	9	9	4	5	10
Personal weapons	5	4	2	4	7
Total	273	328	331	351	356

Weapons

Comments Studies suggest that Federal Bureau of Investigation counting methods underestimate the number of justifiable homicides each year.

Several criminologists have studied statistics to more accurately measure the number of criminals annually killed by civilians in self-defense. These estimates implied that 7–13% of all homicides committed in 1980 by private citizens were justifiable.

If this range is applied to the 24,526 homicides reported in 1993, the number of justifiable cases may have been between 1,700 and 3,200. This is significantly higher than the FBI's count of 356.

The FBI's Uniform Crime Report system says a justifiable homicide happens when a private citizen kills a criminal in the act of the felony. Such incidents are counted separately and are not included in annual murder totals.

These numbers may seem tiny compared to the annual number of murders, which ranged between about 21,500 in 1989 and 24,700 in 1991.

Reporting differences help account for why the FBI counts so few homicides by private citizens as justifiable. First, law enforcement agencies often underreport the number of homicides committed by civilians in self-defense. Police often avoid prosecuting these civilians to save time and resources. Also, FBI reports are based on preliminary investigations. Whenever a self-defense homicide takes place but police initially report it as a criminal murder, the FBI records it as such. The FBI does not adjust its records to account for the later change.

Source U.S. Department of Justice, Federal Bureau of Investigation, *Crime in the United States, 1993* (Washington, DC: U.S. Government Printing Office, 1994), p. 22.

Kleck, Gary. *Point Blank: Guns and Violence in America* (New York: Aldine De Gruyter, 1991), pp. 111–119.

Contact U.S. Department of Justice, Federal Bureau of Investigation, Uniform Crime Reports, Criminal Justice Information Services Division, Washington, DC 20535. Information Dissemination: (202) 324-5015.

Gun Owners of America, 8001 Forbes Place, Suite 102, Springfield, VA 22151. (703) 321-8585.

Handgun Control Inc., 1225 I St. NW, Suite 1100, Washington, DC 20005. (202) 898-0792.

Self-Protective Measures Employed by Victims

Percent distribution of various aggressive and passive self-protective measures used by U.S. victims in 1992.

Self-Protective Measure	Male	Female	White	Black	Total
Ran away or hid	19.4	19.9	19.0	21.0	19.6
Resisted or captured offender	21.9	15.4	18.8	19.5	19.0
Persuaded or appeased offender	14.3	13.4	14.6	12.3	13.9
Got help or gave alarm	7.2	16.3	10.8	12.7	11.3
Attacked offender without weapon	13.8	7.8*	11.1	11.2*	11.1
Took another method	11.0	10.0	11.4	8.2	10.6
Scared or warned offender	6.1	10.8	8.3	7.1	8.3
Screamed from pain or fear	0.7*	4.7	2.1	4.9	2.5
Threatened offender without weapon	2.3	0.7	1.7*	1.0	1.6*
Attacked offender with weapon	1.7	0.8	1.1	1.6	1.3
Threatened offender with weapon	1.6	0.2	1.1*	0.3	1.0*
Total number of self-protective measures	3,858,440	3,184,850	5,597,820	1,232,150	7,043,300

* Estimate based on about 10 or fewer sample cases.

Weapons

Comments

About 72% of all victims of violent crime took some self-protective measures in 1992, according to the National Crime Victimization Survey (NCVS). There were 7,043,300 of these self-protective cases, 5,597,820 of them involving whites. Males were more likely than women to take self-protective action (3,858,440 cases, versus 3,184,850).

Self-protective methods ranged from running away to physically attacking the criminal.

The most frequent self-protective measure taken was one of the more passive methods — running away or hiding. It was used in 19.6% of all cases. This was the most common method used among females, and for both blacks and whites. It was the second most common method used by males.

Resisting or capturing an offender can employ both passive and aggressive tactics and was the most common method used by males. Blacks were slightly more likely to use this self-protective method than whites (19.5% of cases, versus 18.8%).

The most aggressive methods, such as attacking or threatening an offender either with or without a weapon were used least often. The openly aggressive self-protective method used most often was attacking an offender without a weapon (11.1% of all cases).

NCVS annually polls over 100,000 U.S. resident citizens over age 12 about their experiences with reported and unreported violent crimes. Homicides are not included because the victims cannot be interviewed.

Source

U.S. Department of Justice, Bureau of Justice Statistics. *Criminal Victimization in the United States, 1992* (Washington, DC: U.S. Government Printing Office, 1994),

Contact

U.S. Department of Justice, Bureau of Justice Statistics Clearinghouse, Box 6000, Rockville, MD 20850. (800) 732-3277.

Weapons

Self-Defense with Firearms, 1987–92

The average annual number of victimizations throughout the U.S. in which victims used guns to defend themselves or their property.

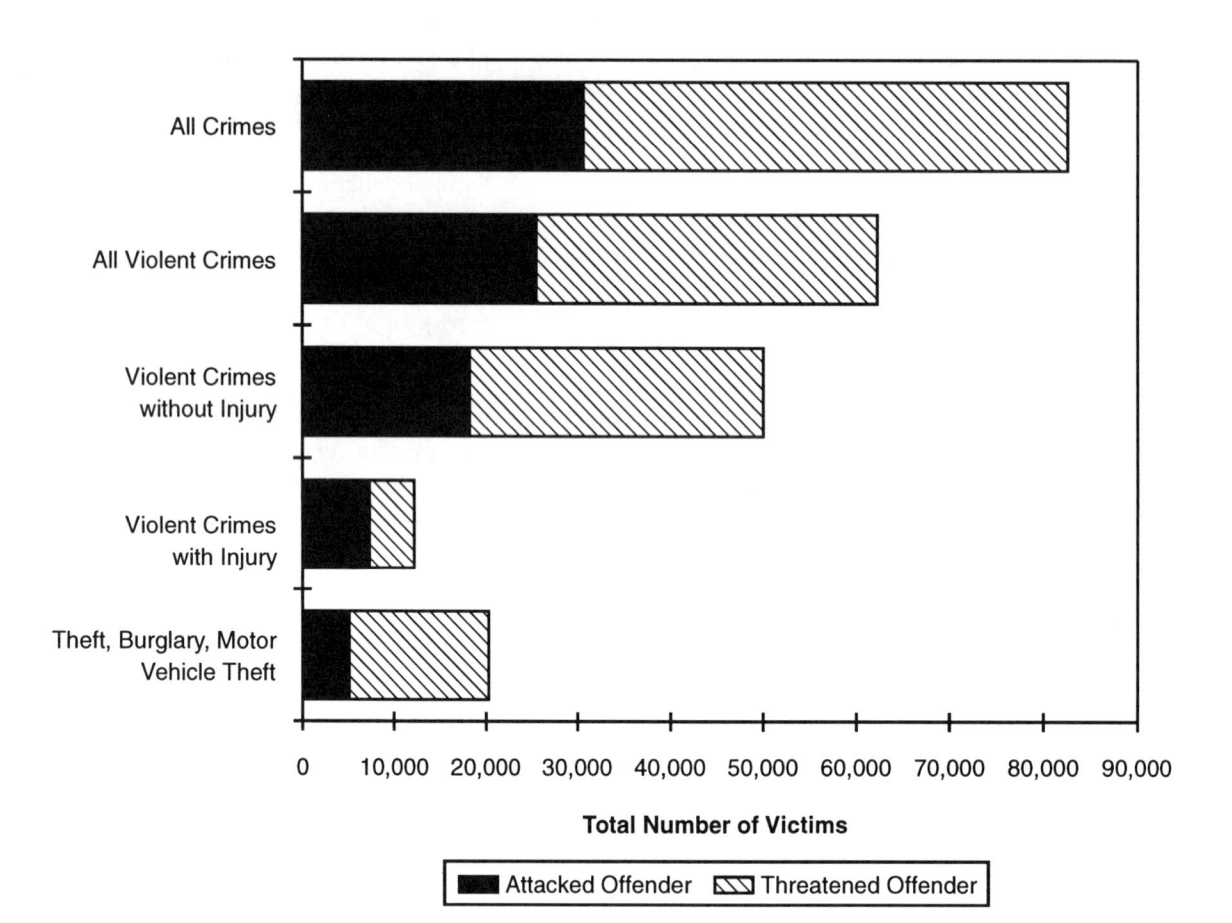

Total Number of Victims

■ Attacked Offender ▨ Threatened Offender

Type of Crime	Attacked Offender	Threatened Offender	Total *
All crimes	30,600	51,900	82,500
Theft, burglary, motor vehicle theft	5,100	15,200	20,300
Violent crimes	25,500	36,700	62,200
With injury	7,300	4,900	12,100
Without injury	18,200	31,800	50,000

* Details may not add to total because of rounding. Includes victimizations in which offenders were unarmed. Excludes homicides.

Weapons

Comments Victims who use firearms to defend themselves often prevent crimes from being completed. Therefore, incidents involving the self-defensive use of firearms often go unrecorded. Criminologists have estimated that law-abiding citizens use firearms to protect themselves against criminals 606,000 to 2,400,000 times per year.

The National Crime Victimization Survey (NCVS) reports that from 1987 to 1992 there were about 82,500 incidents annually in which victims with guns defended themselves against lawbreakers. These statistics do not include incidents in which the victims just showed guns to the offenders as a method of self-protection. NCVS says about 37%, or 30,600, of the victims using guns for self-defense attacked offenders. The remaining 63% used their firearms to threaten offenders.

Victims of violent crimes were more likely to attack criminals with weapons than were those involved in property crimes. Victims attacked using firearms in 25,500 of 62,200 violent crime cases. They attacked in only 5,100 of 20,300 property crimes.

There were 12,100 victims injured during the 62,200 violent crimes in which they defended themselves. They were more likely to be hurt while attacking the criminals rather than just using their guns as threats (7,300 cases, versus 4,900). Those escaping injury were more likely to use guns only as threats.

It is important to remember that the information presented here is a generalization. Many factors can affect individual crimes and their results — including injuries.

NCVS annually polls over 100,000 U.S. resident citizens over age 12 about their experiences with reported and unreported violent crimes. Homicides are not included because the victims cannot be interviewed.

Source U.S. Department of Justice, Bureau of Justice Statistics, "Guns and Crime" (Washington, DC: U.S. Government Printing Office, April 1994).

Kleck, Gary. *Point Blank: Guns and Violence in America* (New York: Aldine De Gruyter, 1991), pp. 106–108.

Suter, Edgar A., M.D. "'Assault Weapons' Revisited—An Analysis of the AMA Report," Journal of the Medical Association of Georgia, May 1994, pp. 281–289.

Contact U.S. Department of Justice, Bureau of Justice Statistics Clearinghouse, Box 6000, Rockville, MD 20850. (800) 732-3277.

Weapons

What Kinds of Weapons Do Robbers Like to Use?

Percent distribution* of robberies in the U.S. known to police, by type of weapon used, 1974–93.

Year	Total Number of Robberies	Firearm	Knife or Other Cutting Instrument	Other Weapon	Strong-Armed
1974	422,989	45	13	8	34
1975	444,937	45	12	8	35
1976	410,651	43	13	8	36
1977	391,128	42	13	8	37
1978	408,358	41	13	9	37
1979	458,759	40	13	9	38
1980	530,070	40	13	9	38
1981	548,038	40	13	9	38
1982	522,823	40	14	9	37
1983	489,227	37	14	10	40
1984	435,732	36	13	9	42
1985	461,725	35	13	9	42
1986	531,468	34	14	10	43
1987	498,632	33	14	10	44
1988	485,522	33	14	10	43
1989	562,340	33	13	10	43
1990	608,464	37	12	10	42
1991	653,432	40	11	9	40
1992	672,478	40	11	10	40
1993	659,757	42	10	10	38

* Details may not add to 100% because of rounding.

Weapons

Comments Firearms were the most common weapons used for robberies from the mid-1970s to early 1980s, according to Federal Bureau of Investigation statistics. The likelihood of a firearm being used to commit a robbery declined throughout the 1980s as the frequency of strong-arm tactics increased. Strong-arm methods include things like punching, beating, and shoving.

The total number of robberies also declined during the 1980s. By the late 1980s, however, the frequency of firearms usage in robberies again began to rise, as did the total number of robberies.

There may be a relationship between how often firearms are used in robberies and the total number of robberies. But it is not really possible to tell by these statistics which factor (if either) caused the other to change first.

For example, someone might claim that robberies have increased in recent years because firearms are being used more often to commit the crimes. The use of a gun might make the robbery seem easier to complete for someone who otherwise would not try it. However, if that were the only reason, the number of robberies should have fallen from the mid-1970s to the early 1980s, because firearms use in robberies fell during that period.

The FBI annually compiles statistics regarding weapon usage in robberies committed across the United States through its Uniform Crime Reporting System. Although the number of reporting agencies and the population represented varies from year to year, it is possible to get an idea about which weapons are used most frequently to commit robberies.

Source U.S. Department of Justice, Federal Bureau of Investigation, *Crime in the United States, 1974*, pp. 26, 160; *1975*, pp. 26, 160; *1976*, pp. 21, 153; *1977*, pp. 19, 153; *1978*, pp. 19, 170; *1979*, pp. 18, 170; *1980*, pp. 19, 173; *1981*, pp. 18, 144; *1982*, pp. 18, 149; *1983*, pp. 18, 152; *1984*, pp. 18, 145; *1985*, pp. 18, 147; *1986*, pp. 18, 147; *1987*, pp. 18, 146; *1988*, pp. 21, 150; *1989*, pp. 20, 154; *1990*, pp. 21, 156; *1991*, pp. 29, 192; as cited by Bureau of Justice Statistics, *Sourcebook of Criminal Justice Statistics—1992* (Washington, DC: U.S. Government Printing Office), p. 396, table 3.154. U.S. Department of Justice, Federal Bureau of Investigation, *Crime in the United States, 1992*, pp. 26, 194; *1993*, pp. 26, 194 (Washington, DC: U.S. Government Printing Office).

Contact Federal Bureau of Investigation, Criminal Justice Information Services Division, Programs Support Section, Washington, DC 20535. Information Dissemination: (202) 324-5015

Weapons

Robberies by State and Type of Weapon Used in 1993

The number of robberies committed in each state during 1993 and the percent distribution of weapons used to commit the robberies.

State	Number of Reporting Law Enforcement Agencies	Population Served (1,000s)	Total Robberies	Robbery Rate per 100,000 Residents	Firearms	Knives or Cutting Instruments	Other Weapons	Strong-Armed
Alabama	5	954	3,883	407.0	27%	24%	24%	25%
Alaska	27	576	713	123.8	37%	11%	8%	44%
Arizona	85	3,738	6,267	167.7	41%	9%	9%	41%
Arkansas	180	2,415	3,017	124.9	48%	8%	8%	36%
California	736	31,154	126,314	405.5	41%	10%	12%	37%
Colorado	197	3,236	4,065	125.6	35%	11%	11%	43%
Connecticut	100	2,786	6,454	231.7	39%	10%	8%	43%
Delaware	3	377	209	55.4	22%	8%	8%	62%
District of Columbia	2	578	7,107	1,229.6	44%	7%	4%	45%
Florida	415	12,622	46,523	366.4	40%	7%	7%	46%
Georgia	340	5,849	15,689	268.2	54%	6%	13%	27%
Hawaii	5	1,172	1,214	103.6	11%	8%	2%	79%
Idaho	69	859	137	15.9	32%	20%	12%	36%
Illinois *	422	9,793	46,619	476.0	43%	9%	7%	41%
Indiana	219	3,702	5,999	162.0	47%	9%	6%	38%
Iowa	140	1,814	621	34.2	21%	15%	16%	48%
Kansas *	257	2,389	3,255	136.2	42%	9%	15%	34%
Kentucky	465	3,325	3,006	90.4	39%	11%	9%	41%
Louisiana	76	2,954	10,764	364.4	64%	6%	7%	23%
Maine	140	1,196	263	22.0	25%	11%	7%	57%
Maryland	150	4,964	21,580	434.7	56%	7%	6%	31%
Massachusetts	221	4,934	9,328	189.1	25%	20%	10%	45%
Michigan	555	8,789	22,028	250.6	54%	6%	15%	25%
Minnesota	294	4,466	5,085	113.9	25%	9%	8%	58%
Mississippi	74	1,078	2,555	237.0	50%	6%	7%	37%
Missouri	208	4,160	12,310	295.9	50%	7%	7%	36%
Montana	51	377	34	9.0	50%	21%	3%	26%
Nebraska	244	1,209	252	20.8	21%	12%	7%	60%
Nevada	21	1,206	4,281	355.0	51%	9%	6%	34%
New Hampshire	89	957	284	296.7	16%	14%	6%	64%
New Jersey	516	7,873	23,319	296.2	35%	10%	8%	47%
New Mexico	39	905	1,772	195.8	46%	14%	9%	31%
New York	619	17,238	101,505	588.8	37%	15%	10%	38%
North Carolina	432	6,651	13,110	197.1	44%	9%	10%	37%
North Dakota	83	587	50	8.5	12%	12%	60%	16%
Ohio	290	7,399	18,585	251.2	42%	6%	9%	43%
Oklahoma	281	3,188	3,933	123.4	41%	8%	7%	44%

[Continued]

Weapons

Robberies by State and Type of Weapon Used in 1993

[Continued]

State	Number of Reporting Law Enforcement Agencies	Population Served (1,000s)	Total Robberies	Robbery Rate per 100,000 Residents	Firearms	Knives or Cutting Instruments	Other Weapons	Strong-Armed
Oregon	185	2,930	3,896	133.0	32%	11%	9%	48%
Pennsylvania	664	9,067	19,562	215.8	43%	8%	5%	44%
Rhode Island	43	971	1,007	103.7	25%	12%	8%	55%
South Carolina	181	3,587	6,785	189.2	37%	11%	11%	41%
South Dakota	60	546	97	17.8	26%	7%	8%	59%
Tennessee	141	3,569	10,776	301.9	53%	7%	7%	33%
Texas	874	17,980	40,375	224.6	48%	9%	8%	35%
Utah	103	1,791	1,090	60.9	32%	9%	12%	47%
Vermont	12	366	23	6.3	9%	22%	43%	26%
Virginia	406	6,491	9,216	142.0	48%	8%	8%	36%
Washington	199	4,897	7,076	144.5	33%	9%	9%	49%
West Virginia	297	1,818	781	43.0	37%	8%	6%	49%
Wisconsin	319	5,016	5,709	113.8	53%	8%	5%	34%
Wyoming	61	398	57	14.3	44%	12%	11%	33%

*Information for 1993 was incomplete or unavailable. Figures shown are for 1992.

Comments The District of Columbia (1,229.6), New York (588.8), Maryland (434.7), and Alabama (407.0) ranked the highest in robberies per 100,000 inhabitants during 1993. Illinois also ranked high at 476.0 but the numbers listed are from 1992, said the Federal Bureau of Investigation.

The states that had the lowest frequencies of robberies per 100,000 residents were Vermont (6.3), North Dakota (8.5), Montana (9.0), Wyoming (14.3), and Idaho (15.9). Many of the states with low robbery rates also had very few robberies take place. Since the populations of the states vary, it is possible for one state to have more robberies than another but a lower robbery rate.

The usage of certain weapons to commit robbery is more common in some states than in others. For instance, the percentage of robberies committed with guns was highest in Louisiana (64%), Maryland (56%), Georgia (54%), Michigan (54%), and Tennessee (53%). Guns were used least frequently in Vermont (9%), Hawaii (11%), North Dakota (12%), New Hampshire (16%), and Iowa (21%).

Some states, like Maryland, had high robbery rates and many robberies involving guns. Other states, like Michigan, had much lower robbery rates, even though high percentages of those robberies involved guns.

Source U.S. Department of Justice, Federal Bureau of Investigation, *Crime in the United States, 1992* (Washington, DC: U.S. Government Printing Office, 1993), p. 203; *1993* (1994), p. 202.

Contact U.S. Department of Justice, Federal Bureau of Investigation, Uniform Crime Reports, Criminal Justice Information Services Division, Washington, DC 20535. Information Dissemination: (202) 324-5015.

What Kinds of Weapons Are Used in Aggravated Assaults?

Aggravated assaults in the U.S. by type of weapon used, 1964–93.
Percent distribution of aggravated assaults known to police.*

Year	Total Number of Assaults	Firearms	Knives or Cutting Instruments	Other Weapons (Clubs, Blunt Objects, etc.)	Personal Weapons
1964	203,050	15	40	23	22
1965	215,330	17	36	22	25
1966	235,330	19	34	22	25
1967	257,160	21	33	22	24
1968	286,700	23	31	24	22
1969	311,090	24	30	25	22
1970	334,970	24	28	24	23
1971	368,760	25	27	24	24
1972	393,090	25	26	23	25
1973	420,650	26	25	23	27
1974	456,210	25	24	23	27
1975	492,620	25	24	25	27
1976	500,530	24	24	26	27
1977	534,350	23	23	27	26
1978	571,460	22	23	28	27
1979	629,480	23	22	28	27
1980	672,650	24	22	28	27
1981	663,900	24	22	28	26
1982	669,480	22	23	28	26
1983	653,290	21	24	29	26
1984	685,350	21	23	31	25
1985	723,250	21	23	31	25
1986	834,320	21	22	32	25
1987	855,090	21	21	32	25
1988	910,090	21	20	31	27
1989	951,710	22	20	32	27
1990	1,054,860	23	20	32	26
1991	1,092,740	24	18	31	27
1992	1,126,970	25	18	31	26
1993	1,135,100	25	18	31	26

* May not add to 100% because of rounding.

Comments

Firearms grew as the weapon of choice in aggravated assaults from 15% of cases in 1964 to 25% in 1993, according to the Federal Bureau of Investigation. Firearm use showed the greatest rate of increase among the arms categories, which also included personal weapons such as fists and feet, clubs, and knives.

Personal weapons topped the list, just ahead of firearms at 26% of cases in 1993. Knives and other sharp objects, which led the list at 40% of cases in 1964, fell to 18% usage by 1993. Clubs and other blunt objects rose from 23% of cases in 1964 to 31% in 1993.

The increases and decreases in weapons use were not steadily up or down. Use of particular weapons rose and fell during the survey period. The number of aggravated assaults increased more than five-fold during the period of the study, from 203,050 in 1964 to 1,135,100 in 1993.

An aggravated assault is an unlawful attack aimed at inflicting severe injury. This type of assault usually involves a weapon or the means to inflict great injury or even death.

The totals also include attempted assaults since it is not necessary that an injury result when a weapon is present. If an attempted assault were successfully completed, the use of a gun, knife, or other weapon could and probably would have resulted in serious personal injury.

Source

U.S. Department of Justice, Federal Bureau of Investigation, *Crime in the United States*, 1964 to 1993 annuals (Washington, DC: U.S. Government Printing Office). Number of assaults provided by FBI's Programs Support Section, Criminal Justice Information Services Division.

U.S. Department of Justice, Bureau of Justice Statistics, *Sourcebook of Criminal Justice Statistics—1992* (Washington, DC: U.S. Government Printing Office, 1993), p. 398.

Contact

U.S. Department of Justice, Federal Bureau of Investigation, Uniform Crime Reports, Criminal Justice Information Services Division, Washington, DC 20535. Information Dissemination: (202) 324-5015.

U.S. Department of Justice, Bureau of Justice Statistics Clearinghouse, Box 6000, Rockville, MD 20850. (800) 732-3277.

Aggravated Assaults by State and Type of Weapon Used, 1993

Percent distribution of weapon types used to commit aggravated assaults in each state.

State	Reported Aggravated Assaults *	Firearms	Knives or Cutting Instruments	Other Weapons	Personal Weapons
Alabama	23,144	11.2%	9.0%	9.2%	70.6%
Alaska	3,124	23.3%	21.5%	21.9%	33.3%
Arizona	19,052	37.6%	15.4%	26.1%	20.9%
Arkansas	9,989	31.4%	14.4%	22.5%	31.7%
California	193,773	23.2%	12.6%	26.9%	37.4%
Colorado	13,451	29.5%	16.9%	30.5%	23.1%
Connecticut	7,507	14.2%	16.3%	36.0%	33.5%
Delaware	981	19.0%	26.8%	39.0%	15.2%
District of Columbia	9,003	24.1%	23.7%	42.7%	9.5%
Florida	100,977	25.3%	18.7%	40.7%	15.3%
Georgia	25,710	29.8%	20.8%	31.2%	18.2%
Hawaii	1,408	12.4%	10.2%	21.3%	56.0%
Idaho	2,066	31.2%	20.1%	22.5%	26.2%
Illinois †	—	—	—	—	—
Indiana	13,896	19.1%	12.8%	24.2%	43.9%
Iowa	3,810	13.9%	17.8%	25.1%	43.2%
Kansas ‡	—	—	—	—	—
Kentucky	9,868	23.7%	13.3%	32.1%	30.8%
Louisiana	21,222	37.6%	17.7%	27.3%	17.5%
Maine	927	5.1%	17.0%	27.2%	50.8%
Maryland	25,133	24.7%	20.6%	38.8%	15.9%
Massachusetts	30,122	8.6%	16.6%	33.9%	40.8%
Michigan	42,800	29.3%	17.0%	40.5%	13.2%
Minnesota	7,915	26.2%	25.8%	28.6%	19.3%
Mississippi	3,537	41.4%	18.2%	19.7%	20.7%
Missouri	21,861	39.1%	14.8%	29.1%	17.0%
Montana	381	38.9%	13.7%	15.5%	32.0%
Nebraska	1,654	7.9%	19.2%	46.7%	26.2%
Nevada	4,912	21.0%	13.8%	33.5%	31.8%
New Hampshire	624	11.5%	16.8%	19.1%	52.6%
New Jersey	23,438	17.3%	23.0%	31.5%	28.2%
New Mexico	7,276	27.0%	15.8%	38.4%	18.8%
New York	84,169	19.9%	24.1%	33.7%	22.3%
North Carolina	29,724	31.7%	19.0%	27.2%	22.1%
North Dakota	227	7.9%	14.5%	44.1%	33.5%
Ohio	22,660	27.5%	17.5%	27.0%	28.1%
Oklahoma	14,662	27.3%	14.3%	28.3%	30.2%

[Continued]

Aggravated Assaults by State and Type of Weapon Used, 1993

[Continued]

State	Reported Aggravated Assaults *	Firearms	Knives or Cutting Instruments	Other Weapons	Personal Weapons
Oregon	9,484	23.6%	16.3%	34.0%	26.1%
Pennsylvania	19,672	21.0%	15.5%	23.3%	40.3%
Rhode Island	2,542	13.4%	18.3%	34.3%	34.1%
South Carolina	27,931	25.4%	22.5%	38.4%	13.7%
South Dakota	881	20.0%	24.0%	18.2%	37.9%
Tennessee	21,839	27.5%	17.1%	31.2%	24.2%
Texas	84,474	29.3%	19.1%	24.8%	26.8%
Utah	3,532	18.8%	17.6%	35.9%	27.7%
Vermont	189	25.4%	18.5%	28.0%	28.0%
Virginia	12,322	19.9%	22.5%	27.9%	29.8%
Washington	15,837	27.3%	16.1%	30.6%	26.0%
West Virginia	2,517	17.0%	19.6%	22.3%	41.2%
Wisconsin	6,076	22.9%	15.4%	16.6%	45.1%
Wyoming	893	14.0%	17.3%	22.0%	46.7%

* Includes only the reports of aggravated assault in 1993 that detailed weapon type. Percentages may not total 100.0% because of rounding.
† Information for 1993 was unavailable. In 1992, there were 57,395 aggravated assaults in Illinois that listed weapon type. Firearms accounted for 34.9%; knives and other cutting instruments, 22.5%; other weapons, 35.9%; and personal weapons, 6.8%.
‡ Information for 1993 was unavailable. In 1992, there were 8,273 aggravated assaults in Kansas that listed weapon type. Firearms accounted for 33.0%; knives and other cutting instruments, 16.1%; other weapons, 33.1%; and personal weapons, 17.7%.

Comments

Federal Bureau of Investigation state-by-state figures on aggravated assaults during 1993 show no clear leader as a weapon of choice among offenders. Other weapons, which include clubs and other blunt objects, were used most often in twenty-four states. Personal weapons such as fists and feet were used most often in nineteen states plus the District of Columbia.

Aggravated assaults are defined as unlawful physical attacks intended to cause severe bodily injury. Aggravated assaults usually are committed with weapons or by some other potentially lethal method. The FBI includes attempted as well as completed assaults in these statistics. The presence of a weapon implies a willingness to seriously injure the victim, even if the crime is unsuccessful.

Source

Federal Bureau of Investigation, *Crime in the United States, 1993* (Washington, DC: U.S. Government Printing Office, 1994), p. 204.

Contact

U.S. Department of Justice, Federal Bureau of Investigation, Uniform Crime Reports, Criminal Justice Information Services Division, Washington, DC 20535. Information Dissemination: (202) 324-5015.

Weapons

Weapons Violation Arrests in 1992 & 1993 by Age Group

The number of arrests made for breaking weapons violations laws throughout the U.S. in 1992 and 1993. Details are for age groups.

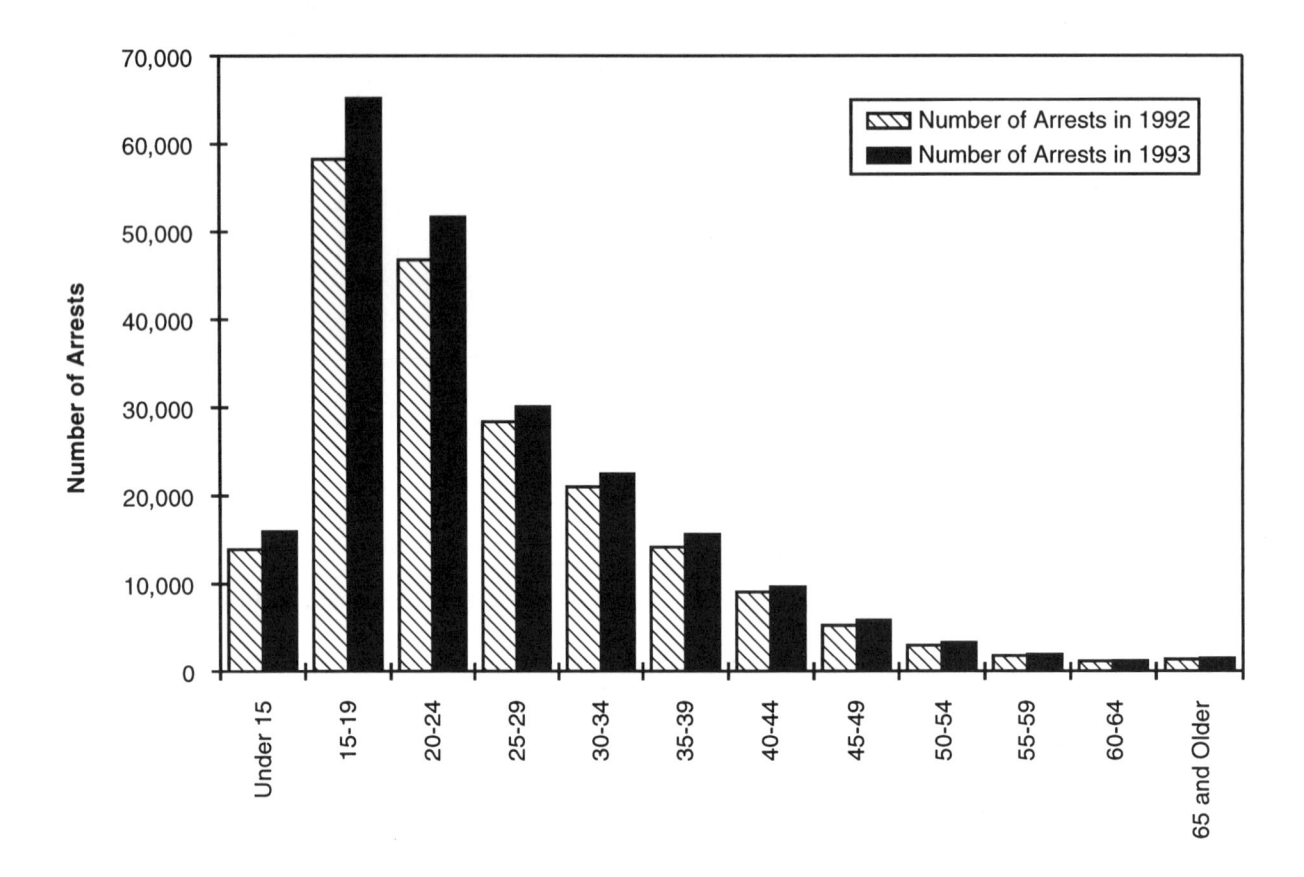

Age	Number of Arrests in 1992	Number of Arrests in 1993
Under 15	13,893	15,950
15–19	58,245	65,218
20–24	46,756	51,658
25–29	28,381	30,095
30–34	21,056	22,481
35–39	14,142	15,598
40–44	9,064	9,629
45–49	5,293	5,899
50–54	3,018	3,331
55–59	1,778	1,901
60–64	1,145	1,188
65 and older	1,345	1,447
Total	204,116	224,395

Weapons

Comments

The 15–19 and 20–24 age groups were the leaders in weapons violations during 1992 and 1993, according to the Federal Bureau of Investigation. There were 58,245 weapons arrests among those aged 15–19 in 1992 and 65,218 in 1993. The 20–24 group followed with 28,381 arrests in 1992 and 51,658 in 1992.

These groups accounted for a large part of the 204,116 total weapons violation arrests in 1992 and 224,395 in 1993.

After the 20–24 age group, numbers of violations dropped with age. The only variation was among those 65 and older. There were 1,345 violations in 1992 and 1,447 in 1993 for people 65 and older. This compares to 1,145 in 1992 and 1,188 in 1993 for those aged 60–64. The under 15 group was No. 6 in numbers of violations in 1992 and No. 5 in 1993.

Weapons violations deal with breaking laws that control deadly weapons like firearms. These violations, however, can include other things like knives, martial arts weapons, and explosives. Weapons violations involve the illegal carrying, use, possession, furnishing, and manufacture of deadly weapons or silencers. Certain types of weapons are illegal in some places or may require special licenses. Weapons violations often involve illegal firearms deals.

According to federal law, minors cannot purchase guns and firearm dealers must have federal licenses. The sale of guns through the mail and black market dealing in various weapons are also illegal. The illegal production or alteration of firearms (such as sawed-off shotguns) or prohibited accessories (such as silencers) and making illegal ammunition also are weapons violations. Carrying a weapon (openly or concealed) in public often requires a special permit, and many urban areas ban shooting firearms within city limits.

Source

U.S. Department of Justice, Federal Bureau of Investigation, *Crime in the United States, 1992* (Washington, DC: U.S. Government Printing Office, 1993), pp. 227–8; *1993* (1994), pp. 227–8.

Contact

U.S. Department of Justice, Federal Bureau of Investigation, Uniform Crime Reports, Criminal Justice Information Services Division, Washington, DC 20535. Information Dissemination: (202) 324-5015.

U.S. Department of the Treasury, Bureau of Alcohol, Tobacco, and Firearms, Washington, DC 20226. (202) 927-8500.

Weapons

Thefts of Firearms, 1987–92

Average annual number of U.S. incidents in which firearms were stolen, 1987–92.*

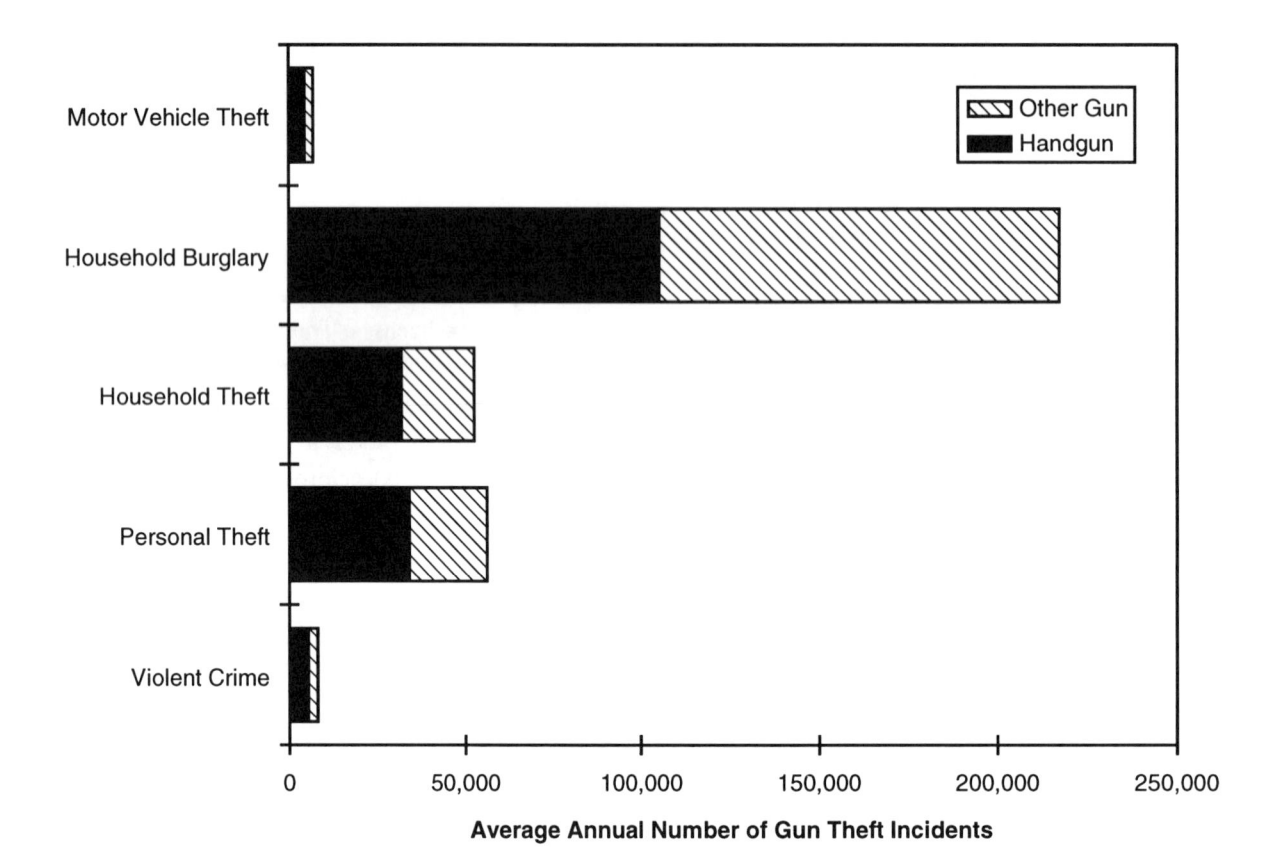

Type of Crime	Handgun	Other Gun	Total
Violent crime	5,300	2,600	7,900
Personal theft	33,900	22,300	56,200
Household theft	31,700	20,900	52,600
Household burglary	105,300	112,000	217,200
Motor vehicle theft	4,400	2,400	6,700
Total	180,500	160,200	340,700

*Detail may not add to total because of rounding. The table measures theft incidents, not the number of guns stolen.

Weapons

Comments The National Crime Victimization Survey (NCVS) reports firearms most often were stolen during home burglaries in 1987–92. Such thefts accounted for an average 217,200 of the 340,700 total gun theft incidents each year during the period.

Stolen guns are used often in violent crimes. A stolen gun often circulates through a black market network, where it can be sold or traded illegally many times. The possession of stolen guns is also common among violent juvenile criminals, since it is illegal for minors to buy guns.

NCVS only asks for types of stolen items and not item counts. Therefore, the annual number of firearms stolen probably was greater than the number of incidents.

In 53% of the firearm theft incidents, handguns were stolen (180,500 of 340,700 total). About 64% of gun thefts occurred during household burglaries (217,000). However, 32% occurred during personal or household thefts (108,800). Theft of a firearm through a larceny like personal or household theft was about equally as likely to happen at the victim's home as it was away from the home.

NCVS annually polls over 100,000 U.S. resident citizens over age 12 about their experiences with reported and unreported violent crimes. Homicides are not included because the victims cannot be interviewed.

Source U.S. Department of Justice, Bureau of Justice Statistics, "Guns and Crime" (Washington, DC: U.S. Government Printing Office, April 1994).

Contact U.S. Department of Justice, Bureau of Justice Statistics Clearinghouse, Box 6000, Rockville, MD 20850. (800) 732-3277.

Weapons

The Role of Firearms in Federal Sentences

Firearms involvement for convicted federal offenders in the U.S. whose sentences were imposed during the 12 months ending September 30, 1993.

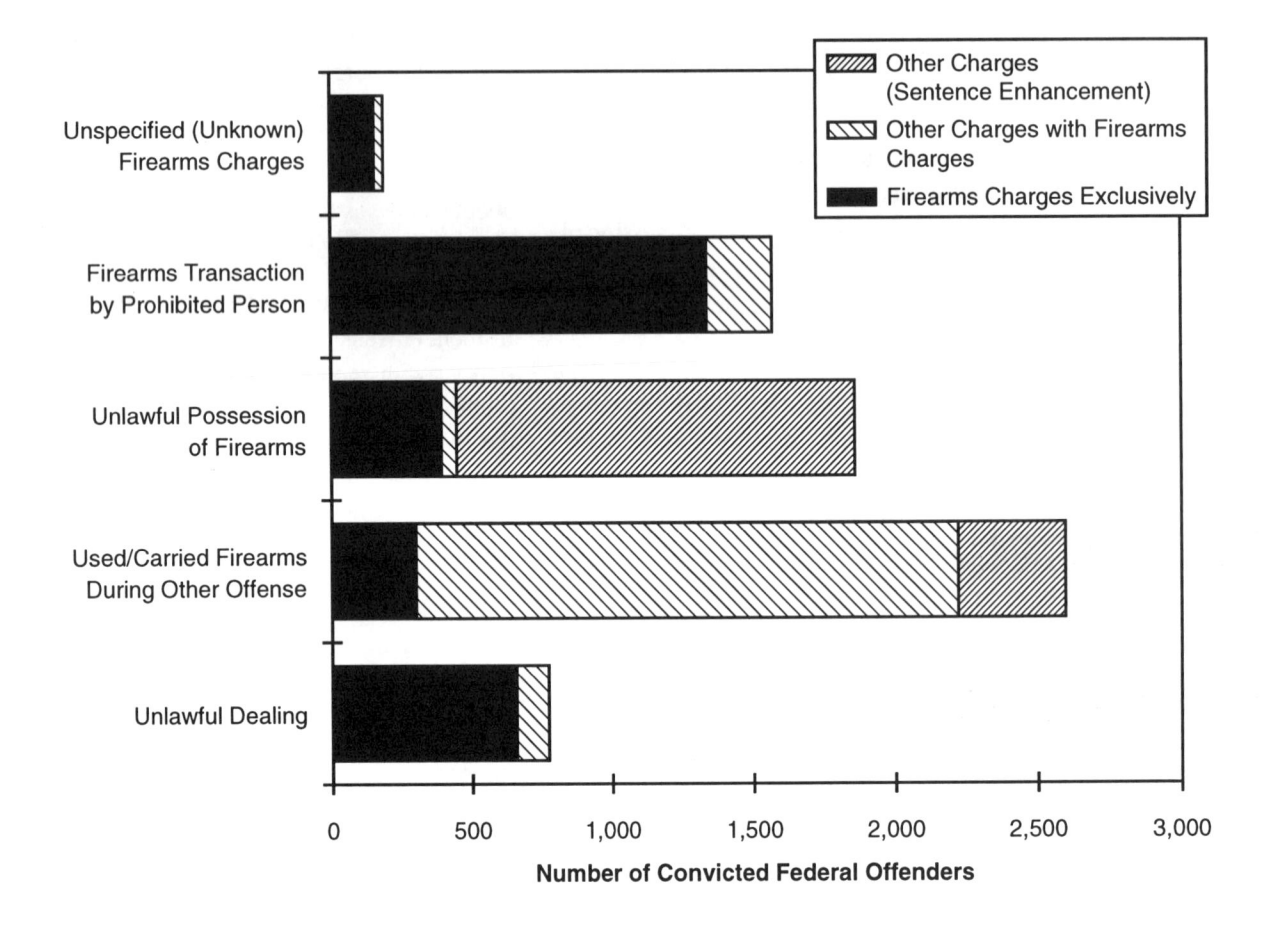

Type of Offense	Firearms Charges Exclusively	Other Charges With Firearms Charges	Other Charges (Sentence Enhancement)	Total	Percent
All offenses	—	—	—	42,107	100.0
No firearms involvement	—	—	—	35,120	83.4
Firearms involvement	2,849	2,352	1,786	6,987	16.6
Unlawful dealing	657	116	0	773	1.8
Used/carried firearms during other offense	302	1,918	376	2,596	6.2
Unlawful possession of firearms	395	53	1,410	1,858	4.4
Firearms transaction by prohibited person	1,337	232	0	1,569	3.7
Unspecified (unknown) firearms charges	158	33	0	191	0.5

Statistics on Weapons & Violence

Weapons

Comments Firearms use in federal offenses tends to increase the severity of sentences, according to the Bureau of Justice Statistics (BJS). It also said 93% of the federal offenders involved with firearms were sentenced to prison. However, only 72% of those not using firearms received prison sentences.

BJS bases its report on convictions of federal offenders charged with illegal firearms use from September 1992 to September 1993. During that period, the crimes of 6,987 federal offenders involved firearms, or about 16.6% of all federal sentences imposed during that period.

BJS said that during 1982–92 the number of federal defendants sentenced to prison with weapons offenses as their most serious crimes increased 175%, from 1,000 to 2,755. These numbers, however, do not include firearms use when a weapons offense was not the most serious crime.

The information gathered by the BJS shows several trends. For example, among all federal offenders convicted only of firearms violations, 47%, or 1,337, were persons barred from having firearms. Also, 23%, or 657, of those sentenced only on firearms charges violated federal laws that govern dealing in firearms. For those federal offenders convicted of firearms violations and who were convicted of other more serious offenses, 81.5%, or 1,918, used or carried firearms during other crimes. And 10%, or 232, were persons prohibited from having firearms.

The firearms use of offenders convicted in U.S. district courts usually is either of two types. The first includes defendants sentenced for weapons offenses, either as the most serious charges or as offenses accompanying more serious crimes, such as robbery or homicide. The other type includes defendants who received more severe sentences for carrying or possessing firearms during their crimes. This type would include sentence enhancements, used primarily for those who unlawfully possess firearms. A sentence enhancement typically occurs when a firearm is present but the person is convicted of a different offense.

Source U.S. Department of Justice, Bureau of Justice Statistics, "Federal Firearms-Related Offenses" (Washington, DC: U.S. Government Printing Office, June 1995).

Contact U.S. Department of Justice, Bureau of Justice Statistics Clearinghouse, Box 6000, Rockville, MD 20850. (800) 732-3277.

Statistics on Weapons & Violence

Weapons

Which Weapons Do Criminals Use Most Often?

Percent distribution of types of weapons used in incidents by armed offenders.
Details are for type of violent crime and weapon in the U.S. during 1992.

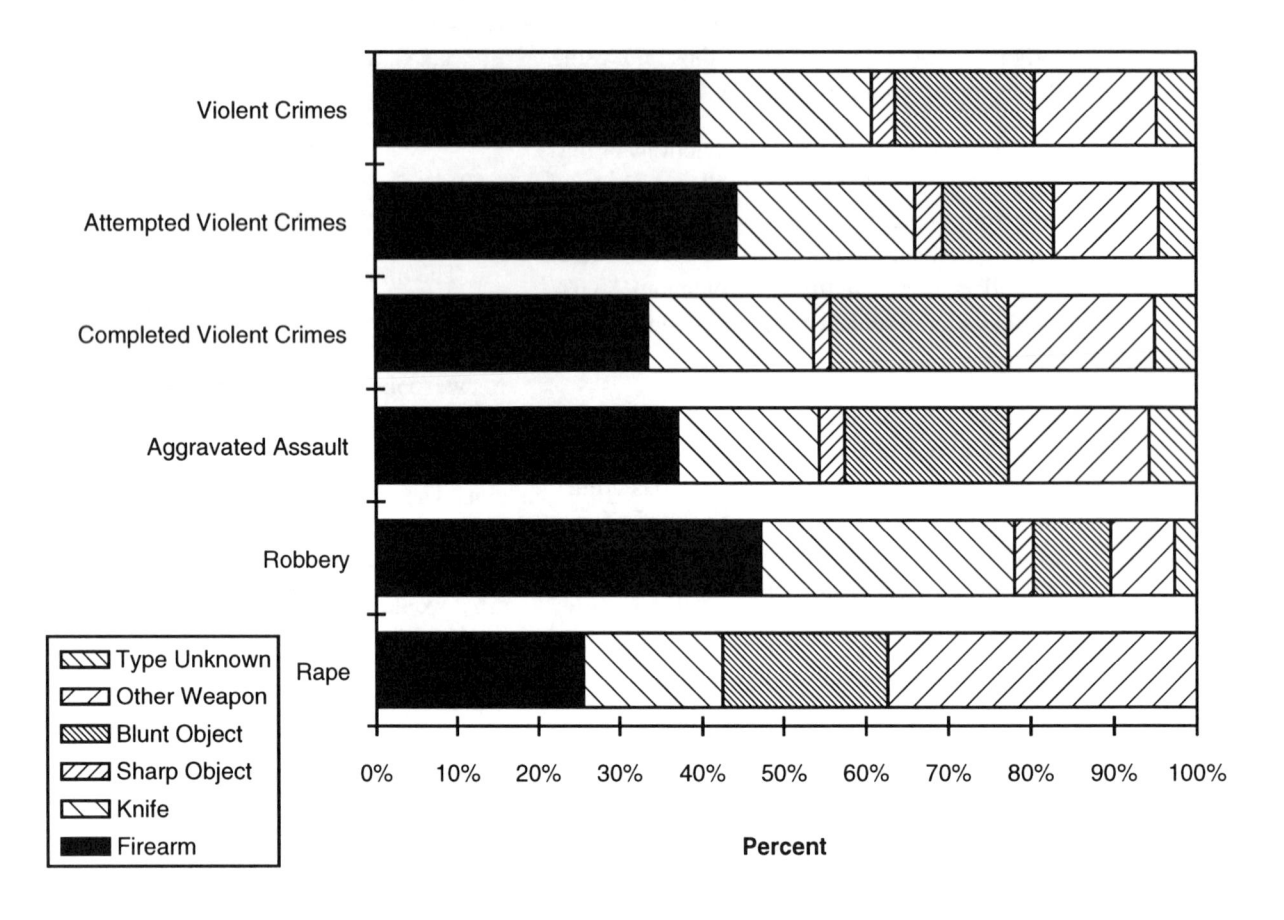

Weapon	Rape	Robbery	Aggravated Assault	Completed Violent Crimes	Attempted Violent Crimes	Violent Crimes
Firearm	25.6	47.2	37.1	33.5	44.3	39.7
Handgun	25.6	42.4	28.5	29.1	34.7	32.3
Other gun	0.0	4.9	8.6	4.3	9.6	7.4
Knife	16.9	30.8	17.3	20.2	21.7	21.1
Sharp object	0.0	2.3	3.1	2.0	3.4	2.8
Blunt object	20.2	9.3	19.9	21.6	13.4	16.9
Other weapon	37.4	7.7	16.9	17.6	12.6	14.7
Type unknown	0.0	2.7	5.8	5.1	4.6	4.8
Total number of weapons used	46,050	645,920	1,598,780	968,880	1,321,880	2,290,770

Weapons

Comments

The 1992 National Crime Victimization Survey (NCVS) found the handgun to be the weapon of choice in all categories of violent crime it studied. Handguns were used in 32.2% of violent crimes. The use of other firearms was just 7.4%

Robbery was the category in which handguns were used most often: 42.4% of cases.

After handguns, knives (21.2% of cases) and blunt objects (16.9%) were the weapons of choice overall. In specific violent crime categories, knives and blunt objects took turns ranking second and third in usage.

Of the 2,290,770 weapons used in violent crimes studied in the survey, 1,598,780 were used in aggravated assaults. Following was the robbery category, with 645,920.

NCVS annually polls over 100,000 U.S. resident citizens over age 12 about their experiences with reported and unreported violent crimes. Homicides are not included because the victims cannot be interviewed.

Source

U.S. Department of Justice, Bureau of Justice Statistics, *Criminal Victimization in the United States, 1992* (Washington, DC: U.S. Government Printing Office), p. 83.

Contact

Bureau of Justice Statistics Clearinghouse, Box 6000, Rockville, MD 20850. (800) 732-3277

Statistics on Weapons & Violence

Weapons

How Likely Is It that Someone Will Be Shot and Killed or Injured During a Crime?

Average annual number of fatal handgun crimes and nonfatal handgun crimes, 1979–87.

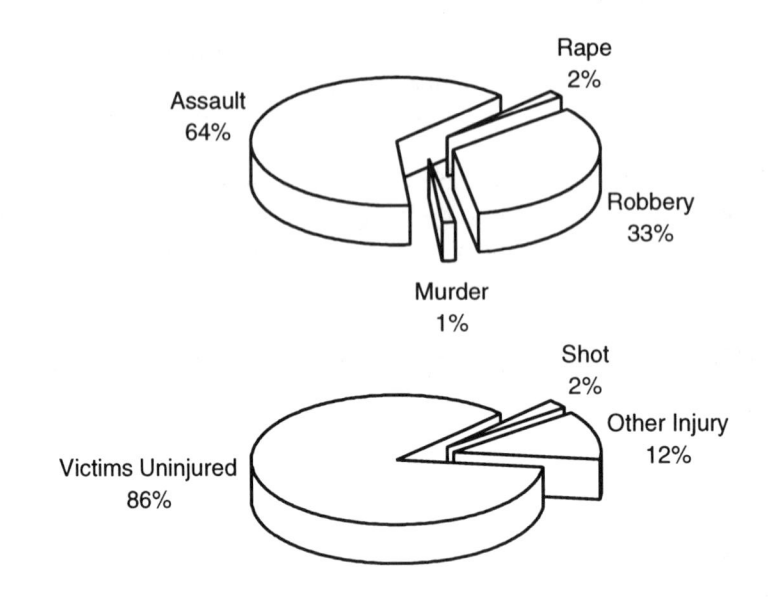

Type of Crime	Average Annual Number, 1979–87
Handgun crimes	638,900
Fatal handgun crimes	9,200
Murder	9,200
Nonfatal handgun crimes	629,700
Rape	12,100
Robbery	210,000
Assault	407,600
Victims injured	91,500
Shot	15,000
Other injury	76,400
Victims uninjured	538,200

Weapons

Comments Between 1979 and 1987, there were an average of 638,900 crimes per year involving handguns in the United States. Of those, 9,200 resulted in deaths, said the National Crime Victimization Survey (NCVS). There were 91,500 people injured, 15,000 by gunshots and the rest by other causes.

NCVS found that between 1979 and 1987 handgun crimes represented 10% of all violent crimes and 27% of all violent crimes by violent offenders. During the period, offenders with handguns committed about 7% of all rapes, 18% of all robberies, 8% of all assaults, and 22% of all aggravated assaults.

About 3.8% of all handgun crimes resulted in shootings: 9,200 gunshot murders and 15,000 people shot during other crimes among the 638,900 annual total.

Of the annual average number of people invloved in handgun crimes during 1979–87 shown here, 629,700 out of 638,900, or about 98%, survived the victimization. About 91,500 of those 629,700 surviving persons, or about 15%, were injured. Only about 16% (15,000 out of 91,500) of all injured persons got hurt from a shooting.

It is not possible, using the NCVS data, to tell what the proportions of firearms injuries and other injuries were for the specific crimes listed (rape, robbery, assault). All injuries are tallied under the general heading of "nonfatal handgun crimes."

NCVS annually polls over 100,000 U.S. resident citizens over age 12 about their experiences with reported and unreported violent crimes. Homicides are not included because the victims cannot be interviewed.

Source U.S. Department of Justice, Bureau of Justice Statistics. *Highlights from 20 Years of Surveying Crime Victims* (Washington, DC: U.S. Government Printing Office, 1993), p. 29.

Contact U.S. Department of Justice, Bureau of Justice Statistics Clearinghouse, Box 6000, Rockville, MD 20850. (800) 732-3277.

Weapons

Who Is the Victim of a Handgun Crime?

Average annual rate of crimes committed with handguns (per 1,000 persons)* in the United States.

Age of Victim	White Males	Black Males	Total Males	White Females	Black Females	Total Females
All ages	3.7	14.2	4.9	1.6	5.8	2.1
12–15	3.1	14.1	5.0	2.1	4.7	2.5
16–19	9.5	39.7	14.2	3.6	13.4	5.1
20–24	9.2	29.4	11.8	3.5	9.1	4.3
25–34	4.9	12.3	5.7	2.1	9.0	3.1
35–49	2.7	8.7	3.3	1.4	3.3	1.7
50–64	1.2	3.5	1.5	0.7	1.6	0.8
65 and older	0.6	3.7	0.8	0.2	2.3	0.3

* Rates are for persons age 12 and older in each category. Rates do not include murder and nonnegligent manslaughter committed with handguns. Totals include persons of other races not shown separately.

Weapons

Comments Black males 16–24 years old stood the greatest risk of being victims of crimes using handguns between 1987 and 1992. The National Crime Victimization Survey (NCVS) found 39.7 black males per 1,000 in the 16–19 age group were victims of handgun crimes each year during the period. For black males ages 20–24, the rate was 29.4% per 1,000.

No white male category got above 9.5 per 1,000 for its victim rate (ages 16–19). White females were even less at risk, with the 16–19 age group topping the list at 3.6 per 1,000.

Black females in the 16–19 age group were victims 13.4 times per 1,000.

Overall, the most at-risk group was males ages 16–19. They were victims 14.2 times per 1,000. For women overall, those aged 16–19 also were most at risk, with 5.1 cases per 1,000.

NCVS annually polls over 100,000 U.S. resident citizens over age 12 about their experiences with reported and unreported violent crimes. Homicides are not included because the victims cannot be interviewed.

Source U.S. Department of Justice, Bureau of Justice Statistics, "Guns and Crime" (Washington, DC: U.S. Government Printing Office, April 1994).

Contact U.S. Department of Justice, Bureau of Justice Statistics Clearinghouse, Box 6000, Rockville, MD 20850. (800) 732-3277.

Weapons

If a Gun is Present During a Violent Crime, How Often Is a Shot Fired?

Percentage of state inmates in the U.S. who carried and fired a gun during the crime for which they were sentenced to prison.

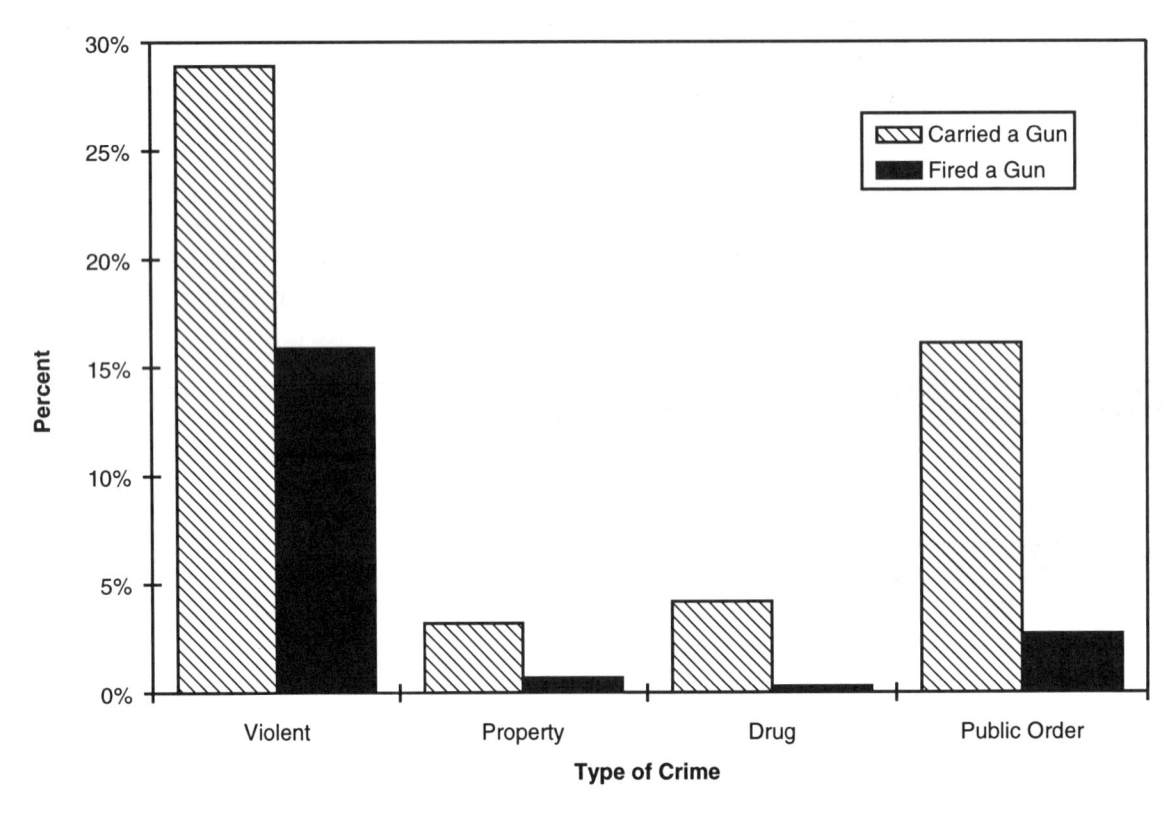

Type of Crime	Carried a Gun	Fired a Gun	Ratio of Gun Shooting to Presence at Crime
Violent	28.9	15.9	1 : 1.8
Murder	43.6	37.9	1 : 1.2
Rape	5.2	0.4	1 : 13.0
Robbery	34.4	5.5	1 : 6.3
Assault	31.1	24.9	1 : 1.2
Property	3.2	0.7	1 : 4.6
Burglary	3.8	0.9	1 : 4.2
Larceny	2.1	0.3	1 : 7.0
Motor vehicle theft	3.3	0.3	1 : 11.0
Drug	4.2	0.3	1 : 14.0
Possession	4.4	0.2	1 : 22.0
Trafficking	4.0	0.3	1 : 13.3
Public order *	16.1	2.7	1 : 6.0
Total	16.3	7.8	1 : 2.1

* Public order offenses include weapons possession or trafficking, driving while intoxicated, gambling and commercial vice, offense against nature and decency, and other such crimes.

Weapons

Comments Murder and assault were the categories in which offenders were most likely to fire guns during their crimes, a 1991 federal Bureau of Justice Statistics study shows.

In 43.6% of murder cases, the offenders carried guns; they fired them 37.9% of the time for a shooting ratio of 1:1.2. Assaults had the same ratio, with guns being carried 31.1% of the time and fired in 24.9% of the cases.

Approximately 16.3% of surveyed state prison inmates reported that they carried a firearm when committing the crimes for which they were jailed. Nearly half of those carrying guns each fired at least one shot during their crimes.

Likelihood that a gun would be fired was smallest for drug, rape, and motor vehicle theft cases.

It is important to remember that this survey only includes prisoners who gave information about carrying and using guns during the crimes for which they were sentenced. This survey does not consider gun use by these same prisoners for previous crimes. It is also possible that the ratio of using firearms to carrying firearms during a crime is higher among state prison inmates.

Firing a gun during a crime is more serious than just carrying a gun. As a result, those who fire guns during crimes are likely to receive longer prison sentences.

Source U.S. Department of Justice, Bureau of Justice Statistics, *Survey of State Prison Inmates, 1991* (Washington, DC: U.S. Government Printing Office, March 1993).

Department of Justice, Bureau of Justice Statistics, "Firearms and Crimes of Violence: Selected Findings" (Washington, DC: U.S. Government Printing Office, February 1994).

Contact U.S. Department of Justice, Bureau of Justice Statistics Clearinghouse, Box 6000, Rockville, MD 20850. (800) 732-3277.

Weapons

Inmates' Gun Usage in Crimes

Percentage of state inmates in the U.S. who carried or fired a gun during the crime for which they went to prison. Details are given for first-time offenders and recidivists (repeat criminals).

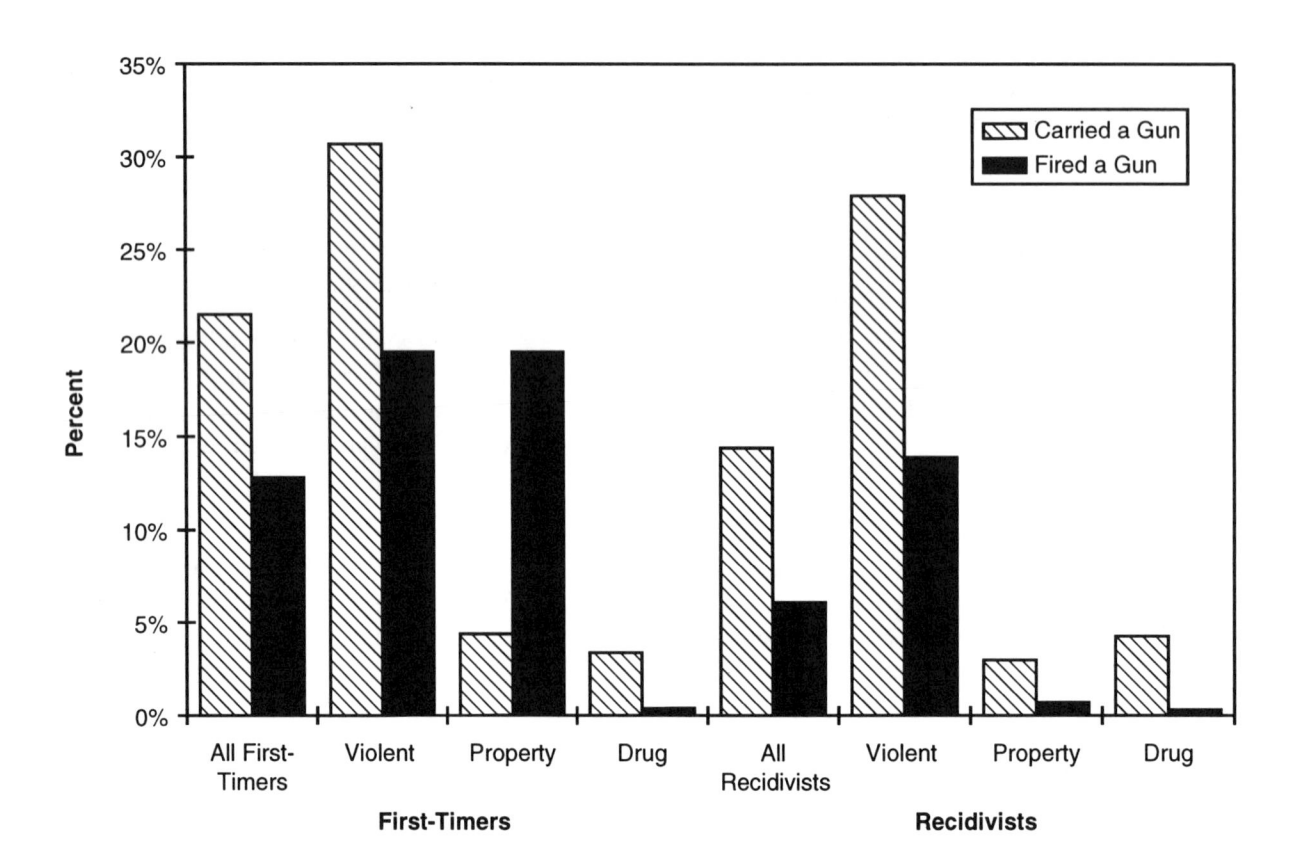

Offense	Carried a Gun	Fired a Gun
First-timers	21.5%	12.8%
Violent	30.7%	19.5%
Property	4.4%	19.5%
Drug	3.4%	0.4%
Recidivists	14.4%	6.1%
Violent	27.9%	13.9%
Property	3.0%	0.7%
Drug	4.3%	0.3%

Weapons

Comments A 1991 study by the Federal Bureau of Justice Statistics found 21.5% of all first-time inmates had carried guns in their crimes, compared to 14.4% of all repeat inmates. Among inmates who fired guns during their crimes, 12.8% were first-timers and 6.1% were repeaters.

Inmates serving time for violent crimes were more likely to have carried guns: 30.7% for first-timers and 27.9% for repeat offenders. Guns were fired during the offenses by 12.8% of the first timers and 6.1% of the repeaters.

It may seem strange that the first-timers were more likely to have carried and used guns. However, a first-time offender often receives a prison sentence because the crime was very serious. If someone has no prior criminal record, the sentencing usually will try to avoid prison time.

Repeat offenders, however, typically are given prison sentences more liberally. Possession or use of a firearm during a crime often can be the deciding factor leading to an initial prison sentence.

Source U.S. Department of Justice, Bureau of Justice Statistics, *Survey of State Prison Inmates, 1991* (Washington, DC: U.S. Government Printing Office, 1993).

U.S. Department of Justice, Bureau of Justice Statistics, "Firearms and Crimes of Violence: Selected Findings" (Washington, DC: U.S. Government Printing Office, February 1994).

Contact U.S. Department of Justice, Bureau of Justice Statistics Clearinghouse, Box 6000, Rockville, MD 20850. (800) 732-3277.

Weapons

Murders, Robberies, and Aggravated Assaults in Which Firearms Were Used

Estimated number of offenses and rates (per 100,000 inhabitants) in the U.S., 1980–92.

Year	Total Firearm Crimes	Firearm Crimes Rate	Murders with Firearms *	Murders with Firearms Rate	Robberies with Firearms	Robberies with Firearms Rate	Aggravated Assaults with Firearms	Aggravated Assaults with Firearms Rate
1980	392,083	174.0	14,377	6.4	221,170	98.1	156,535	69.5
1981	396,197	172.9	14,052	6.1	230,226	100.5	151,918	66.3
1982	372,477	160.9	12,648	5.5	214,219	92.5	145,609	62.9
1983	330,419	141.2	11,258	4.8	183,581	78.5	135,580	57.9
1984	329,232	139.4	10,990	4.7	173,634	73.5	144,609	61.2
1985	340,942	142.8	11,141	4.7	175,748	73.6	154,052	64.5
1986	376,064	156.0	12,181	5.1	186,174	77.2	177,710	73.7
1987	365,709	150.3	11,879	4.9	170,841	70.2	182,989	75.2
1988	385,934	157.0	12,553	5.1	181,352	73.8	192,029	78.1
1989	410,039	165.2	13,416	5.4	192,006	77.3	204,618	82.4
1990	492,671	198.1	15,025	6.0	233,973	94.1	243,673	98.0
1991	548,667	217.6	16,376	6.5	274,404	108.8	257,887	102.3
1992	565,575	221.7	16,204	6.4	271,009	106.2	278,362	109.1
Percent change 1980–92	+44.2	+27.4	+12.7	0.0	+22.5	+8.3	+77.8	+57.1

*Includes nonnegligent manslaughters (killings that were not accidental).

Weapons

Comments

The rates at which firearms were used in aggravated assaults and robberies rose between 1980 and 1992, according to the Federal Bureau of Investigation. For aggravated assaults, the rate rose 57% to 109 per 100,000 people. Robberies with firearms saw an 8.3% increase to 106.2 per 100,000.

For murders, the rate remained unchanged at 6.4 per 100,000 people.

Every year the FBI tabulates the number of murders and other crimes occurring throughout the country with its Uniform Crime Reporting system (UCR). It collects data from state and local police. These numbers provide preliminary estimates for crime rates, although the statistics only include incidents reported to police.

Although the numbers of crimes show how many times a certain offense occurred during a year, the rates show how often that crime occurred. This is important since population numbers change from year to year.

By studying the data over several years, it is possible to see how often guns are used for specific types of violent crimes. For example, although the number of murders committed with firearms steadily increased from 1980 to 1992, the rate remained unchanged.

Source

U.S. Department of Justice, Federal Bureau of Investigation, *Crime in the United States*, 1980 to 1992 annuals (Washington, DC: U.S. Government Printing Office).

U.S. Department of Justice, Bureau of Justice Statistics, "Firearms and Crimes of Violence: Selected Findings" (Washington, DC: U.S. Government Printing Office, February 1994).

Contact

U.S. Department of Justice, Bureau of Justice Statistics Clearinghouse, Box 6000, Rockville, MD 20850. (800) 732-3277.

U.S. Department of Justice, Federal Bureau of Investigation, Uniform Crime Reports, Criminal Justice Information Services Division, Washington, DC 20535. Information Dissemination: (202) 324-5015.

Weapons

Murder Victims, by Specific Type of Weapon Used, 1989–93

Victims of murder in the U.S. according to type of murder weapon.

Type of Weapon	1989	1990	1991	1992	1993
Total Firearms	11,832	13,035	14,373	15,489	16,189
Handguns	9,013	10,099	11,497	12,580	13,252
Shotguns	1,173	1,245	1,124	1,111	1,059
Rifles *	865	746	745	706	754
Other guns	34	25	30	42	38
Firearms, not stated	747	920	977	1,050	1,086
Knives or cutting instruments	3,458	3,526	3,430	3,296	2,957
Personal weapons (hands, fists, feet) †	1,050	1,119	1,202	1,131	1,164
Blunt objects (clubs, hammers, etc.)	1,128	1,085	1,099	1,040	1,024
Strangulation	366	312	327	314	329
Fire	234	288	195	203	217
Asphyxiation	101	96	113	115	113
Explosives	16	13	16	19	26
Drowning	60	36	40	29	23
Narcotics	17	29	22	24	22
Poison	11	11	12	13	9
Other weapons or weapons not stated	681	723	847	1,043	1,198
Total	18,954	20,273	21,676	22,716	23,271

* Includes so-called "assault weapons."
† Includes pushing someone to their death.

Comments

Handguns have overwhelmingly been the preferred weapon of murderers in recent years, according to this information collected by the FBI through its Uniform Crime Reporting system. Each year, the FBI gathers preliminary data regarding the type of murder weapon used to commit an offense. However, the number of reporting agencies and the population represented varies from year to year.

Handguns are often used to commit murder. Shotguns and rifles, however, are used less frequently to commit murder than knives and cutting instruments, personal weapons, and blunt objects. The recent controversial political debate concerning so-called "assault weapons" may seem out of context considering the minority of total murders committed with rifles.

Some people believe that these firearms need to be more strictly controlled because assault-type weapons make up an estimated 1% of all firearms in the U.S. but are believed to be used in up to 10% of all crimes. Others believe that such imposition is unnecessary, because these "assault weapons" in question are not machine guns but can only fire one bullet per squeeze of the trigger, just like any other rifle. Since the National Firearms Act of 1934 came into force, the legal acquisition of real machine guns by U.S. citizens has required a federal license that is very difficult to earn.

According to U.S. Army ballistics research, assault weapons are actually less deadly than many traditional hunting firearms, such as 12-gauge shotguns. Hunting weapons by definition are designed to kill their targets. Proponents of government control on assault weapons have indicated that many of these guns can easily be converted to fire fully automatically (like a machine gun). On the other hand, the Bureau of Alcohol, Tobacco, and Firearms (ATF) has stated that no guns available to the public can be so easily converted.

Source

U.S. Department of Justice, Federal Bureau of Investigation. *Crime in the United States, 1993*, (Washington, DC: U.S. Government Printing Office, 1994) p. 18.

Kopel, David B. "The Violence of Gun Control." *Policy Review*, No. 63 (Winter 1993).

Contact

Federal Bureau of Investigation, Uniform Crime Reports, Criminal Justice Information Services Division, Washington DC 20535. Information Dissemination: (202) 324-5015

Coalition to Stop Gun Violence, 100 Maryland Ave., Washington, DC 20002. (202) 544-7190

The Heritage Foundation, 214 Massachusetts Ave. NE, Washington, DC 20002. (202) 546-4400

Weapons

Deaths Due to Firearms and Nonfirearms by Manner of Death for Persons 1–34 Years of Age in the United States, 1985–90

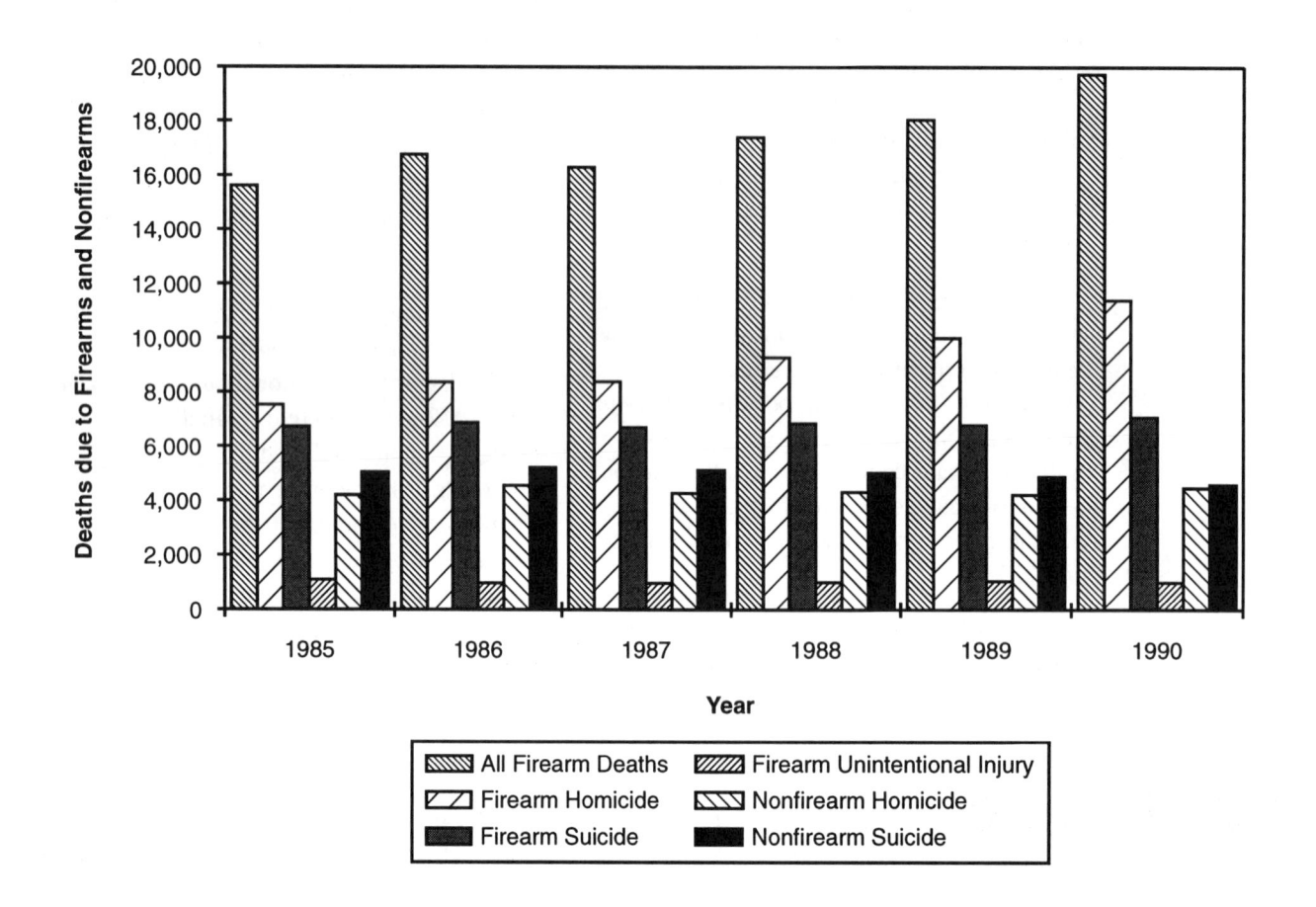

Manner of Death	1985	1986	1987	1988	1989	1990
All firearm deaths	15,614	16,764	16,295	17,398	18,053	19,722
Firearm homicide	7,527	8,360	8,381	9,281	10,005	11,415
Firearm suicide	6,729	6,865	6,702	6,846	6,786	7,080
Firearm unintentional injury	1,094	973	970	1,007	1,059	1,012
All nonfirearm deaths	—	—	—	—	—	—
Nonfirearm homicide	4,200	4,557	4,260	4,322	4,218	4,472
Nonfirearm suicide	5,043	5,216	5,127	5,030	4,885	4,597
Nonfirearm unintentional injury	—	—	—	—	—	—

Weapons

Comments   The National Center for Health Statistics (NCHS) collects information regarding births and deaths (and its various causes such as diseases, accidents, and homicides) on a monthly basis. Each year, the NCHS produces a report which analyzes the causes of all deaths occurring within that year. Deaths occurring from firearms consist of three types: homicides, suicides, and unintentional injuries.

The numbers of all deaths caused by firearms for persons ages 1 to 34 increased from 1985 to 1990, according to these statistics. Of all firearm deaths, homicides increased most significantly within the five year period. Suicides and unintentional injuries from firearms remained fairly stable over the same period. Homicides and suicides not caused by firearms were in the minority for both cases during 1985–90.

Obviously absent from these statistics, however, are the number of deaths caused by unintentional injuries not related to firearms. If such information were included, it would help give a real indication as to how often a death from a firearm accident occurs relative to all accidental deaths.

In 1992 for example, there were 12,017 deaths caused by accidents and adverse effects for persons ages 1 to 34 years (not including 21,298 motor vehicle accident deaths). Of those deaths, 991 were from firearm accidents (some 264 more were undetermined whether accidentally or purposely inflicted). Therefore during 1992, somewhere between 8.2% (or 991 ÷ 12,017) and 10.4% (or [991 + 264] ÷ 12,017) of all accidental deaths for persons aged 1–34 not involving motor vehicles were caused by firearms.

Source   U.S. Department of Health and Human Services, Public Health Service, Centers for Disease Control and Prevention, National Center for Health Statistics, "Firearm Mortality Among Children, Youth, and Young Adults 1–34 Years of Age, Trends and Current Status: United States, 1985–90" (Hyattsville, MD: National Center for Health Statistics, 1993) no. 231.

U.S. Department of Health and Human Services, Public Health Service, Centers for Disease Control and Prevention, National Center for Health Statistics, "Advance Report of Final Mortality Statistics, 1992" (Hyattsville, MD: National Center for Health Statistics, 1994) vol. 43, no. 6, suppl.

Contact   U.S. Department of Health and Human Services, Public Health Service, Centers for Disease Control and Prevention, National Center for Health Statistics, 6525 Belcrest Rd., Hyattsville, MD 20782. Data dissemination: (301) 436-8500.

Weapons

Murder Circumstances by Weapon in 1993

Conditions or reasons why murders occurred in the U.S. during 1993.

Murder Circumstance	Firearms	Knives or Cutting Instruments	Blunt Objects (Clubs, Hammers, Etc.)	Personal Weapons (Hands, Fists, Feet, Etc.)	Other Weapons *	Total Murder Victims
Total	16,189	2,957	1,024	1,161	1,985	23,271
Felony type total	3,222	416	231	175	407	4,451
Rape	15	29	20	24	25	116
Robbery	1,748	243	137	75	98	2,301
Burglary	88	28	31	11	21	179
Larceny-theft	20	3	1	2	6	32
Motor vehicle theft	42	9	4	1	5	61
Arson	9	2	2	0	138	151
Prostitution and commercialized vice	3	7	2	0	5	17
Other sex offenses	5	3	6	4	7	25
Narcotic drug laws	1,153	68	16	15	35	1,287
Gambling	10	0	0	0	0	10
Other, not specified	129	24	12	43	64	272
Suspected felony type	85	16	5	9	29	144
Other than felony type total	8,424	1,871	496	765	679	12,235
Romantic triangle	320	79	9	14	17	439
Child killed by baby-sitter	0	1	1	28	3	33
Brawl due to influence of alcohol	211	104	23	35	8	381
Brawl due to influence of narcotics	214	24	8	7	9	262
Argument over money or property	318	68	25	21	13	445
Other arguments	4,284	1,242	271	251	244	6,292
Gangland killings	131	2	6	1	7	147
Juvenile gang killings	1,093	37	9	5	3	1,147
Institutional killings	2	6	1	3	3	15
Sniper attacks	7	0	0	0	0	7
Other, not specified	1,844	308	143	400	372	3,067
Unknown	4,458	654	292	212	1,453	6,441

* Includes murders by poison, pushing or throwing from a precipice, explosives, fire, narcotics, drowning, strangulation, asphyxiation, and other methods.

Comments

The FBI annually tabulates murders according to the weapon used and the circumstances surrounding the murder, when such information is available. Firearms accounted for about 70% of all murders in 1993 (16,189 of 23,271). When a felony was the situation leading to murder, guns were involved 72% of the time (3,222 of 4,551).

Some weapons, however, were used more often than firearms, depending upon the circumstances behind the murder. For example, firearms were used in 13% of the incidents when rapes resulted in murders (15 of 116 cases). Knives, blunt objects, personal, and other weapons all were used more often than firearms in rapes.

For situations that did not also involve felonies, firearms were used most often when the murder was the result of an argument. Arguments also led up the largest murder totals in other weapons categories.

Guns were used in 69% of murders not related to felonies (8,424 of 12,235). Knives and other sharp objects were used just 9% of the time in felony-related murders (416 of 4,451) but accounted for 15% of those not related to felonies (1,871 of 12,235). Likewise, personal weapons accounted for about only 4% of the felony-related murders (175), but made up over 6% of the nonfelony-related murders (765).

Source

U.S. Department of Justice, Federal Bureau of Investigation, *Crime in the United States, 1993* (Washington, DC: U.S. Government Printing Office, 1994), p. 19.

Contact

U.S. Department of Justice, Federal Bureau of Investigation, Uniform Crime Reports, Criminal Justice Information Services Division, Washington, DC 20535. Information Dissemination: (202) 324-5015.

Murder in the States by Weapon, 1992 & 1993

The number of murders in the states during 1992 and 1993 according to type of weapon used.

State	Total Murders 1992	Total Murders 1993	Total Firearms Murders 1992	Total Firearms Murders 1993	Handguns 1992	Handguns 1993	Knives or Cutting Instruments 1992	Knives or Cutting Instruments 1993	Other Weapons 1992	Other Weapons 1993	Hands, Fists, Feet, Etc. 1992	Hands, Fists, Feet, Etc. 1993
Alabama	391	473	230	284	196	234	64	66	80	105	17	18
Alaska	43	54	24	27	15	20	10	11	7	14	2	2
Arizona	304	330	210	230	165	168	31	45	47	33	16	22
Arkansas	249	244	185	175	137	125	38	26	15	31	11	12
California	3,921	4,094	2,851	3,007	2,442	2,609	544	473	353	476	173	138
Colorado	214	206	119	132	88	111	46	32	37	30	12	12
Connecticut	166	206	114	139	99	117	31	28	19	30	2	9
Delaware	20	20	8	12	4	10	4	4	6	2	2	2
District of Columbia	442	417	368	350	368	350	36	32	38	35	0	0
Florida	1,176	1,223	712	753	507	486	131	143	265	270	68	57
Georgia	671	750	443	506	373	435	104	114	88	94	36	36
Hawaii	42	43	15	16	10	12	8	12	8	5	11	10
Idaho	35	31	21	17	12	14	5	7	6	4	3	3
Illinois	1,217	*	832	*	689	*	196	*	131	*	58	*
Indiana	355	357	239	260	190	225	56	35	46	46	14	16
Iowa	23	45	9	18	7	10	3	13	6	9	5	5
Kansas	133	*	73	*	63	*	15	*	28	*	17	*
Kentucky	211	236	128	161	99	115	33	17	35	48	15	10
Louisiana	659	721	507	586	445	520	80	52	57	55	15	28
Maine	*	7	*	5	*	4	*	0	*	2	*	0
Maryland	596	632	428	458	392	427	90	80	60	65	18	29
Massachusetts	178	210	89	110	71	60	41	57	28	33	20	10
Michigan	934	922	655	681	388	379	133	90	117	112	29	39
Minnesota	133	131	72	69	54	51	33	29	16	17	12	16
Mississippi	203	218	133	161	113	141	35	32	25	14	10	11
Missouri	458	546	296	410	189	324	57	57	94	56	11	23
Montana	18	*	12	*	11	*	0	*	3	*	3	*
Nebraska	42	28	26	13	18	7	4	3	10	8	2	4
Nevada	130	129	70	84	61	79	27	17	24	10	9	18
New Hampshire	18	20	12	10	10	5	1	7	3	2	2	1
New Jersey	397	418	190	213	151	182	99	93	65	68	43	44
New Mexico	89	95	53	49	42	39	17	26	14	9	5	11
New York	2,378	2,415	1,760	1,739	1,643	1,604	297	310	199	262	122	104
North Carolina	708	771	450	493	340	368	114	107	108	126	36	45
North Dakota	12	11	8	5	2	3	1	2	3	3	0	1
Ohio	647	599	428	431	367	375	92	62	84	58	43	48
Oklahoma	206	272	126	170	98	131	44	39	19	48	17	15
Oregon	137	143	60	76	36	57	19	31	42	26	16	10
Pennsylvania	684	804	450	573	371	486	105	93	88	82	41	56
Rhode Island	35	39	17	21	11	16	5	7	13	9	0	2

[Continued]

Weapons

Murder in the States by Weapon, 1992 & 1993

[Continued]

State	Total Murders 1992	Total Murders 1993	Total Firearms Murders 1992	Total Firearms Murders 1993	Handguns 1992	Handguns 1993	Knives or Cutting Instruments 1992	Knives or Cutting Instruments 1993	Other Weapons 1992	Other Weapons 1993	Hands, Fists, Feet, Etc. 1992	Hands, Fists, Feet, Etc. 1993
South Carolina	361	375	251	264	180	213	56	53	35	37	19	21
South Dakota	4	18	0	10	0	8	4	0	0	4	0	4
Tennessee	434	450	301	322	250	271	66	58	55	49	12	21
Texas	2,239	2,142	1,627	1,535	1,164	1,107	299	281	230	234	83	92
Utah	51	58	23	23	19	17	9	13	12	6	7	16
Vermont	10	12	6	8	2	5	2	1	2	3	0	0
Virginia	563	539	407	394	336	325	69	71	54	48	33	26
Washington	255	264	137	155	115	127	57	45	39	49	22	15
West Virginia	114	125	82	85	57	53	16	12	9	18	7	10
Wisconsin	184	222	113	117	84	88	34	29	19	51	18	25
Wyoming	17	16	7	10	5	6	4	2	2	1	4	3

* Information was incomplete or unavailable.

Comments

Not only do the numbers of murders vary by state from one year to the next, but the manner in which the murders were committed varies as well. This chart categorizes the number of murders in each state during 1992 and 1993. The FBI annually records the number of reported murders in the U.S. and compiles information on how those murders were committed. The "firearms" category shown here includes a subtotal indicating the frequency of murder by a handgun. "Other weapons" includes blunt objects, drowning, fire, and other methods.

Murders committed with firearms typically made up the majority of all murders among the states in both years. Handguns were usually the firearm of choice, but the frequency of handgun use in murder varied as well. For example, handgun murders accounted for 100% of firearm murders in the District of Columbia (where legal handgun ownership is difficult) during 1992 and 1993. In Texas, however, handgun murders only accounted for 72% of firearm murders during those years.

There are several differences between the District of Columbia and Texas that might explain the frequency of handgun use in murder. Texas is a geographically large area, much of which is rural and sparsely populated. Long guns (shotguns and rifles) are more common in rural areas for hunting and security purposes. Rifles are more accurate over long distances than handguns.

Source

U.S. Department of Justice, Federal Bureau of Investigation, *Crime in the United States, 1992* (Washington, DC: U.S. Government Printing Office, 1993), p. 202; *1993* (1994), p. 202.

Contact

U.S. Department of Justice, Federal Bureau of Investigation, Uniform Crime Reports, Criminal Justice Information Services Division, Washington, DC 20535. Information Dissemination: (202) 324-5015.

Weapons

Firearm Accident Fatality Rates, 1903–93

Rate of deaths per 100,000 inhabitants caused by accidental discharges from firearms in the U.S. during the 20th century.

Year	Unintentional Injury Deaths from Firearms per 100,000 Population	Year	Unintentional Injury Deaths from Firearms per 100,000 Population	Year	Unintentional Injury Deaths from Firearms per 100,000 Population
1903	3.1	1934	2.4	1965	1.2
1904	3.4	1935	2.2	1966	1.3
1905	2.4	1936	2.2	1967	1.5
1906	2.4	1937	2.0	1968	1.2
1907	2.0	1938	2.1	1969	1.2
1908	2.1	1939	2.0	1970	1.2
1909	1.8	1940	1.8	1971	1.1
1910	2.1	1941	1.8	1972	1.2
1911	2.2	1942	2.0	1973	1.2
1912	2.2	1943	1.7	1974	1.2
1913	2.5	1944	1.8	1975	1.1
1914	2.3	1945	1.8	1976	0.9
1915	2.1	1946	2.0	1977	0.9
1916	2.2	1947	1.7	1978	0.8
1917	2.2	1948	1.6	1979	0.9
1918	2.4	1949	1.6	1980	0.9
1919	2.7	1950	1.4	1981	0.8
1920	2.5	1951	1.5	1982	0.8
1921	2.6	1952	1.4	1983	0.7
1922	2.6	1953	1.4	1984	0.7
1923	2.6	1954	1.4	1985	0.7
1924	2.5	1955	1.3	1986	0.6
1925	2.4	1956	1.3	1987	0.6
1926	2.4	1957	1.4	1988	0.6
1927	2.5	1958	1.3	1989	0.6
1928	2.4	1959	1.3	1990	0.6
1929	2.6	1960	1.3	1991	0.6
1930	2.6	1961	1.2	1992	0.6
1931	2.5	1962	1.1	1993	0.6
1932	2.4	1963	1.2		
1933	2.4	1964	1.2		

Weapons

Comments

The rate of fatalities caused by accidental shootings has fallen gradually throughout the 20th century, according to the National Safety Council. There were 3.1 accidental shooting deaths per 100,000 of population in 1903 and 0.6 in 1993. The rate generally declined between those two years.

The fatality rate was highest in 1904, at 3.4 per 100,000 U.S. residents. That year, there were about 2,800 accidental shooting deaths. However, the actual number of deaths caused by firearms injuries was at its highest in 1929 and 1930, at 3,200. Because the U.S. population had grown by then, the rate per 100,000 was lower than in 1904.

The fatality rate from accidental gun injuries has held steady at 0.6 since 1986. There are several possible explanations for this. A general increase in training and respect for firearms may have an effect. Better gun design could mean greater safety. Also as people move into the cities and away from rural areas, there is less daily use of firearms.

Source

National Safety Council, *Accident Facts 1994* (Chicago: National Safety Council, 1995) pp. 32, 33.

Edgar A. Suter, M.D. "Guns in the Medical Literature—A Failure of Peer Review," The Journal of the Medical Association of Georgia, (March 1994) 83; pp. 133–147.

Contact

National Safety Council, 1121 Spring Lake Dr., Itasca, IL 60143. (708) 285-1121.

Weapons

Deaths from Firearm Accidents, 1993 & 1994

Accidental firearm deaths as a portion of all firearm deaths.

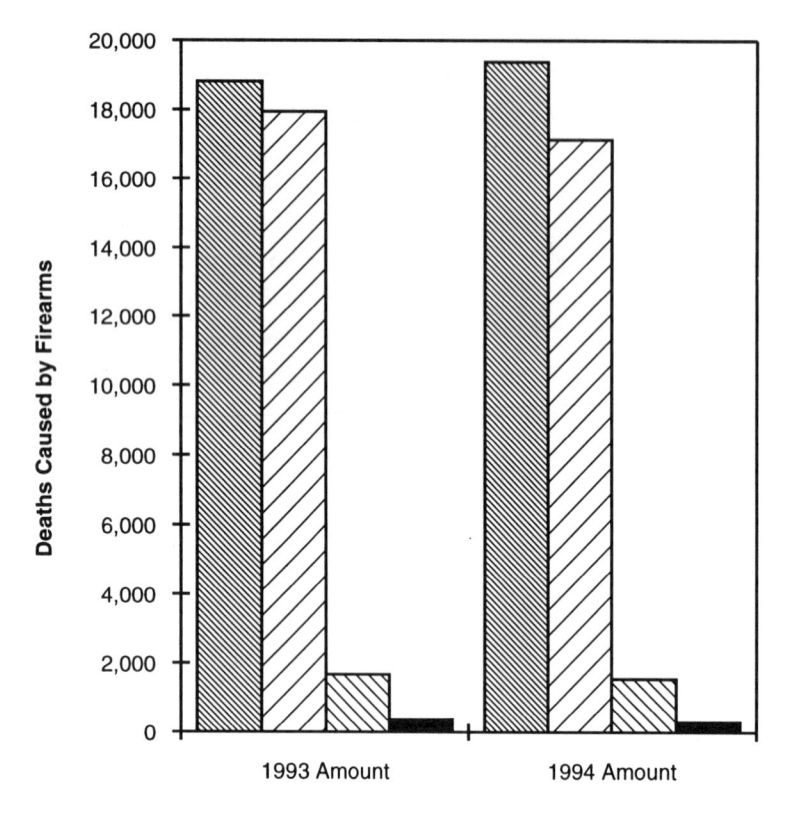

[Bar chart showing Deaths Caused by Firearms for 1993 and 1994, with categories: Suicides, Homicides and Legal Interventions, Accidents, Injuries Undetermined whether Accidentally or Purposely Inflicted]

Deaths Caused by Firearms	1993 Amount	1993 Rate*	1994 Amount	1994 Rate*
Suicides	18,810	7.3	19,380	7.4
Homicides and legal interventions**	17,940	7.0	17,140	6.6
Accidents	1,680	0.7	1,550	0.6
Injuries, undetermined whether accidentally or purposely inflicted	370	0.1	290	0.1
Total deaths caused by firearms	38,800	15.0	38,360	14.7

* Per 100,000 estimated population.
**Legal intervention deaths occur when law enforcement personnel kill someone in the line of duty.

Weapons

Comments Suicide was the leading cause for all deaths caused by firearms in 1993 and 1994, according to the National Center for Health Statistics. Suicides accounted for 48% of all deaths caused by firearms in 1993 and for just over 50% in 1994. There were 7.3 suicides per 100,000 of estimated population in 1993 and 7.4 in 1994.

Each year, the center tabulates the number of fatal firearms injuries, both intentionally and accidentally inflicted. Intentional firearms injuries (suicides and homicides) make up the vast majority of all deaths caused by guns.

Homicides accounted for most of the other deaths caused by guns. They comprised 46% of all deaths by guns in 1993 and nearly 45% in 1994. Together, homicides and suicides accounted for about 95% of all gun deaths in both 1993 and 1994.

The number of accidental shooting deaths represented only about 4.3% of all firearms-related deaths in 1993 and 4.0% in 1994.

However, the reasons behind some shooting deaths could not be learned. These uncertain cases accounted for less than 1% of all gun deaths in both years. Some of these shooting deaths could have been accidents, but some could have been homicides or suicides set up to look like accidents.

Source U.S. Department Of Health and Human Services, Public Health Service, Centers for Disease Control and Prevention, National Center for Health Statistics, *Monthly Vital Statistics Report,* 44; 1, p. 19.

Contact U.S. Department of Health and Human Services, Public Health Service, Centers for Disease Control and Prevention, National Center for Health Statistics, 6525 Belcrest Rd., Hyattsville, MD 20782. Data dissemination: (301) 436-8500.

Gun Owners of America, 8001 Forbes Place, Suite 102, Springfield, VA 22151. (703) 321-8585.

National Rifle Association, 1600 Rhode Island Ave. NW, Washington, DC 20036. (800) 672-3888.

Weapons

Deaths Caused by Firearms Injuries, 1993

Provisional age distribution of deaths from accidental firearm discharge injury and undetermined fatal firearm injury in the U.S. in 1993.

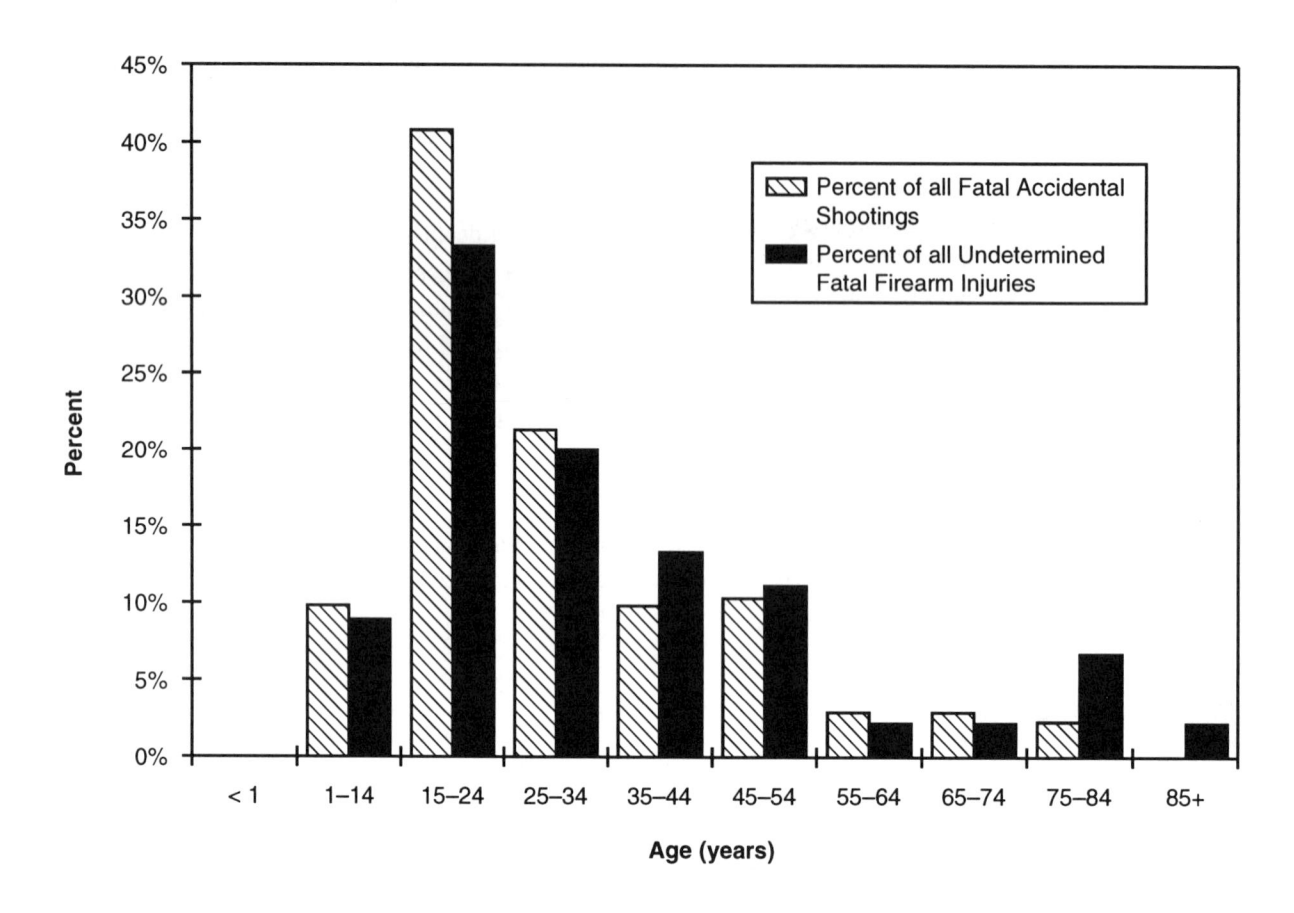

Age (years)	Fatal Accidental Shootings	Percent of All Fatal Accidental Shootings*	Fatal Injuries by Firearms, Undetermined whether Accidentally or Purposely Inflicted	Percent of All Undetermined Fatal Firearm Injuries*
< 1	0	0.0	0	0.0
1–14	170	9.8	40	8.9
15–24	710	40.8	150	33.3
25–34	370	21.3	90	20.0
35–44	170	9.8	60	13.3
45–54	180	10.3	50	11.1
55–64	50	2.9	10	2.2
65–74	50	2.9	10	2.2
75–84	40	2.3	30	6.7
85+	0	0.0	10	2.2

* Does not add to 100% because of rounding.

Weapons

Comments In 1993, persons 15–34 years old accounted for 62.1% of accidental shooting deaths, according to the National Center for Health Statistics. There were 710 deaths among those aged 15–24 (40.8% of the total) and 370 for the 25–34 group (21.3%).

On both sides of these high-risk groups, deaths generally dropped off with decreasing or increasing age. The 1–14 age group accounted for 9.8% of deaths. There were none for children under age 1. Between ages 35 and 85-plus, the death rate generally tapered from 9.8% to zero, with an uptick to 10.3% at 45–54 years old.

Shooting accidents among children often receive much publicity, even though only 9.8% of fatal gun accidents in 1993 involved children 14 and younger. Most children accidentally killed with guns found the firearms within their homes. The center indicated that in 1993 there were over 7,000 deaths caused by all kinds of accidents for children under age 14. The 170 accidental shooting cases accounted for about 2.4% of the total. Motor vehicle accidents typically account for well over 50% of all accidental deaths of those under age 14.

In most cases, the unintentional nature of a death resulting from an accidental shooting is obvious. In some cases, however, there is not enough information to determine whether the shooting was totally unplanned. Some of these cases may include suicides and murders made to resemble accidents. The statistics presented here only count fatalities caused by accidental shootings. Accidental gun injuries that are not fatal often result in permanent disabilities like blindness, lost limbs, or paralysis.

Source U.S. Department Of Health and Human Services, Public Health Service, Centers for Disease Control and Prevention, National Center for Health Statistics, *Monthly Vital Statistics Report,* 42; 13, p. 29.

Contact U.S. Department of Health and Human Services, Public Health Service, Centers for Disease Control and Prevention, National Center for Health Statistics, 6525 Belcrest Rd., Hyattsville, MD 20782. Data dissemination: (301) 436-8500.

Gun Owners of America, 8001 Forbes Place, Suite 102, Springfield, VA 22151. (703) 321-8585.

The Children's Safety Network at the National Center for Education in Maternal and Child Health, 2000 15th St. N., Suite 701, Arlington, VA 22201. (703) 524-7802.

National Rifle Association, 1600 Rhode Island Ave. NW, Washington, DC 20036. (800) 672-3888.

Weapons

Firearm Accident Fatalities by Type of Gun Involved, 1979–91

The number of people accidentally killed by guns in the U.S. from 1979 to 1991, according to the type of gun that caused the accidental killing.

Year	Handguns	Shotguns*	Hunting Rifles	Unspecified†	Total	Percent Handguns‡
1979	311	254	145	1,294	2,004	44%
1980	288	283	129	1,255	1,995	41%
1981	224	273	140	1,234	1,871	35%
1982	219	232	127	1,178	1,756	38%
1983	209	260	132	1,094	1,695	35%
1984	225	214	118	1,111	1,668	40%
1985	190	215	113	1,131	1,649	37%
1986	183	190	108	971	1,452	37%
1987	206	178	105	951	1,440	42%
1988	202	185	93	1,021	1,501	42%
1989	231	175	86	997	1,489	47%
1990	251	160	73	942	1,416	51%
1991	255	163	94	929	1,441	50%

* Includes semi-automatics.
† Includes a small number of "military rifle" fatalities.
‡ Does not include unspecified cases.

Comments

From 1979 to 1991, the annual number of accidental gun injury deaths declined by about 28%, from 2,004 to 1,441, according to the National Safety Council.

Although the numbers of deaths declined in every firearms category, the rate of deaths involving handguns rose from 15.5% of the total in 1979 to 17.7% in 1991. This is because handgun involvement in firearms fatalities fell only 18.0%, compared to drops of 35.8% for shotguns, 35.2% for hunting rifles, and 28.2% when the gun was not identified. The last category accounted for 64.5% of fatal firearms accidents in 1993.

The number of firearms—especially handguns—kept at home significantly increased during the survey period. Guns kept loaded at home frequently are the cause of accidental firearms injuries. Approximately nine out of every ten guns kept loaded at home are handguns.

Source

National Safety Council. *Accident Facts 1994*.

Kates, Don B., et al. "Guns and Public Health: Epidemic of Violence or Pandemic of Propaganda?" 62 *Tennessee Law Review* 513 (1995) (forthcoming, August 1995). Used by permission of the Tennessee Law Review Association, Inc., College of Law—Dunford Hall, 915 Volunteer Blvd., Knoxville, TN 37996.

Contact

National Safety Council, 1121 Spring Lake Dr., Itasca, IL 60143. (708) 285-1121.

Weapons

Percentage of High School Students in 1993 Who Carried a Weapon or a Gun

Frequency of weapon-carrying per 100 students within the past month, by sex, race/ethnicity, and grade.

Student Characteristic	Carried a Weapon Female	Carried a Weapon Male	Carried a Weapon Total	Carried a Gun Female	Carried a Gun Male	Carried a Gun Total	30-Day Incidence of Weapon-Carrying* Female	30-Day Incidence of Weapon-Carrying* Male	30-Day Incidence of Weapon-Carrying* Total
White, non-Hispanic	6.9	33.4	20.6	1.2	12.0	6.8	25.6	143.0	86.4
Black, non-Hispanic	18.9	38.2	28.5	3.8	20.9	12.3	80.9	152.7	116.6
Hispanic	11.5	37.3	24.4	3.1	17.0	10.1	40.0	152.5	96.3
9th grade	11.1	39.0	25.5	2.2	15.6	9.1	41.8	161.7	103.4
10th grade	9.8	32.5	21.4	2.2	14.6	8.6	34.1	135.9	86.4
11th grade	9.1	33.0	21.5	1.3	13.0	7.4	35.8	139.9	90.0
12th grade	6.9	32.6	19.9	1.3	11.8	6.6	29.9	143.0	86.7
Total	9.2	34.3	22.1	1.8	13.7	7.9	35.9	144.8	92.0

* Students who replied that they carried a weapon 2 or 3 days were assigned a weapon-carrying frequency of 2.5; 4 or 5 days, 4.5; and 6 days or more, 6.0.

Confidence intervals for data

Student Characteristic	Carried a Weapon Female	Carried a Weapon Male	Carried a Weapon Total	Carried a Gun Female	Carried a Gun Male	Carried a Gun Total	30-Day Incidence of Weapon-Carrying* Female	30-Day Incidence of Weapon-Carrying* Male	30-Day Incidence of Weapon-Carrying* Total
White, non-Hispanic	±1.8	±3.8	±2.8	±0.5	±2.6	±1.4	±6.9	±26.5	±15.3
Black, non-Hispanic	±3.7	±5.2	±2.4	±1.2	±3.0	±1.5	±24.0	±34.5	±24.0
Hispanic	±1.9	±4.9	±2.6	±1.3	±4.0	±1.9	±14.3	±44.9	±28.0
9th grade	±2.7	±3.7	±2.8	±1.0	±3.2	±1.9	±13.4	±21.5	±13.9
10th grade	±2.0	±3.7	±2.2	±0.9	±2.4	±1.4	±9.4	±27.0	±16.0
11th grade	±1.8	±5.4	±3.2	±0.6	±3.1	±1.7	±8.0	±30.2	±16.2
12th grade	±1.7	±4.2	±2.9	±0.7	±3.1	±1.7	±8.0	±30.2	±16.2
Total	±1.7	±3.3	±2.3	±0.4	±2.2	±1.3	±7.4	±22.0	±13.0

* Students who replied that they carried a weapon 2 or 3 days were assigned a weapon-carrying frequency of 2.5; 4 or 5 days, 4.5; and 6 days or more, 6.0.

Weapons

Comments

In 1993, 22.1% of U.S. students had carried weapons (such as guns, knives, or clubs) to school during the 30 days preceding a survey on such behavior. The Youth Risk Behavior Surveillance System (YRBSS) found that 7.9% of students carried guns.

An estimated 92.0 weapons-carrying incidents occurred monthly per 100 students. This means that for every 100 students who attended a school, there were 92 times that someone had brought a weapon to school within the 30 days. This does not mean that 92 of every 100 students carried weapons during the month. Some students carried weapons more than once and were counted accordingly.

Males were between 2 and 4.8 times more likely than females to carry weapons. Blacks (38.2%) were more likely to carry weapons than Hispanics (37.3%), or whites (33.4%). The carrying of weapons generally dropped off as high school grade levels rose, going from 25.5% in 9th grade to 19.9% in 12th grade.

All of these figures are subject to confidence intervals which could affect the rankings.

The survey was based on samples designed to represent all U.S. students. Since it is unlikely that such sampling will be 100% accurate, the second table shows the confidence intervals for the first table. For example, if a category has a value of 45% and a confidence interval of ±3, that group's value could be as high as 48% or as low as 42%. It is predicted that 95% of all cases would fall into the range. As the confidence interval narrows, the likelihood that the estimate is accurate and valid increases.

Homicide accounts for 19% of all deaths between ages 5 and 24, according to the Centers for Disease Control and Prevention (CDC). In order to monitor behaviors that contribute to youth homicide (as well as other health risk factors) the CDC developed YRBSS. The survey uses national, state (including U.S. territories), and local school-based surveys of high school students.

Source

Department of Health and Human Services, Public Health Service, Centers for Disease Control and Prevention,

"Youth Risk Behavior Surveillance, United States, 1993," *Morbidity and Mortality Weekly Report*, 1995; 44, SS-1, pp. 23–25.

Contact

U.S. Department of Health and Human Services, Public Health Service, Centers for Disease Control and Prevention, 1600 Clifton Rd. NE, Atlanta, GA 30333. (404) 332-4555. The CDC also maintains a World-Wide Web server at http://www.cdc.gov/.

Weapons

Gun Possession Among Juvenile Inmates and Students in 1991

The percentages of surveyed juvenile inmates and students in the U.S. who possessed guns.

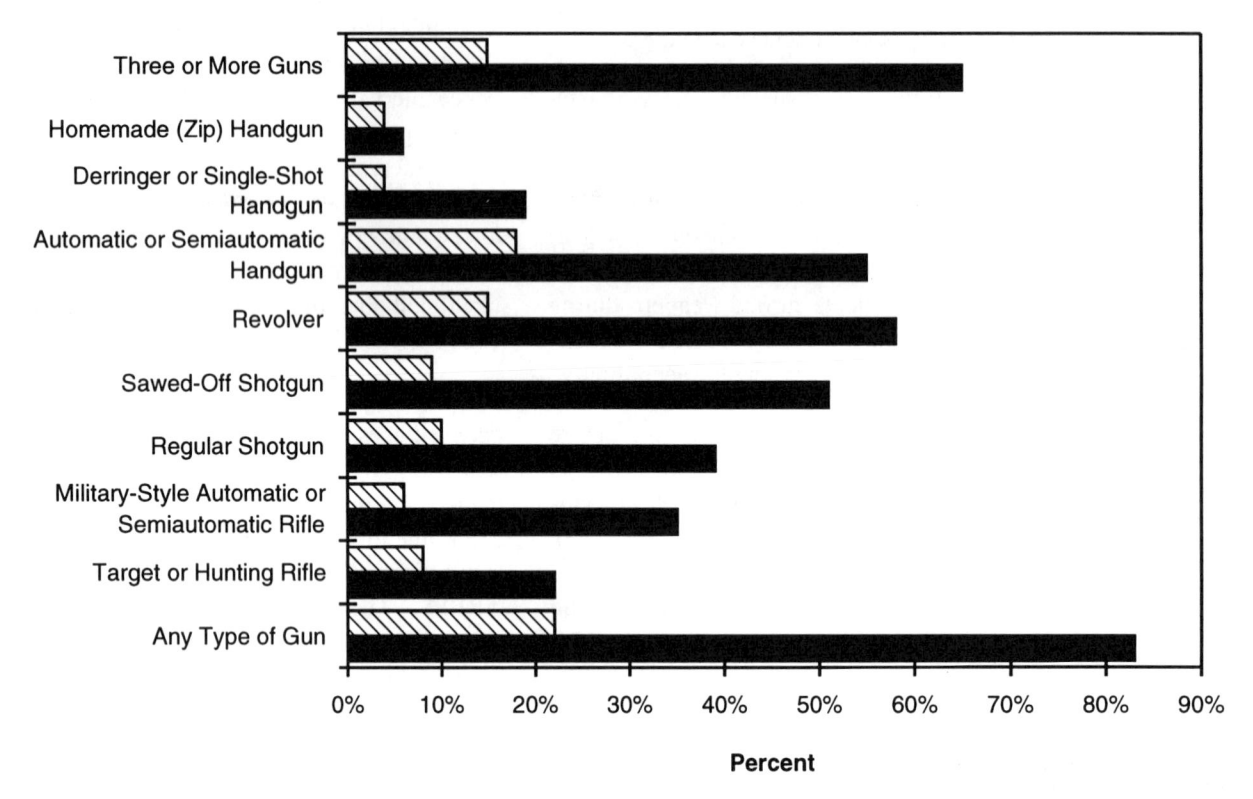

Percent of students who owned at time of survey
Percent of inmates who owned just prior to confinement

Type of Gun	Percent of Inmates Who Owned just Prior to Confinement	Percent of Students Who Owned at Time of Survey
Any type of gun	83	22
Target or hunting rifle	22	8
Military-style automatic or semiautomatic rifle	35	6
Regular shotgun	39	10
Sawed-off shotgun	51	9
Revolver	58	15
Automatic or semiautomatic handgun	55	18
Derringer or single-shot handgun	19	4
Homemade (zip) handgun	6	4
Three or more guns	65	15

Comments Handguns were found to be the weapons of choice among juvenile inmates and high school students in a 1991 National Institute of Justice (NIJ) study.

Among the juvenile inmates, revolvers were the most commonly owned firearms, with .38- and .357-caliber weapons the most popular. Closely following the revolver in popularity were automatic and semiautomatic handguns, typically 9mm or .45-caliber weapons. Shotguns, both unmodified and sawed-off, also were popular among those juvenile inmates surveyed.

Among the high school students surveyed, automatic or semiautomatic handguns, followed by revolvers, were the most popular firearms. Students owned shoulder weapons (such as rifles and shotguns) of all sorts much less frequently than they owned handguns. Still, 9% of the students surveyed owned sawed-off shotguns; 10% had unmodified shotguns; and 6% had military-style rifles.

NIJ questioned selected samples of male inmates (mostly in urban areas) in juvenile correctional facilities in California, Louisiana, and Illinois. The survey also included male students in ten inner-city public high schools near the correctional institutions.

The research focused on serious juvenile offenders and on inner-city students. Many people think these groups participate in and experience violence more frequently than other groups. The media often depict the relationship between firearms and juveniles as one in which guns of all types, even sophisticated military-style weapons, are widely and easily available. Much of this perception lacks hard evidence. Prior to this survey, few statistics existed about the types of guns youths were obtaining.

Source U.S. Department of Justice, National Institute of Justice, Office of Juvenile Justice and Delinquency Prevention, "Gun Acquisition and Possession in Selected Juvenile Samples" (Washington, DC: U.S. Government Printing Office, 1993), p. 4.

Contact U.S. Department of Justice, National Institute of Justice, National Criminal Justice Reference Service, Box 6000, Rockville, MD 20849. (800) 851-3420.

Weapons

Where Juveniles Obtain Handguns

The person or place from which surveyed students and juvenile correctional facility inmates in the U.S. obtained their most recent handguns.

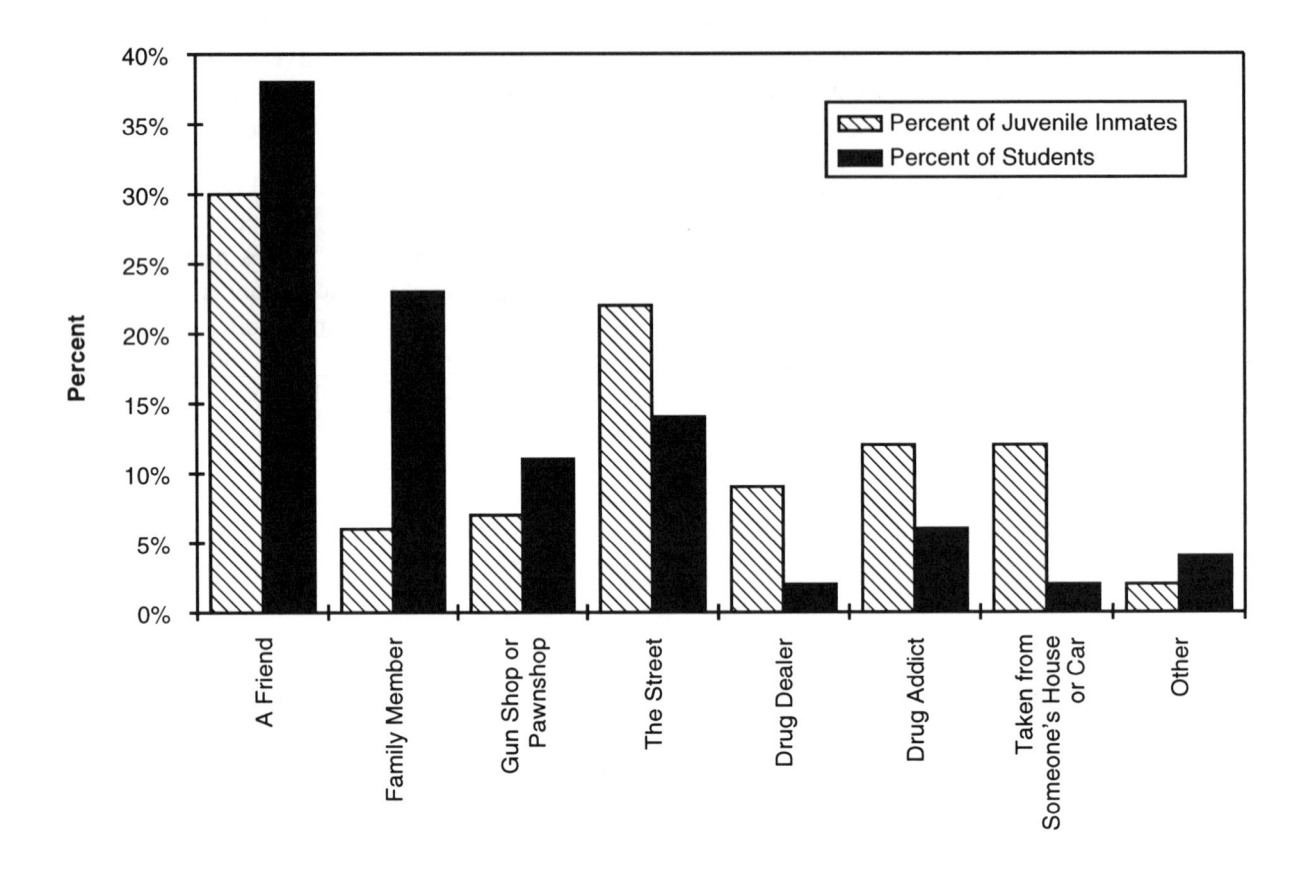

Source of Handgun	Percent of Juvenile Inmates	Percent of Students
A friend	30%	38%
Family member	6%	23%
Gun shop or pawnshop	7%	11%
The street	22%	14%
Drug dealer	9%	2%
Drug addict	12%	6%
"Taken" from someone's house or car	12%	2%
Other	2%	4%

Weapons

Comments A 1991 National Institute of Justice (NIJ) survey found friends were the main source of handguns for juvenile inmates (30%) and a selected group of students (38%). Among the juvenile inmates, 52% had gotten handguns from friends or off the street. Drug dealers and addicts were the sources of 21% of the handguns acquired by the juvenile inmates.

The picture was different for the students. Friends (38%) and street sources (14%) were important, but family members also were a primary source. Drug dealers and addicts were the sources for only 8% of handguns acquired by the students.

NIJ surveyed male inmates (mostly in urban areas) in juvenile correctional facilities in California, Louisiana, and Illinois to learn how they had gotten their handguns. Before this survey, little reliable data existed about the types of guns youths were obtaining and how they got them. The research focused on serious juvenile offenders and on inner-city students. The survey included male students in ten inner-city public high schools near the correctional institutions. Many people believe that these groups engage in and encounter violence more often than other groups.

The survey helps show that youths often use an informal network of family, friends, and street sources to obtain guns. If, for example, family or friends cannot supply a gun, then a juvenile can utilize a broad black market. Federal law prohibits minors from purchasing firearms, but youths often get older friends or relatives to purchase guns for them. Stolen guns also circulate widely and possession often passes through a series of many juveniles. Therefore, theft and burglary are often the ultimate sources of guns.

Source U.S. Department of Justice, National Institute of Justice, Office of Juvenile Justice and Delinquency Prevention, "Gun Acquisition and Possession in Selected Juvenile Samples" (Washington, DC: U.S. Government Printing Office, 1993), p. 6.

Contact U.S. Department of Justice, National Institute of Justice, National Criminal Justice Reference Service, Box 6000, Rockville, MD 20849. (800) 851-3420. Inquiries can also be sent by e-mail to askncjrs@aspensys.com.

U.S. Department of Justice, Juvenile Justice Clearinghouse, P.O. Box 6000, Rockville, MD 20849. (800) 638-8736.

Reasons Juveniles in the U.S. Obtain Firearms

Percent stating that each reason was "very important."

Gun Type	Juvenile Inmates	Students
Military-Style Guns		
Protection	73	75
Enemies had guns	60	42
Use in crimes	40	*
To get someone	43	25
Friends had one	20	16
To impress people	10	9
To sell	11	6
Handguns		
Protection	74	70
Enemies had guns	52	28
Use in crimes	36	*
To get someone	37	13
Friends had one	16	7
To impress people	10	10
To sell	10	4
Rifles or Shotguns		
Protection	64	59
Enemies had guns	47	29
Use in crimes	35	*
To get someone	37	20
Friends had one	16	5
To impress people	10	7
To sell	10	8

* Item not asked.

Comments

"Protection" and the fact that "enemies had guns" were the main reasons a sampling of male juvenile inmates and high school students gave for obtaining guns. The reasons were given in that order by both groups in a 1993 National Institute of Justice (NIJ) survey.

Youth involvement with firearms is another facet of the violence proliferation problem in America. To understand the issue, NIJ's Office of Juvenile Justice and Delinquency Prevention conducted a study to learn the types of firearms that juveniles own. The study also was to determine where, how, and why juveniles get and carry guns. Under federal law, minors cannot own firearms.

The study surveyed male juvenile correctional inmates from mostly urban areas in California, New Jersey, Louisiana, and Illinois. It also questioned male students in ten inner-city public high schools near the correctional institutions surveyed. Because the study focused on serious juvenile offenders and students from schools in high-risk areas, it is not possible to generalize the results to the entire population.

Source

U.S. Department of Justice, National Institute of Justice, Office of Juvenile Justice and Delinquency Prevention, "Gun Acquisition and Possession in Selected Juvenile Samples" (Washington, DC: U.S. Government Printing Office, December 1993).

Contact

U.S. Department of Justice, National Institute of Justice, National Criminal Justice Reference Service, Box 6000, Rockville, MD 20849. (800) 851-3420.

U.S. Department of Justice, Juvenile Justice Clearinghouse, P.O. Box 6000, Rockville, MD 20849. (800) 638-8736.

vIoLEnce

Violence

Suicide and Homicide Rates, 1900–93

Rate of deaths per 100,000 population caused by intentional violence during the 20th century.

Year	Suicides	Homicides	Year	Suicides	Homicides	Year	Suicides	Homicides
1900	10.2	1.2	1932	17.4	9.0	1964	10.8	5.1
1901	10.4	1.2	1933	15.9	9.7	1965	11.1	5.5
1902	10.3	1.2	1934	14.9	9.5	1966	10.9	5.9
1903	11.3	1.1	1935	14.6	8.3	1967	10.8	6.8
1904	12.2	1.3	1936	14.3	8.0	1968	10.7	7.3
1905	13.5	2.1	1937	15.0	7.6	1969	11.1	7.7
1906	12.8	3.9	1938	15.3	6.8	1970	11.6	8.3
1907	14.5	4.9	1939	14.1	6.4	1971	11.7	9.1
1908	16.8	4.8	1940	14.4	6.2	1972	12.0	9.4
1909	16.0	4.2	1941	12.8	6.0	1973	12.0	9.8
1910	15.3	4.6	1942	12.0	5.8	1974	12.1	10.2
1911	16.0	5.5	1943	10.2	5.0	1975	12.7	10.1
1912	15.6	5.4	1944	10.0	4.9	1976	12.5	9.1
1913	15.4	6.1	1945	11.2	5.6	1977	13.3	9.2
1914	16.1	6.2	1946	11.5	6.3	1978	12.5	9.4
1915	16.2	5.9	1947	11.5	6.0	1979	12.4	10.0
1916	13.7	6.3	1948	11.2	5.8	1980	11.9	10.7
1917	13.0	6.9	1949	11.4	5.4	1981	12.0	10.3
1918	12.3	6.5	1950	11.4	5.3	1982	12.2	9.6
1919	11.5	7.2	1951	10.3	4.9	1983	12.1	8.6
1920	10.2	6.8	1952	10.0	5.2	1984	12.4	8.4
1921	12.4	8.1	1953	10.1	4.8	1985	12.3	8.3
1922	11.7	8.0	1954	10.1	4.8	1986	12.8	9.0
1923	11.5	7.8	1955	10.2	4.5	1987	12.7	9.7
1924	11.9	8.1	1956	10.0	4.6	1988	12.4	9.0
1925	12.0	8.3	1957	9.8	4.5	1989	12.6	9.3
1926	12.6	8.4	1958	10.7	4.5	1990	12.4	10.0
1927	13.2	8.4	1959	10.6	4.6	1991	12.2	10.5
1928	13.5	8.6	1960	10.6	4.7	1992	12.0	10.0
1929	13.9	8.4	1961	10.4	4.7	1993*	12.1	9.9
1930	15.6	8.8	1962	10.9	4.9			
1931	16.8	9.2	1963	11.0	4.9			

* Estimated.

Violence

Comments   The table shown here follows the rates of homicides and suicides in the United States since the turn of the century. The rates for homicide and suicide, the two methods of willfully killing a person, have risen and fallen throughout the 20th century.

During the first half of the century, the rate of suicide widely fluctuated. The frequency of suicide skyrocketed in the early years of the 1900s, and stood at 16.8 per 100,000 in 1908. But by 1920, the suicide rate had fallen back to 10.2 per 100,000. The suicide rate steadily climbed throughout the prohibition years, and increased even more quickly at the onset of the Great Depression (1929–41). The suicide rate peaked during the early years of the Depression. Perhaps the worst year of the Depression was 1932, because widespread joblessness and economic collapse were rampant. The rate of suicide in 1932 stood at 17.4 per 100,000, the highest rate any time during this century. After 1932, however, the suicide rate gradually declined until the end of the Depression and throughout World War II (1941–45). After World War II, the suicide rate hovered in the 10–11 per 100,000 range until the 1970s. Since the 1970s, the annual suicide rate has typically been slightly higher than 12 per 100,000.

The rate for homicide quickly elevated throughout the first two decades of this century. As with other crimes, homicide also became more frequent during the alcohol prohibition years of the 1920s. During the Great Depression, the homicide rate reached a half-century peak in 1933. After 1933, however, the rate of homicide plummeted throughout the remainder of the Depression and declined further during World War II. After a brief rise immediately after World War II, the homicide rate fell to its lowest point in the second half of this century. That low point happened during the late 1950s, when the homicide rate stood at 4.5 per 100,000. The frequency of homicide consistently increased in the early 1960s. The increase of the 1960s brought about legislation like the Gun Control Act of 1968 as a response to rising violence. However, the homicide rate kept climbing until the mid-1970s. The frequency of homicide fell during the early 1980s but wandered upward in the late 1980s.

Source   U.S. Department Of Health and Human Services, Public Health Service, Centers for Disease Control and Prevention, National Center for Health Statistics, *Vital Statistics Rates in the United States 1900–1960* (Washington, DC: U.S. Government Printing Office, 1968).

U.S. Department Of Health and Human Services, Public Health Service, Centers for Disease Control and Prevention, National Center for Health Statistics, *Vital Statistics of the United States* (Hyattsville, Md.: National Center for Health Statistics). Individual volumes for 1961 through 1991.

Edgar A. Suter, M.D. "Guns in the Medical Literature—A Failure of Peer Review," The Journal of the Medical Association of Georgia, (March 1994) 83; pp. 133–147.

Contact   U.S. Department of Health and Human Services, Public Health Service, Centers for Disease Control and Prevention, National Center for Health Statistics, 6525 Belcrest Rd., Hyattsville, MD 20782. Data dissemination: (301) 436-8500.

Statistics on Weapons & Violence

Violence

Violent Crime Index Rate in the United States, 1960–93

Number of offenses per 100,000 inhabitants.

Year	Violent Crime	Property Crime	Total Crime Index*
1960	160.9	1,726.3	1,887.2
1961	158.1	1,747.9	1,906.1
1962	162.3	1,857.5	2,019.8
1963	168.2	2,012.1	2,180.3
1964	190.6	2,197.5	2,388.1
1965	200.2	2,248.8	2,449.0
1966	220.0	2,450.9	2,670.8
1967	253.2	2,736.5	2,989.7
1968	298.4	3,071.8	3,370.2
1969	328.7	3,351.3	3,680.0
1970	363.5	3,621.0	3,984.5
1971	396.0	3,768.8	4,164.7
1972	401.0	3,560.4	3,961.4
1973	417.4	3,737.0	4,154.4
1974	461.1	4,389.3	4,850.4
1975	487.8	4,810.7	5,298.5
1976	467.8	4,819.5	5,287.3
1977	475.9	4,601.7	5,077.6
1978	497.8	4,642.5	5,140.3
1979	548.9	5,016.6	5,565.5
1980	596.6	5,353.3	5,950.0
1981	594.3	5,263.9	5,858.2
1982	571.1	5,032.5	5,603.6
1983	537.7	4,637.4	5,175.0
1984	539.2	4,492.1	5,031.3
1985	556.6	4,650.5	5,207.1
1986	617.7	4,862.6	5,480.4
1987	609.7	4,940.3	5,550.0
1988	637.2	5,027.1	5,664.2
1989	663.1	5,077.9	5,741.0
1990	731.8	5,088.5	5,820.3
1991	758.1	5,139.7	5,897.8
1992	757.5	4,902.7	5,660.2
1993	746.1	4,736.9	5,483.0

* Numbers may not add due to rounding.

Violence

Comments Each year, the FBI compiles statistics regarding the frequency of violent and property crimes. According to the FBI's definition, violent crime is composed of four offenses: murder and nonnegligent manslaughter, forcible rape, robbery, and aggravated assault. All violent crimes involve force or the threat of force. Although the rate for property crime (burglary, larceny-theft, and motor-vehicle theft) far outnumbers that of violent crime, the frequency of violent crime has significantly increased since the early 1960s. The proportion of violent crime to total crime has increased as well.

For instance, in 1962 violent crime accounted for just over 8% of all reported crime per 100,000 inhabitants (162.3 ÷ 2,019.8). But in 1993, violent crime represented over 13.6% of all reported crime per 100,000 inhabitants (746.1 ÷ 5,483.0). Initially, it may seem that this does not represent an enormous increase. Since these statistics only measure reported crimes, perhaps some crimes are reported more frequently now than in the past, while others are more rarely reported now.

Suppose that for some reason property crimes are less likely to be reported now than in the past. Then perhaps the proportion of violent crime to total crime actually might not have changed much during the past three decades. This would only be true however if violent crimes are just as likely to be reported now as in the past.

Source Federal Bureau of Investigation, Criminal Justice Information Services Division.

Contact U.S. Department of Justice, Federal Bureau of Investigation, Uniform Crime Reports, Criminal Justice Information Services Division, Washington, DC 20535. Information Dissemination: (202) 324-5015.

Violence

Violent Crime Is Increasing

Crime rate index (number of offenses per 100,000 inhabitants) in the U.S. for specific violent crimes, 1960–93.

Year	Murder	Forcible Rape	Robbery	Aggravated Assault	Violent Crime Total *
1960	5.1	9.6	60.1	86.1	160.9
1961	4.8	9.4	58.3	85.7	158.1
1962	4.6	9.4	59.7	88.6	162.3
1963	4.6	9.4	61.8	92.4	168.2
1964	4.9	11.2	68.2	106.2	190.6
1965	5.1	12.1	71.7	111.3	200.2
1966	5.6	13.2	80.8	120.3	220.0
1967	6.2	14.0	102.8	130.2	253.2
1968	6.9	15.9	131.8	143.8	298.4
1969	7.3	18.5	148.4	154.5	328.7
1970	7.9	18.7	172.1	164.8	363.5
1971	8.6	20.5	188.0	178.8	396.0
1972	9.0	22.5	180.7	188.8	401.0
1973	9.4	24.5	183.1	200.5	417.4
1974	9.8	26.2	209.3	215.8	461.1
1975	9.6	26.3	220.8	231.1	487.8
1976	8.8	26.6	199.3	233.2	467.8
1977	8.8	29.4	190.7	247.0	475.9
1978	9.0	31.0	195.8	262.1	497.8
1979	9.7	34.7	218.4	286.0	548.9
1980	10.2	36.8	251.1	298.5	596.6
1981	9.8	36.0	258.7	289.7	594.3
1982	9.1	34.0	238.9	289.2	571.1
1983	8.3	33.7	216.5	279.2	537.7
1984	7.9	35.7	205.4	290.2	539.2
1985	7.9	37.1	208.5	302.9	556.6
1986	8.6	37.9	225.1	346.1	617.7
1987	8.3	37.4	212.7	351.3	609.7
1988	8.4	37.6	220.9	370.2	637.2
1989	8.7	38.1	233.0	383.4	663.1
1990	9.4	41.2	257.0	424.1	731.8
1991	9.8	42.3	272.7	433.3	758.1
1992	9.3	42.8	263.6	441.8	757.5
1993	9.5	40.6	255.8	440.1	746.1

* Numbers may not add due to rounding.

Violence

Comments The FBI classifies criminal offenses as either property crime or violent crime, of which violent crime consists of offenses committed with the use or threat of force (murder, forcible rape, robbery, and aggravated assault). A crime rate is simply a measurement that gives an indication of how frequently a crime occurs within a given population.

These numbers are calculated by taking the total number of crime offenses and dividing by the total population number. Then the remaining fraction is multiplied by 100,000 to obtain the frequency of the crime per every 100,000 inhabitants. The rate is shown by the following equation: [crime offenses ÷ total population] × 100,000 = crime rate per 100,000. By measuring the rates for specific crimes, it is possible to see how the frequency of the crime changes over time regardless of changes in the total population size.

Using only year-to-year changes in the number of criminal offenses, it is not possible to tell if the frequency of crime is changing without also knowing the population size. In other words, if population increases, the frequency of crime will remain the same if the number of crimes increases proportionally.

Source Federal Bureau of Investigation, Criminal Justice Information Services Division.

Contact U.S. Department of Justice, Federal Bureau of Investigation, Uniform Crime Reports, Criminal Justice Information Services Division, Washington, DC 20535. Information Dissemination: (202) 324-5015.

Violence

How Much Does Violent Crime Change from One Year to the Next?

Crime index rate yearly percent change in the U.S., 1960–93. Annual percent variation in the number of specific violent offenses per 100,000 inhabitants.

Year	Murder	Forcible Rape	Robbery	Aggravated Assault	Violent Crime Total
1960					
1961	-5.9	-2.1	-3.0	-0.5	-1.7
1962	-4.2	0.0	2.4	3.4	2.7
1963	0.0	0.0	3.5	4.3	3.6
1964	6.5	19.1	10.4	14.9	13.3
1965	4.1	8.0	5.1	4.8	5.0
1966	9.8	9.1	12.7	8.1	9.9
1967	10.7	6.1	27.2	8.2	15.1
1968	11.3	13.6	28.2	10.4	17.9
1969	5.8	16.4	12.6	7.4	10.2
1970	8.2	1.1	16.0	6.7	10.6
1971	8.9	9.6	9.2	8.5	8.9
1972	4.7	9.8	-3.9	5.6	1.3
1973	4.4	8.9	1.3	6.2	4.1
1974	4.3	6.9	14.3	7.6	10.5
1975	-2.0	0.4	5.5	7.1	5.8
1976	-8.3	1.1	-9.7	0.9	-4.1
1977	0.0	10.5	-4.3	5.9	1.7
1978	2.3	5.4	2.7	6.1	4.6
1979	7.8	11.9	11.5	9.1	10.3
1980	5.2	6.1	15.0	4.4	8.7
1981	-3.9	-2.2	3.0	-2.9	-0.4
1982	-7.1	-5.6	-7.7	-0.2	-3.9
1983	-8.8	-0.9	-9.4	-3.5	-5.8
1984	-4.8	5.9	-5.1	3.9	0.3
1985	0.0	3.9	1.5	4.4	3.2
1986	8.9	2.2	8.0	14.3	11.0
1987	-3.5	-1.3	-5.5	1.5	-1.3
1988	1.2	0.5	3.9	5.4	4.5
1989	3.6	1.3	5.5	3.6	4.1
1990	8.0	8.1	10.3	10.6	10.4
1991	4.3	2.7	6.1	2.2	3.6
1992	-5.1	1.2	-3.3	2.0	-0.1
1993	2.2	-5.1	-3.0	-0.4	-1.5

Violence

Comments A crime rate, as calculated by the FBI, is a measurement that indicates how frequently a particular type of crime occurs within the general population. The FBI classifies violent crime as consisting of those offenses committed with the use or threat of force (murder, forcible rape, robbery, and aggravated assault). The FBI's crime rate index relates annual changes in the frequency of a particular type of crime.

The information presented here shows year-to-year percentage changes in annual crime rates. By observing the annual fluctuations in the crime rates, the statistics single out each year's frequency of crime. This makes it possible to determine how often crime occurred compared to the previous year.

The reason why the entry for 1960 is empty is because each year is compared only with the preceding year. The crime rates under analysis are for the 1960–93 period. The first year in this series where the crime rates of one year can be compared with the previous year's rates occurs in 1961.

This information only allows year-to-year comparisons, and can not be used to make any general observations of the changes in the number of crimes occurring overall during the 1960–93 period.

Source Federal Bureau of Investigation, Criminal Justice Information Services Division.

Contact U.S. Department of Justice, Federal Bureau of Investigation, Uniform Crime Reports, Criminal Justice Information Services Division, Washington, DC 20535. Information Dissemination: (202) 324-5015.

Violence

How Do Violent Crime Rates Compare with the Rates of Other Life Events?

Annual rates of violent incidents (per 1,000 adults) compared with the annual rates of other serious events in the U.S. during 1991.

Events (Note: violent events are in boldface)	Rate per 1,000 Adults per Year
Accidental injury, all circumstances	220
Accidental injury at home	66
Personal theft	61
Accidental injury at work	47
Violent victimization	**31**
Assault (aggravated and simple)	**25**
Injury in motor vehicle accident	22
Death, all causes	11
Victimization with injury	**11**
Serious (aggravated) assault	**8**
Robbery	**6**
Heart disease death	5
Cancer death	3
Rape (women only)	**1**
Accidental death, all circumstances	0.4
Pneumonia/influenza death	0.4
Motor vehicle accident death	0.2
Carjacking	**0.2**
Suicide	**0.2**
Homicide/legal intervention	**0.1**

Violence

Comments Since 1973, the National Crime Victimization Survey (NCVS) has measured the amount and features of crime by asking an extensive amount of people whether they had been crime victims. The NCVS provides long-term information about crime victims including the kinds of crime they have experienced, the context of the crime, and impact on victims. The NCVS also provides a glimpse into what the 1967 President's Commission on Law Enforcement and Administration of Justice called the two "dark figures" of crime. These hidden figures include crimes that are not reported to law enforcement agencies and reported crimes that go unrecorded.

For this table, results from the 1991 NCVS were gathered and compared with the results of other surveys and estimates that measure vital and health statistics. Since each survey differs slightly in construction, frequency rates make comparisons possible. A frequency rate tells how often an event occurs within a given population group or over a period of time. In this case, it is possible to make some general comparisons because the whole population of the U.S. is the group being studied, even though the various surveys utilized may have counted different individuals.

According to this table, personal theft is the most common crime event that occurs in a given year. When comparing the rates, the rate of personal theft is about two times larger than the rate of any violent victimization. For any sample group of 1,000 people polled within the course of one year, there should be about twice as many people who were victims of theft than there were victims of violent crimes. The rates for specific violent crimes are lower because the violent victimization rate includes all the specific crimes added together.

Source U.S. Department of Justice, Bureau of Justice Statistics. *Highlights from 20 Years of Surveying Crime Victims* (Washington, DC: U.S. Government Printing Office, 1993), p. 6.

U.S. Department of Justice, Bureau of Justice Statistics, "Carjacking" (Washington, DC: U.S. Government Printing Office, March 1994).

Contact U.S. Department of Justice, Bureau of Justice Statistics Clearinghouse, Box 6000, Rockville, MD 20850. (800) 732-3277.

Violence

Number of State Prisoners in Custody for Violent Offenses, 1979–92

Estimated number of prisoners in state correctional institutions in the U.S., by most serious violent offense.

Year	Murder *	Man-slaughter	Rape	Other Sexual Assault	Robbery	Assault	Other Violent †	Total, Violent Offenses	Total, All Offenses
1979	34,600	11,200	12,100	5,600	70,600	21,700	7,000	162,800	281,233
1980	34,700	11,900	13,200	7,300	75,000	23,300	7,800	173,300	295,819
1981	36,100	13,300	15,000	9,400	84,000	26,600	9,000	193,300	333,251
1982	42,300	14,900	16,500	11,400	90,500	29,900	9,700	215,300	375,603
1983	43,600	13,400	17,000	12,000	88,300	31,300	9,000	214,600	394,953
1984	46,800	13,000	18,400	14,200	89,800	34,000	11,100	227,300	417,389
1985	50,600	14,500	19,400	20,300	94,000	36,100	11,300	246,200	451,812
1986	54,300	14,600	19,800	25,500	94,500	38,600	11,200	258,600	486,655
1987	59,100	14,200	21,000	29,700	95,200	40,800	11,200	271,300	520,336
1988	63,600	13,700	22,100	32,500	96,000	43,100	11,700	282,700	562,605
1989	67,600	13,600	22,600	35,400	97,900	45,500	11,500	293,900	629,995
1990	72,000	13,200	24,500	39,100	99,200	53,300	12,400	313,600	684,544
1991	77,200	13,100	25,500	43,000	107,800	59,000	13,100	339,500	728,605
1992	85,000	14,100	29,500	46,400	113,400	67,900	15,200	370,300	778,495

* Includes nonnegligent manslaughter. Manslaughter is the killing of a person (like murder) but without the hostile or malicious intent.
† Includes extortion, intimidation, criminal endangerment, and other violent offenses.

Violence

Comments

Numbers of inmates in state prisons nearly tripled—from 281,233 to 778,495—between 1979 and 1992, according to the federal Bureau of Justice Statistics. During the period, inmates serving time for violent offenses more than doubled from 162,800 to 370,300.

All categories of violent crime showed increases during the period. Largest percentage increases were for sexual assaults other than rape (729%), assault (213%), murder (146%), and rape (144%).

Prisoners counted here include only inmates in state custody and exclude those housed outside of state facilities. Although the number of prisoners sentenced for violent offenses has risen, inmates kept for violent crimes actually have decreased as a percentage of all state prisoners.

In 1979, violent offenders in custody represented about 58% of all state prisoners. By 1992, this had fallen to 47%. Most of the change was caused by a nearly ten-fold increase in the number of drug offenders.

There are several possible explanations for the changing trends. Changes in criminal acts, as well as arrests, prosecution, sentencing, and release procedures all can affect how many and what kinds of criminals are in prison. First, some crimes may be more widespread now than they once were. Second, some laws might be more strictly enforced than they were before, while enforcement of other laws may have eased. Third, some crimes may carry stiffer penalties now, while other crimes now may have milder penalties. Next, the possibility for an early release from prison might be more common now for some crimes and less common for others. Finally, some crimes may be reported more often now than in the past (allowing police the chance to arrest more criminals), while other crimes might be reported less frequently.

Source

U.S. Department of Justice, Bureau of Justice Statistics. *Correctional Populations in the United States, 1992* (Washington, DC: U.S. Government Printing Office, 1995), p. 53.

Contact

U.S. Department of Justice, Bureau of Justice Statistics Clearinghouse, Box 6000, Rockville, MD 20850. (800) 732-3277.

Violence

Percent of State Prisoners in Custody for Violent Offenses, 1979–92

Estimated percent of inmates in state correctional institutions in the U.S. who where sentenced for a violent offense, by most serious violent offense.

Year	Murder *	Man-slaughter	Rape	Other Sexual Assault	Robbery	Assault	Other Violent †	Total Violent Offenses ‡
1979	12.3	4.0	4.3	2.0	25.1	7.7	2.5	57.9
1980	11.7	4.0	4.4	2.5	25.4	7.9	2.7	58.6
1981	10.8	4.0	4.5	2.8	25.2	8.0	2.7	58.0
1982	11.3	4.0	4.4	3.0	24.1	8.0	2.6	57.3
1983	11.0	3.4	4.3	3.0	22.4	7.9	2.3	54.3
1984	11.2	3.1	4.4	3.4	21.5	8.1	2.7	54.5
1985	11.2	3.2	4.3	4.5	20.8	8.0	2.5	54.5
1986	11.2	3.0	4.1	5.2	19.4	7.9	2.3	53.1
1987	11.4	2.7	4.0	5.7	18.3	7.8	2.1	52.1
1988	11.3	2.4	3.9	5.8	17.1	7.7	2.1	50.3
1989	10.7	2.2	3.6	5.6	15.5	7.2	1.8	46.7
1990	10.5	1.9	3.6	5.7	14.5	7.8	1.8	45.8
1991	10.6	1.8	3.5	5.9	14.8	8.1	1.8	46.6
1992	10.9	1.8	3.8	6.0	14.6	8.7	2.0	47.6

* Includes nonnegligent manslaughter. Manslaughter is the killing of a person (like murder) but without the hostile or malicious intent.
† Includes extortion, intimidation, criminal endangerment, and other violent offenses.
‡ Numbers may not add to total due to rounding.

Violence

Comments

Inmates serving time for violent crimes declined from 57.9% of the state prison population in 1979 to 47.6% in 1992, according to the Bureau of Justice Statistics.

This does not mean that the number of state prisoners serving sentences for violent crimes has fallen; actually, it has grown. What the figures reflect is a sharp increase in people imprisoned for nonviolent crimes, primarily drug offenses. They account for a growing percentage of the inmate population.

However, there are two categories of violent crime for which the percentage of inmates in state prisons grew between 1979 and 1992. Inmates serving time for sexual assaults other than rape went from 2.0% of the prison population in 1979 to 6.0% in 1992. And those sentenced in assault cases rose from 7.7% of the total in 1979 to 8.7% in 1992.

Source

U.S. Department of Justice, Bureau of Justice Statistics. *Correctional Populations in the United States, 1992* (Washington, DC: U.S. Government Printing Office, 1995), p. 52.

Contact

U.S. Department of Justice, Bureau of Justice Statistics Clearinghouse, Box 6000, Rockville, MD 20850. (800) 732-3277.

Violence

Does Locking Up Violent Criminals Help Reduce Violent Crime?

Incarceration of state prisoners compared to violent crime and arrests for violent crime, 1980–92.

Year	Violent Victimizations*	Violent Crimes Reported to the Police †	Adults Arrested for Violent Crimes ‡	Total New Prisoners ¤	Per 1,000 Violent Victimizations	Per 1,000 Violent Crimes Reported to the Police	Per 1,000 Adults Arrested for Violent Crime
1980	3,112,810	1,344,520	383,700	55,200	18	41	144
1981	3,376,660	1,361,820	400,100	52,500	16	39	131
1982	3,261,580	1,322,390	436,400	58,100	18	44	133
1983	2,839,960	1,258,090	416,000	57,000	20	45	137
1984	3,042,560	1,273,280	411,100	54,000	18	42	131
1985	2,747,450	1,328,800	414,600	58,700	21	41	142
1986	2,702,580	1,489,170	468,700	61,700	23	44	132
1987	2,801,970	1,484,000	462,500	65,200	23	41	141
1988	2,937,430	1,566,220	532,600	66,400	23	42	125
1989	2,913,450	1,646,040	578,000	74,200	25	45	128
1990	2,904,080	1,820,130	591,200	79,700	27	44	135
1991	3,036,120	1,911,770	596,000	83,400	27	44	140
1992	3,238,730	1,932,270	612,500	87,600	27	45	143

* Violent victimizations include the number of rapes, robberies, and aggravated assaults, as measured by the National Crime Victimization Survey (NCVS), and the number of murders and nonnegligent manslaughters, as reported in the Uniform Crime Reports (UCR).
† Violent crimes in the UCR include murder, nonnegligent manslaughter, forcible rape, robbery, and aggravated assault.
‡ For each year, the number of adult arrests for violent crimes was estimated by multiplying the proportion of persons age 18 or older who were arrested by the estimated number of arrests.
¤ Includes murder, nonnegligent manslaughter, rape, sexual assault, robbery, and aggravated assault.

Violence

Comments Violent crime, and resulting prison sentences, generally rose between 1980 and 1992, according to the federal Bureau of Justice Statistics.

During the period, violent crimes reported to police rose from 1,344,520 to 1,932,270, and the annual number of new prisoners rose from 55,200 to 87,600. Total violent crimes (including those not reported to police) rose from 3,112,810 to 3,238,730. Violent crimes include murder, nonnegligent manslaughter, forcible rape, robbery, and aggravated assault.

Prison terms for violent victimizations rose from 18 per 1,000 cases in 1980 to 27 per 1,000 in 1992. During the same period, the rates of imprisonment for violent crimes reported to police and for arrests made failed to show the same general upward movement. Despite year-to-year changes, they were little changed from start to finish of the reporting period.

Crime in the United States is measured by the federal government through two systems: the Uniform Crime Reports (UCR) and the National Crime Victimization Survey (NCVS). The UCR gets crime reports from law enforcement agencies. The NCVS uses a random sampling of over 100,000 individuals to measure both reported and unreported crimes each year. Since the UCR and NCVS count different items to measure crime (criminal offenses and crime victims, respectively), using both systems gives a better picture of crime in the United States. How the figures are viewed is adjusted to allow for the different systems.

Source U.S. Department of Justice, Bureau of Justice Statistics, *Correctional Populations in the United States, 1992* (Washington, DC: U.S. Government Printing Office, 1995), p. 61. Source also cites U.S. Department of Justice, Bureau of Justice Statistics, *Highlights from 20 Years of Surveying Crime Victims* (Washington, DC: U.S. Government Printing Office, 1993).

Contact U.S. Department of Justice, Bureau of Justice Statistics Clearinghouse, Box 6000, Rockville, MD 20850. (800) 732-3277.

Violence

Convictions and Sentences for Violent Crimes, Compared to the Number of Arrests in 1992

The number of adults arrested, felony convictions, and incarceration sentences for certain violent crimes in the U.S. in 1992.

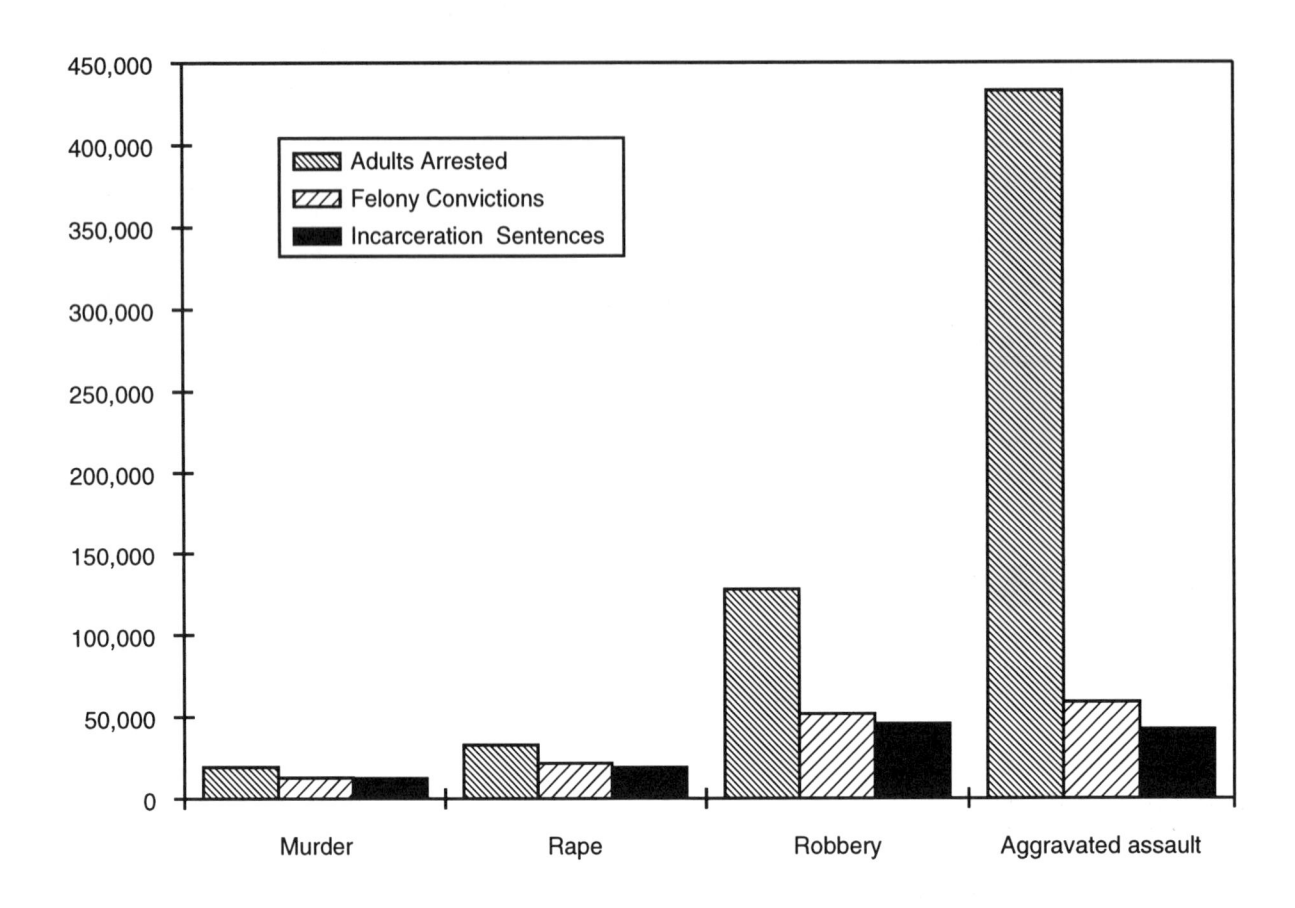

Type of Crime	Number of Adults Arrested	Number of Felony Convictions	Number of Incarceration Sentences	Convictions per 100 Arrests	Incarceration Sentences per 100 Arrests
Murder	19,246	12,548	12,172	65	63
Rape	32,805	21,655	18,840	66	57
Robbery	127,729	51,878	45,653	41	36
Aggravated assault	432,650	58,969	42,458	14	10

Violence

Comments The Bureau of Justice Statistics' National Judicial Reporting Program (NJRP) reports that 63% of the 19,246 murder case arrests in 1992 ended with prison sentences. There were convictions in 65% of the cases.

For rape, 57% of the 32,805 arrests resulted in jail time; there were convictions in 66% of the cases. Next came robbery, with 36% of 127,729 charged going to prison; the conviction rate was 41%.

NJRP compiles detailed information on the sentences and characteristics of convicted felons. Using data from NJRP and the Federal Bureau of Investigation's Uniform Crime Reports (UCR) on arrests, it is possible to compare arrests with convictions. It is important to remember that these numbers are aggregates and should not be interpreted as representing individual cases that went through the legal system. Actually, a person arrested for a specific offense may be convicted of a different crime if charges are changed or a plea bargain is arranged. Also, someone arrested in 1992 may not have been convicted during the same year.

In spite of that, the comparisons show the approximate odds of being convicted and going to prison if one is charged with a violent crime.

Source U.S. Department of Justice, Bureau of Justice Statistics, "Federal Firearms-Related Offenses" (Washington, DC: U.S. Government Printing Office, June 1995).

U.S. Department of Justice, Federal Bureau of Investigation, *Crime in the United States, 1992* (Washington, DC: U.S. Government Printing Office, 1993).

Contact U.S. Department of Justice, Federal Bureau of Investigation, Uniform Crime Reports, Criminal Justice Information Services Division, Washington, DC 20535. Information Dissemination: (202) 324-5015.

U.S. Department of Justice, Bureau of Justice Statistics Clearinghouse, Box 6000, Rockville, MD 20850. (800) 732-3277.

Violence

Released Violent Offenders* in 1992 by Type of Offense and Average Time Served

The average number of months for a prison sentence compared with the average number of months served in prison. Details are for released violent offenders on the U.S. during 1992.

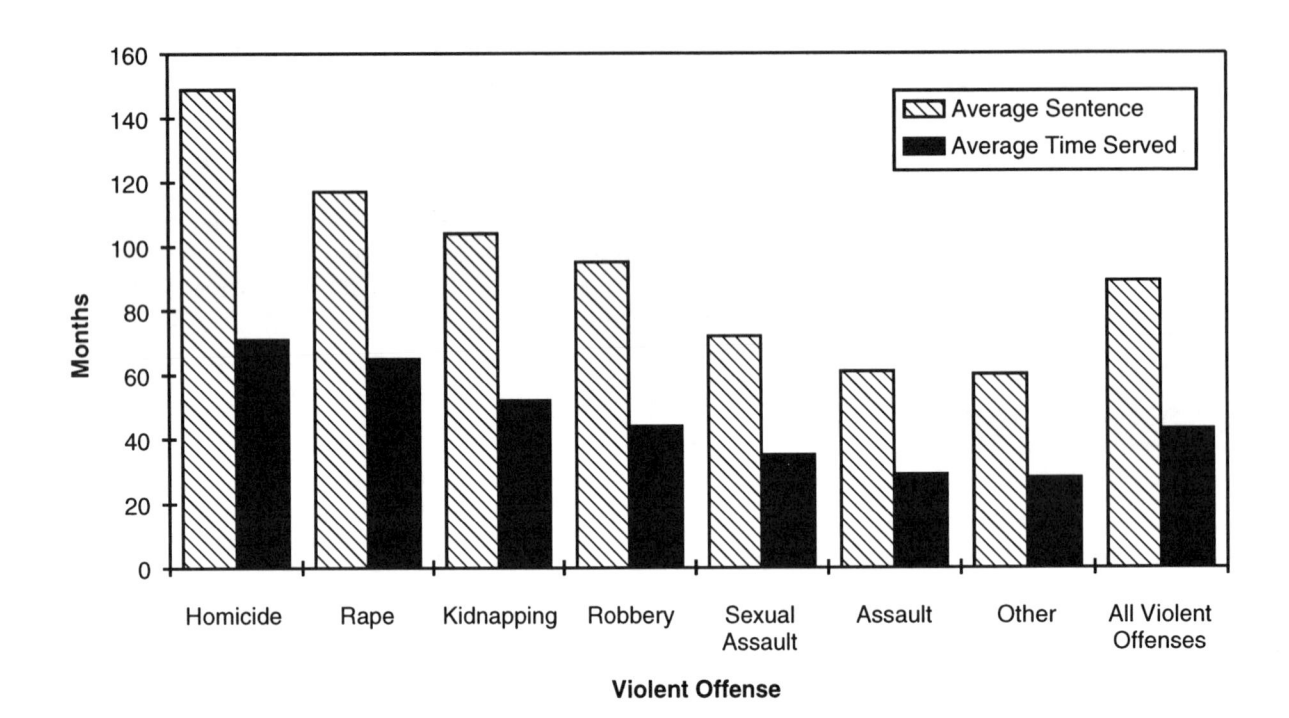

Type of Offense	Average Sentence (months)	Average Time Served† (months)	Portion of Sentence Served
Homicide	149	71	48%
Rape	117	65	56%
Kidnapping	104	52	50%
Robbery	95	44	46%
Sexual assault	72	35	49%
Assault	61	29	48%
Other	60	28	47%
All violent offenses	89	43	48%

* Violent offenders are persons convicted of homicide, kidnapping, forcible rape, sexual assault, robbery, assault, and other crimes involving the threat or imposition of harm upon the victim. Such offenses also include extortion, intimidation, reckless endangerment, hit-and-run driving with injury, and child abuse.
† Includes jail credit and prison time.

Violence

Comments Violent offenders usually served just 48% of an average 89-month sentence, according to the National Corrections Reporting Program (NCRP). Thirty-eight states and the District of Columbia participated in the NCRP, covering 93% of state prison admissions and 86% of state prison releases nationwide during 1992. Although the length of the sentence was gathered for both groups of prisoners, time served (including local jail credits) was only obtainable for those released from prison.

Portions of sentences served showed little variation from one type of violent crime to the next. They ranged from 46% in robbery cases to 56% for rape.

Although state-by-state sentence lengths for violent offenders vary significantly, the actual time spent in confinement changed less severely from one state to the next.

Source Bureau of Justice Statistics, "Prison Sentences and Time Served for Violence," April 1995.

Contact Bureau of Justice Statistics Clearinghouse, Box 6000, Rockville, MD 20850. (800) 732-3277

From 1989 to 1992, although the average sentence dropped from 95 to 89 months, the average time served went from 41 to 43 months. This increase meant that the proportion of the sentence served rose from 43% to 48%. The trend reflects increased truth in sentencing. This means that the sentence imposed upon the prisoner more closely corresponds to the actual amount of time served prior to prison release.

Fixed sentencing, mandatory minimums, and guidelines-based sentencing have all become more common since the mid-1970s. Most state prisoners today can estimate their own probable release dates. In 1977, about 72% of those released from state prisons had served indeterminate sentences (terms with no fixed completion dates), and parole boards decided their release dates. In 1992, less than 40% of prison releases were determined by parole boards.

Violence

Gang-Related Violent Crimes Prosecuted in 1991

Frequency distribution of gang-related violent crimes prosecuted per month in surveyed large and small U.S. cities.

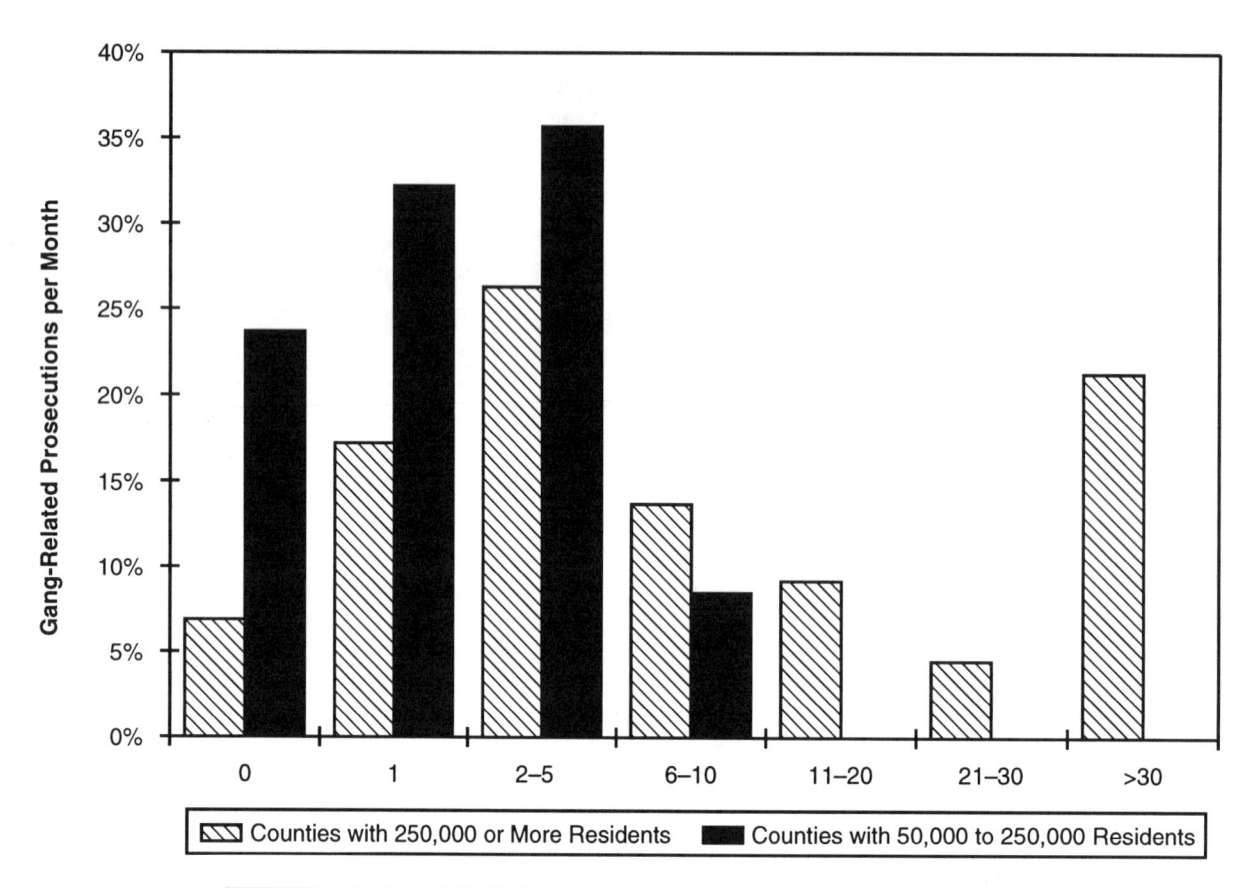

	Counties with 250,000 or More Residents	Counties with 50,000 to 250,000 Residents
0	6.9%	23.7%
1	17.2%	32.2%
2–5	26.3%	35.7%
6–10	13.7%	8.5%
11–20	9.2%	0.0%
21–30	4.5%	0.0%
More than 30	21.3%	0.0%

Comments Extreme violence has become a major part of gang activities. In 1991/92, the National Institute of Justice (NIJ) polled the state prosecutors' offices of 192 large urban counties about gang activities. It found the average number of gang-related homicides prosecuted in 1991 was 8.9 in large counties and 1.75 in small counties.

Large counties were defined as having 250,000 or more residents. Small ones had 50,000-250,000.

NIJ asked about the number of gang-related homicides, driveby shootings, and violent crimes prosecuted per month. It wanted to measure the effects of gang violence on caseloads. Prosecutors in large counties handled an average of 15.1 gang-related violent crimes per month, compared with 3.3 in small counties. About 50% of all the large counties prosecuted fewer than six gang-related violent crime cases per month. But 21.3% of the large counties prosecuted more than 30 such cases per month.

This concentration of percentages at the high and low ends could indicate that gang-related violent crime is a much greater problem in some areas than in others. Or it could mean that some counties are just more aggressive in prosecuting gang-related violent crimes. Prosecution of gang-related crime was less frequent in the smaller counties. Again, this could be the result of either fewer gang-related violent crimes or of lax prosecution. Fewer gang-related crimes is the more likely reason.

Source U.S. Department of Justice, National Institute of Justice, Office of Justice Programs, "Prosecuting Gangs: A National Assessment" (Washington, DC: U.S. Government Printing Office, February 1995).

Contact U.S. Department of Justice, National Institute of Justice, National Criminal Justice Reference Service, Box 6000, Rockville, MD 20849. (800) 851-3420. Inquiries can also be sent by e-mail to askncjrs@aspensys.com.

Violence

How Long Are Violent Criminals Staying in Prison?

Average violent crime sentences for prison admissions and releases during 1988–92.

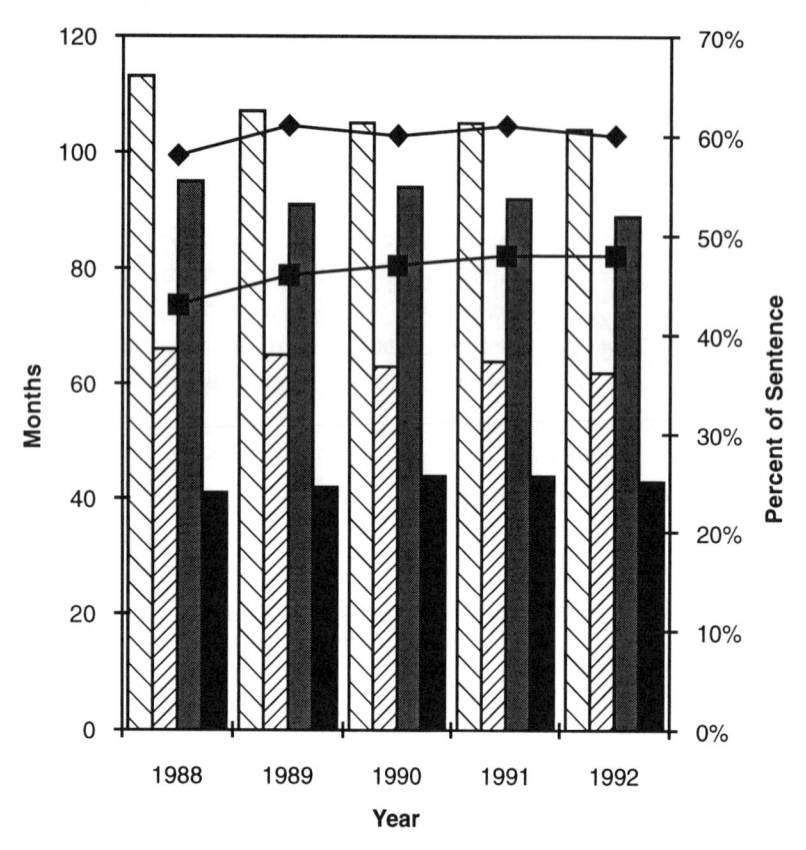

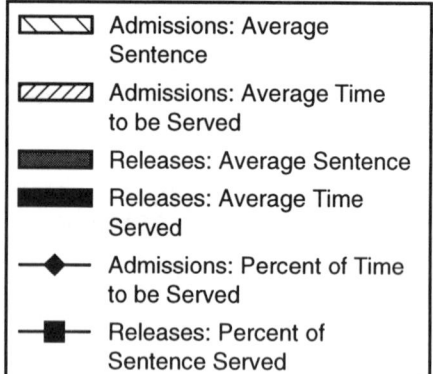

	1988	1989	1990	1991	1992
Prison Admissions					
Average sentence (months)	113	107	105	105	104
Average time to be served (months)	66	65	63	64	62
Percent of time to be served	58%	61%	60%	61%	60%
Prison Releases					
Average sentence (months)	95	91	94	92	89
Average time served (months)	41	42	44	44	43
Percent of sentence served	43%	46%	47%	48%	48%

Statistics on Weapons & Violence

Violence

Comments

Criminals imprisoned for violent offenses generally served less than half of their sentences during 1988–92, says the federal Bureau of Justice Statistics. They also served less time than had been predicted at the times they were imprisoned.

Since 1988, the percentage differences between the estimate of time to be served (upon admission) and percentage of sentence completed (at release) have been narrowing. For example, in 1988 the average estimate of the sentence to be served was 58%, but the prisoners who were released that year had served only 43% of their terms. By 1992, however, this difference had narrowed to 60% predicted and 48% served.

Sentencing of violent criminals has changed within the past twenty years. Since the mid-1970s, the use of sentence lengths determined by parole boards has declined. Most inmates now know about how long their sentences will take when they enter prison.

The sentence length exceeded the actual time served each year from 1988 to 1992 for the prisoners released. For the admissions, the information uses estimates reflecting then-current policies and laws affecting prison sentences. Also, the estimate at admission for percent of time to be served was greater than the percentage of the sentence actually served upon release.

During a prison stay, a prisoner might earn credits against a sentence (such as good time). Reductions in sentence length also might occur (such as sentence rollbacks during prison crowding emergencies).

Source

U.S. Department of Justice, Bureau of Justice Statistics, "Prison Sentences and Time Served for Violence" (Washington, DC: U.S. Government Printing Office, April 1995).

Contact

U.S. Department of Justice, Bureau of Justice Statistics Clearinghouse, Box 6000, Rockville, MD 20850. (800) 732-3277.

Violence

Where Do Violent Crimes Occur?

Percent distribution of where the 5,964,090 violent victimizations of 1992 occurred by location.

Location	Percent of Incidents
At or in respondent's home	12.0%
Near home	7.3%
On the street near home	4.3%
At, in, or near a friend's, relative's, or neighbor's home	7.4%
On street near a friend's, relative's, or neighbor's home	1.2%
Inside a restaurant, bar, or nightclub	4.9%
Other commercial building	5.5%
Parking lot or garage	8.5%
Inside school building	6.2%
On school property	5.9%
In apartment, yard, park, field, or playground	4.9%
On the street not near own or friend's home	24.3%
On public transportation or inside station	1.4%
Other	6.1%
Total *	100.0%

* May not add to total due to rounding.

Violence

Comments

The most frequent location for violent crimes was on the street, away from the victim's own home or a friend's home, according to the 1992 National Crime Victimization Survey (NCVS). At 24.3% of cases, this category easily exceeded the No. 2 location—at or in the victim's home—which was cited 12.0% of the time.

Violent crime often occurs within the victim's own neighborhood or community. Places within the victim's neighborhood where violence occurred included near the victim's home, 7.3%; and on the street near the victim's home, 4.3%. Violence happening "at, in, or near a friend's, relative's, or neighbor's home" accounted for 7.4%. Adding the percentages for these sites together shows about 31% of all the violent crimes occurred within the victim's own neighborhood.

However, some of the cases at a friend's or relative's home might have occurred in other neighborhoods.

NCVS annually collects information by polling over 100,000 U.S. residents over age 12 about reported and unreported violent crimes. In 1992, NCVS estimated the total number of cases in the United States at 5,964,090. Homicides are not included because the victims cannot be interviewed.

Source

U.S. Department of Justice, Bureau of Justice Statistics. *Criminal Victimization in the United States, 1992* (Washington, DC: U.S. Government Printing Office, 1994), p. 75.

Contact

U.S. Department of Justice, Bureau of Justice Statistics Clearinghouse, Box 6000, Rockville, MD 20850. (800) 732-3277.

National Victim Center, 2111 Wilson Blvd., Suite 300, Arlington, VA 22201. (703) 276-2880.

Violence

Where Does Violence Occur When Committed by a Stranger, Friend, Relative, or Acquaintance?

Percent distribution of violent incidents in the U.S. between strangers and nonstrangers in 1992 based on place of occurrence.

Place	Committed by a Stranger	Committed by a Nonstranger
At or in respondent's home	15.3%	84.7%
Near home	51.1%	48.9%
On the street near home	71.4%	28.6%
At, in, or near a friend's, relative's, or neighbor's home	24.2%	75.8%
On street near a friend's, relative's, or neighbor's home	79.0%	21.0%
Inside a restaurant, bar, or nightclub	62.3%	37.7%
Other commercial building	63.5%	36.5%
Parking lot or garage	79.5%	20.5%
Inside school building	30.6%	69.4%
On school property	57.7%	42.3%
In apartment, yard, park, field, or playground	67.6%	32.4%
On the street not near own or friend's home	84.9%	15.1%
On public transportation or inside station	87.9%	12.7%
Other	63.6%	36.4%

Violence

Comments

National Crime Victimization Survey (NCVS) statistics for 1992 show home can be a dangerous place when the crime victim and offender know each other. NCVS found that in violent crimes committed at the victims' homes, the offenders were not strangers 84.7% of the time. Other high-risk places for crimes committed by nonstrangers are at, in, or near a friend's, relative's, or neighbor's home (75.8%) and inside school buildings (69.4%).

The least likely place for a violent crime when the victim and offender know each other was on public transportation or inside a transit station (12.7% of the time).

However, transit facilities do represent high-risk areas when the victim and offender do not know each other. In that case, public transportation or transit stations were crime scenes 87.9% of the time. Other dangerous areas were on the street not near the victim's or a friend's home (84.9%) and in a parking lot or garage (79.5%). However, familiar settings aren't always safe from violent crimes by strangers. In 71.4% of the cases in which people were attacked on the street near home, strangers were the offenders.

The least likely place for an offender to strike if victim and criminal are not acquainted was at the victim's home (15.3% of the time).

The figures challenge the idea that violent crime is a problem in which offenders randomly pick their victims. Although this is often true, many times violent criminals also will attack their own friends, relatives, and acquaintances.

NCVS monitors trends in reported and unreported crime by annually polling over 100,000 U.S. residents 12 and older about cases of rape, robbery, and assault.

Source

U.S. Department of Justice, Bureau of Justice Statistics. *Criminal Victimization in the United States, 1992* (Washington, DC: U.S. Government Printing Office, 1994), p. 78.

Contact

U.S. Department of Justice, Bureau of Justice Statistics Clearinghouse, Box 6000, Rockville, MD 20850. (800) 732-3277.

National Victim Center, 2111 Wilson Blvd., Suite 300, Arlington, VA 22201. (703) 276-2880.

Who Are the Victims of Violent Crime?

Victimization rate in the U.S. from violent crimes per 1,000 persons age 12 and older in 1991.

Sex and Marital Status	
Males	40
Never married	80
Divorced/separated	44
Married	19
Widowed	*
Females	23
Never married	43
Divorced/separated	45
Married	11
Widowed	6
Age	
12–15	63
16–19	91
20–24	75
25–34	35
35–49	20
50–64	10
65 and older	4
Race	
White	30
Black	44
Other	28
Ethnicity	
Hispanic	36
Non-Hispanic	31
Family Income	
Less than $7,500	59
$7,500–$9,999	42
$10,000–$14,999	43
$15,000–$24,999	31
$25,000–$29,999	32
$30,000–$49,999	25
$50,000 and more	20
Education	
0–4 years	18
5–7 years	45
8 years	28
9–11 years	49
High school graduate	28
1–3 years college	36
College graduate	18

[Continued]

Who are the Victims of Violent Crime?

[Continued]

Residence	
Central city	44
1,000,000 or more	39
500,000–99,999	50
250,000–499,999	54
50,000–249,999	38
Suburban	26
Rural	25

* Based on 10 or fewer sample cases.

Comments Males, people 16–19 years old, blacks, the poor, people who did not graduate from high school, and residents of large cities were the likeliest violent crime victims in 1991. The National Crime Victimization Survey, which annually measures rates of reported and unreported crime based on interviews with over 100,000 U.S. residents 12 and older, provided the data.

Forty males per 1,000 of population said they had experienced violent crimes in the previous year. This compares to twenty-three per 1,000 for women. Single people seemed more at risk than those who were married. Eighty per 1,000 of single men and 44 per 1,000 who were divorced or separated were victims. This compares to nineteen per 1,000 for married men. Among women, singles (43 per 1,000) and divorced/separated persons (45 per 1,000) were more at risk than those who were married (eleven per 1,000).

The most dangerous age group, 16–19, had 91 instances of violent crime per 1,000. Next came the 20–24 age group with 75. Blacks were victims at a rate of 44 per 1,000. This compared to 30 per 1,000 for whites and 28 per 1,000 for all others.

Risk generally seemed to diminish as family income grew. For families with annual incomes of less than $7,500, 59 individuals per 1,000 were victims of violent crimes.

There was no easily defined risk pattern based on education levels of the victims. Those with five to seven years of schooling (45 victims per 1,000) and nine to eleven years (49 per 1,000) experienced violent crimes most often.

Among city dwellers, those living in central cities (44 per 1,000) and in cities with populations of 500,000–999,999 (50 per 1,000) and 250,000–499,999 (54 per 1,000) were victims most often. The suburbs (26 per 1,000) and rural areas (25 per 1,000) had the lowest violent crime rates.

Source U.S. Department of Justice, Bureau of Justice Statistics. *Highlights from 20 Years of Surveying Crime Victims* (Washington, DC: U.S. Government Printing Office, 1993), p. 18.

Contact U.S. Department of Justice, Bureau of Justice Statistics Clearinghouse, Box 6000, Rockville, MD 20850. (800) 732-3277.

Violence

Reasons Given for Reporting or Failing to Report Violent Crimes

Reasons victims gave most frequently for reporting or not reporting a violent crime to the police in the U.S. during 1992.

Crime	Most frequent reasons for reporting to the police	Most frequent reasons for failing to report to police
Rape	Prevent further crimes by offender, 23% Punish offender, 12% Prevent crime by offender against anyone, 12%	Private or personal matter, 18% Police inefficient, ineffective, or biased, 13% Offender unsuccessful, 13%
Robbery	Recover property, 20% Prevent further crimes by offender, 12% Catch or find offender, 11%	Object recovered, offender unsuccessful, 19% Lack of proof, 13% Police would not want to be bothered, 11%
Aggravated Assault	Prevent further crimes by offender, 20% Stop or prevent this incident, 15% Because it was a crime, 14%	Private or personal matter, 22% Offender unsuccessful, 16% Lack of proof, 9%
Simple Assault	Prevent further crimes by offender, 25% Stop or prevent this incident, 17% Because it was a crime, 11%	Private or personal matter, 26% Offender unsuccessful, 19% Reported to another official, 13%

Violence

Comments

Preventing further crimes by the offender topped other reasons for reporting violent crimes to police, the National Criminal Victimization Survey (NCVS) found.

That was given as victims' primary reason for reporting simple assaults (25% of the time), rapes (23%), and aggravated assaults (20%). It was the second-leading reason for reporting robberies. Recovery of property (20% of the time) topped the reasons for reporting robberies.

The reason most often given for not reporting violent crimes to the police was that the incidents were private or personal matters. It was cited 26% of the time by simple assault victims, by 22% of those suffering aggravated assaults, and 18% of rape victims. The primary reason for not reporting a robbery (cited 19% of the time) was that the property was recovered or the offender was unsuccessful.

NCVS found that in 1992, victims reported only about 50% of all violent incidents to the police. This proportion excludes murders, because it is impossible to survey such victims. There was no distinguishable difference in reporting an offense that was committed by a stranger or a nonstranger. Violent crime victims who were 12–19 years old generally were less likely than persons in other age groups to report crimes to the police.

According to the NCVS, women are more likely than men to report violent crimes. Women reported about 56% of their cases to the police. Men only reported about 45% of the time.

NCVS annually polls over 100,000 U.S. resident citizens over age 12 about their experiences with reported and unreported violent crimes.

Source

U.S. Department of Justice, Bureau of Justice Statistics. *Highlights from 20 Years of Surveying Crime Victims* (Washington, DC: U.S. Government Printing Office, 1993), pp. 33, 34.

Contact

U.S. Department of Justice, Bureau of Justice Statistics Clearinghouse, Box 6000, Rockville, MD 20850. (800) 732-3277.

National Victim Center, 2111 Wilson Blvd., Suite 300, Arlington, VA 22201. (703) 276-2880.

Violence

How Many Crime Victims Are Violent Crime Victims?

The estimated number of victimizations (in thousands) in the U.S. resulting from violent crime during 1973–92.

Year	Total Number of Crime Victimizations (1,000s)	Violent Crime Victimizations (1,000s)	Violent Crime as a Percent of the Total
1973	35,661	5,350	15.0%
1974	38,411	5,510	14.3%
1975	39,266	5,573	14.2%
1976	39,318	5,599	14.2%
1977	40,314	5,902	14.6%
1978	40,412	5,941	14.7%
1979	41,249	6,159	14.9%
1980	40,252	6,130	15.2%
1981	41,454	6,582	15.9%
1982	39,756	6,459	16.2%
1983	37,001	5,903	16.0%
1984	35,544	6,021	16.9%
1985	34,864	5,823	16.7%
1986	34,118	5,515	16.2%
1987	35,336	5,796	16.4%
1988	35,796	5,910	16.5%
1989	35,818	5,861	16.4%
1990	34,404	6,009	17.5%
1991	35,497	6,587	18.6%
1992	33,649	6,621	19.7%

Violence

Comments

Violent acts, as a percent of all crimes, generally increased between 1972 and 1992, according to the National Crime Victimization Survey (NCVS). Violent crimes peaked at 19.7% of total offenses in 1992 after being as low as 14.2% in 1975 and 1976.

NCVS annually polls over 100,000 resident U.S. citizens 12 and older about experiences with reported and unreported crimes. Based on the responses, NCVS estimates numbers of crimes.

The NCVS classifies crimes three ways: personal theft, household crimes, and violent crimes. Personal theft includes crimes like purse snatching, pocket picking, and stealing items found in cars. Household crimes consist of burglary, household larceny, and motor vehicle theft. Violent crimes included by the NCVS are rape, robbery, and assault. Homicides are not included because the victims cannot be interviewed.

During 1973–92, the total number of crime victims peaked in 1981 at nearly 41.5 million, NCVS said. The total number of crime victims has fallen since the early 1980s, but the percentage of violent crime has continued to rise.

Source

U.S. Department of Justice, Bureau of Justice Statistics, Criminal Victimization in the United States, 1992 (Washington, DC: U.S. Government Printing Office, 1994), p. 4.

Contact

U.S. Department of Justice, Bureau of Justice Statistics Clearinghouse, Box 6000, Rockville, MD 20850. (800) 732-3277.

Violence

Victimization Rates for Violent Crimes, 1973–92

The estimated number of victimizations (per 1,000 persons age 12 and older) for certain crimes of violence in the U.S.

Year	Rape *	Robbery †	Aggravated Assault ‡	Simple Assault ¤	Total Assault	Total
1973	1.0	6.7	10.1	14.8	24.9	32.6
1974	1.0	7.2	10.4	14.4	24.8	33.0
1975	0.9	6.8	9.6	15.6	25.2	32.8
1976	0.8	6.5	9.9	15.4	25.3	32.6
1977	0.9	6.2	10.0	16.8	26.8	33.9
1978	1.0	5.9	9.7	17.2	26.9	33.7
1979	1.1	6.3	9.9	17.3	27.2	34.5
1980	0.9	6.6	9.3	16.5	25.8	33.3
1981	1.0	7.4	9.6	17.3	27.0	35.3
1982	0.8	7.1	9.3	17.1	26.4	34.3
1983	0.8	6.0	8.0	16.2	24.1	31.0
1984	0.9	5.7	9.0	15.7	24.7	31.4
1985	0.7	5.1	8.3	15.9	24.2	30.0
1986	0.7	5.1	7.9	14.4	22.3	28.1
1987	0.8	5.3	8.0	15.2	23.3	29.3
1988	0.6	5.3	8.7	15.0	23.7	29.6
1989	0.7	5.4	8.3	14.7	23.0	29.1
1990	0.6	5.7	7.9	15.4	23.3	29.6
1991	0.9	5.9	8.0	17.5	25.5	32.2
1992	0.7	5.9	9.0	16.5	25.5	32.1

* Sexual contact through the use of force, including attempts. Statutory rape (without force) is excluded. Both heterosexual and homosexual rape are included.

† Completed or attempted theft, directly from a person, of property or cash by force or threat of force, with or without a weapon.

‡ Attack or attempted attack with a weapon, regardless of whether or not an injury occurred, and attack without a weapon when serious injury results.

¤ Attack without a weapon resulting either in minor injury or in undetermined injury requiring less than two days of hospitalization. Also includes attempted assault without a weapon.

Violence

Comments Violent crime rates led an up-and-down existence between 1973 and 1992, according to the National Crime Victimization Survey (NCVS). Total violent crime finished 1992 with 32.1 victims per 1,000 U.S. residents. That is near the 1973 figure of 32.6 per 1,000 but an increase from 28.1 per 1,000 in 1986, when the rate bottomed out.

NCVS annually polls over 100,000 U.S. resident citizens over age 12 about their experiences with reported and unreported violent crimes. Homicides are not included because the victims cannot be interviewed. Increases and decreases in individual crime categories helped to keep the overall totals in balance from beginning of the period to end.

Rapes fell from 1.0 per 1,000 in 1973 to 0.7 in 1992. Robberies also fell—from 6.7 to 5.9 per 1,000. The same was true for aggravated assaults (involving weapons and serious injuries); they went from 10.1 to 9.0 per 1,000.

However, between 1973 and 1992, simple assaults went from 14.8 to 16.5 per 1,000.

Source U.S. Department of Justice, Bureau of Justice Statistics, *Criminal Victimization in the United States, 1992* (Washington, DC: U.S. Government Printing Office, 1994), p. 6.

Contact U.S. Department of Justice, Bureau of Justice Statistics Clearinghouse, Box 6000, Rockville, MD 20850. (800) 732-3277.

Violence

Percent of Victimizations from Crimes of Violence Reported to the Police, 1973–92

The frequency of reporting a violent incident to the police in the U.S.

Year	Rape *	Robbery †	Aggravated Assault ‡	Simple Assault ¤	Total Assault	Total
1973	49	52	52	38	44	46
1974	52	54	53	39	45	47
1975	56	53	55	39	45	47
1976	53	53	58	41	48	49
1977	58	56	51	39	44	46
1978	49	51	53	37	43	44
1979	51	55	51	37	42	45
1980	41	57	54	40	45	47
1981	56	56	52	39	44	47
1982	53	56	58	40	46	48
1983	47	53	56	41	46	47
1984	56	54	55	40	45	47
1985	61	54	58	40	46	48
1986	48	58	59	41	48	50
1987	52	55	60	38	46	48
1988	45	57	54	41	46	48
1989	51	51	52	38	43	45
1990	54	50	59	42	47	48
1991	59	55	58	42	47	49
1992	53	51	62	43	49	50

* Sexual contact through the use of force, including attempts. Statutory rape (without force) is excluded. Both heterosexual and homosexual rape are included.
† Completed or attempted theft, directly from a person, of property or cash by force or threat of force, with or without a weapon.
‡ Attack or attempted attack with a weapon, regardless of whether or not an injury occurred, and attack without a weapon when serious injury results.
¤ Attack without a weapon resulting either in minor injury or in undetermined injury requiring less than two days of hospitalization. Also includes attempted assault without a weapon.

Violence

Comments

Aggravated assaults (involving weapons and serious injuries) are the violent crimes victims are most likely to report to police, according to the National Crime Victimization Survey (NCVS). In 1992, such cases were reported 62% of the time, compared to 52% in 1973, when the data collection began.

Although some rates rose and fell during the survey period, reports to police increased in every category but one. Total reporting also rose, from 46% of cases in 1973 to 50% in 1992. Only robbery reports showed a decline—a slight drop from 52% of cases in 1973 to 51% in 1992. People usually report crimes because they want to prevent the offender from committing another crime, or they want to recover their property. Usually a crime is left unreported when the victim believes the incident was too much of a private or personal matter, or the offender was unsuccessful.

NCVS annually polls over 100,000 U.S. resident citizens over age 12 about their experiences with reported and unreported violent crimes. Homicides are not included because the victims cannot be interviewed.

If many violent crimes are not reported to police, it can be difficult for law enforcement agencies to act effectively. Information missing from unreported incidents could help in setting up strategies to reduce violent crime.

Source

U.S. Department of Justice, Bureau of Justice Statistics, *Criminal Victimization in the United States, 1992* (Washington, DC: U.S. Government Printing Office, 1994), p. 7.

Contact

U.S. Department of Justice, Bureau of Justice Statistics Clearinghouse, Box 6000, Rockville, MD 20850. (800) 732-3277.

Violence

What Kind of Violent Crime Is Most Frequent?

Number, percent distribution, and rate of violent victimizations, 1992

Type of Crime	Number of Victimizations	Percent of All Victimizations	Rate per 1,000 Persons Age 12 and Older
Crimes of violence	6,621,140	19.7	32.1
Completed	2,409,520	7.2	11.7
Attempted	4,211,610	12.5	20.4
Rape	140,930	0.4	0.7
Completed	40,730	0.1	0.2
Attempted	100,200	0.3	0.5
Robbery	1,255,510	3.6	5.9
Completed	806,460	2.4	3.9
With injury	334,040	10.	1.6
From serious assault	173,480	0.5	0.8
From minor assault	160,550	0.5	0.8
Without injury	472,420	1.4	2.3
Attempted	419,040	1.2	2.0
With injury	103,320	0.3	0.5
From serious assault	55,750	0.2	0.3
From minor assault	47,560	0.1	0.2
Without injury	315,720	0.9	1.5
Assault	5,254,690	15.6	25.5
Aggravated	1,848,530	5.5	9.0
Completed with injury	657,550	2.0	3.2
Attempted with weapon	1,190,970	3.5	5.8
Simple	3,406,160	10.1	16.5
Completed with injury	904,770	2.7	4.4
Attempted with weapon	2,501,390	7.4	12.1
Crimes of theft *	12,210,830	36.3	59.2
Other crimes †	14,817,360	44.0	152.2

* Includes personal larceny with contact (purse snatching, pocket picking) and personal larceny without contact.
† Includes all household crimes (burglary, household larceny, motor vehicle theft) and is measured in numbers of households. Rate is measured per 1,000 households.

Violence

Comments Assault was the violent crime committed most often in 1992, according to the National Crime Victimization Survey (NCVS). Assaults accounted for 79.2% of violent crimes and 15.6% of total offenses cited in the survey.

NCVS found 5,254,690 assault cases among the total of 6,621,140 violent crimes.

The violent crime cited next most often was robbery at 18.3% of the violent cases and 3.6% of total crime. Some of the robbery cases included assaults. NCVS annually polls over 100,000 U.S. resident citizens over age 12 about their experiences with reported and unreported violent crimes. Homicides are not included because the victims cannot be interviewed.

Source U.S. Department of Justice, Bureau of Justice Statistics. *Criminal Victimization in the United States, 1992* (Washington, DC: U.S. Government Printing Office, 1994), pp. 16, 17.

Contact U.S. Department of Justice, Bureau of Justice Statistics Clearinghouse, Box 6000, Rockville, MD 20850. (800) 732-3277.

Violence

How Often Does a Violent Crime Involve More Than One Victim?

Number of violent incidents and victimizations, and ratio of victimizations per incident in the U.S. during 1992.

Type of Crime	Incidents	Number of Victimizations	Ratio of Victimizations per Incident
Crimes of violence	5,964,090	6,621,140	1.11
Completed	2,179,600	2,409,520	1.11
Attempted	3,784,490	4,211,610	1.11
Rape	131,530	140,930	1.07
Completed	35,370	40,730	1.15
Attempted	96,160	100,200	1.04
Robbery	1,113,300	1,255,510	1.10
Completed	741,590	806,460	1.09
With injury	312,110	334,040	1.07
From serious assault	154,780	173,480	1.12
From minor assault	157,320	160,550	1.02
Without injury	429,470	472,420	1.10
Attempted	371,710	419,040	1.13
With injury	91,390	103,320	1.13
From serious assault	45,360	55,750	1.23
From minor assault	46,020	47,560	1.03
Without injury	280,310	315,720	1.13
Assault	4,719,250	5,254,690	1.11
Aggravated	1,594,210	1,848,530	1.16
Completed with injury	574,410	657,550	1.14
Attempted with weapon	1,019,790	1,190,970	1.17
Simple	3,125,030	3,406,160	1.09
Completed with injury	828,210	904,770	1.09
Attempted with weapon	2,296,820	2,501,390	1.09

Violence

Comments   Some violent crimes are more likely than others to have multiple victims. Since numbers of crimes and numbers of victims usually are not equal, it is important to consider this information.

National Crime Victimization Survey (NCVS) data for 1992 show that attempted robberies involving injuries from serious assaults most often have multiple victims. NCVS found 1.23 victims per case.

Attempted aggravated assaults (weapons involved) followed with 1.17 victims per case. The crime least likely to produce multiple victims was a completed robbery involving injuries from a minor assault. There were 1.02 victims per case. NCVS annually polls over 100,000 U.S. resident citizens over age 12 about their experiences with reported and unreported violent crimes. Homicides are not included because the victims cannot be interviewed.

Source   U.S. Department of Justice, Bureau of Justice Statistics. *Criminal Victimization in the United States, 1992* (Washington, DC: U.S. Government Printing Office, 1994), p. 70.

Contact   U.S. Department of Justice, Bureau of Justice Statistics Clearinghouse, Box 6000, Rockville, MD 20850. (800) 732-3277.

Violence

Amount of Economic Loss from Violent Crimes, 1992

Percent distribution of economic loss amounts in the U.S. from violent crimes in 1992.

Type of Crime	Number of Victimizations	No Monetary Value	Less Than $50	$50–$99	$100–$249	$250–$499	$500 or More	Not Known and Not Available
Crimes of violence †	1,548,680	5.3%	25.6%	12.3%	19.4%	8.6%	12.7%	16.2%
Robbery	876,800	1.3%*	28.3%	12.0%	19.7%	9.1%	17.9%	11.6%
Completed	806,460	0.0%*	30.5%	12.5%	20.2%	9.5%	17.7%	9.7%
Attempted	70,340	16.6%*	4.0%*	6.8%*	14.6%*	4.5%*	20.2%*	33.3%*
Assault	639,170	10.3%	22.3%	13.3%	19.8%	7.6%	4.0%*	22.8%
Aggravated	319,570	3.5%*	17.8%	14.9%	22.2%	7.7%*	6.1%*	28.3%
Simple	319,590	17.0%	26.7%	11.6%*	17.5%	8.0%*	1.9%*	17.3%

* Percentage estimates based on 10 or fewer sample cases.
† Includes rape, not shown separately because of the relatively few victims reporting monetary loss.

Violence

Comments

In 1992, over 1.5 million Americans were the victims of violent crimes involving economic losses, according to the National Crime Victimization Survey (NCVS). These losses included property theft or damage, cash losses, medical expenses, and earnings lost due to activities and injuries related to the crime.

Many violent crimes generated little monetary reward for the felons in 1992. In 29.6% of 1992 robberies, economic losses were less than $50. However, 17.7% resulted in losses of over $500.

The amount of losses for specific violent crimes varied in 1992. The actual economic loss from a violent crime is often tough to count or may be unknown until long after the crime has occurred.

In 1992, the average loss from a violent crime was $206, including medical expenses and time lost from work. Robbery was by far the most monetarily expensive violent crime, averaging $555 per offense. Other average monetary losses tabulated by the NCVS included rape, $234; and assault, $124.

Even though the average robbery cost a victim over $500, the NCVS indicated that the median loss from robbery was just $89. This means that one-half of all robberies cost more than $89, and the other half cost less than $89.

The average is so much higher than the median probably because there were a small number of robberies in which the losses were high. There also could have been many robberies that had very small losses. Either condition would cause the median and the average to be different.

NCVS annually polls over 100,000 U.S. resident citizens over age 12 about their experiences with reported and unreported violent crimes. Homicides are not included because the victims cannot be interviewed.

Source

U.S. Department of Justice, Bureau of Justice Statistics. *Criminal Victimization in the United States, 1992* (Washington, DC: U.S. Government Printing Office, 1994), p. 94.

U.S. Department of Justice, Bureau of Justice Statistics, "The Costs of Crime to Victims" (Washington, DC: U.S. Government Printing Office, February 1994).

Contact

U.S. Department of Justice, Bureau of Justice Statistics Clearinghouse, Box 6000, Rockville, MD 20850. (800) 732-3277.

Violence

Total Economic Loss to Victims of Crime, 1992

Percent distribution of the $17.6 billion lost by crime victims in the U.S. due to theft, damage, expenses, and losses.

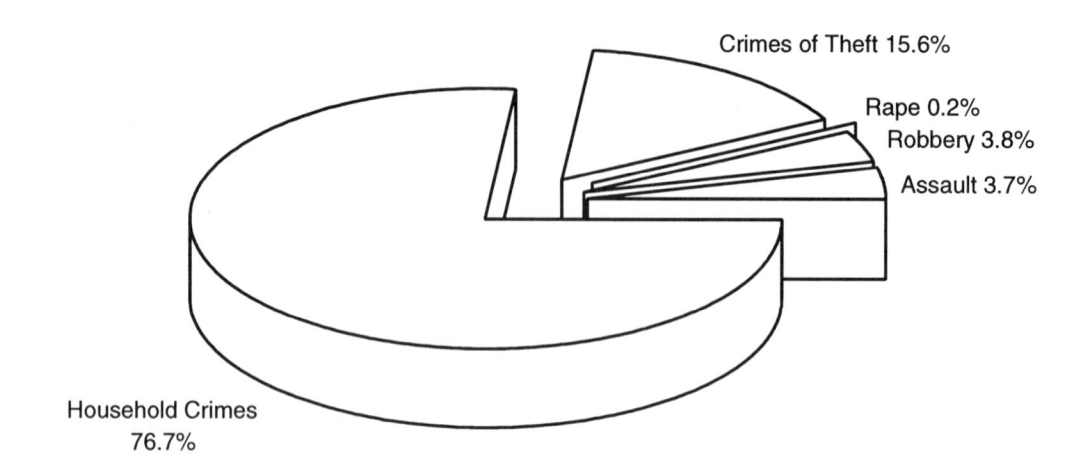

- Crimes of Theft 15.6%
- Rape 0.2%
- Robbery 3.8%
- Assault 3.7%
- Household Crimes 76.7%

Type of Crime	Gross Loss ($ millions)
All crimes	17,646
Household crimes	13,536
Personal crimes	4,110
Crimes of theft	2,748
Crimes of violence	1,362
Rape	33
Robbery	680
Assault	649

Comments

The total estimated cost of crime in 1992 was $17.6 billion, according to the National Crime Victimization Survey. This estimate includes losses from property theft or damage, cash losses, medical expenses, and other costs. This figure combines all the crime victims' estimates of the amount of stolen cash, the value of stolen property, and medical expenses. It also includes the amount of lost pay from work because of injuries, police- and court-related activities, or time spent repairing or replacing property.

Some type of economic loss occurred in 71% of all personal crimes in 1992. These crimes included personal thefts as well as the violent crimes of rape, robbery, and assault. For violent crimes alone, economic loss happened 23% of the time. The economic cost from violent crime accounted for 33% of losses from all personal crimes ($1.36 billion) and 7.7% of losses from all crime in 1992.

The economic costs to victims reported here included only those that had occurred before the interviews, which happened six months or less after the crimes. Medical costs may continue for months or years after a crime. Some victims also may have included psychological counseling as a cost, but it is unclear how frequently such costs were reported.

The estimates also do not include increases in insurance premiums as a result of filing claims, decreased productivity at work, and costs incurred when moving as a result of crime. Also, it is not possible to put into numbers the intangible costs of pain and suffering.

NCVS annually polls over 100,000 U.S. resident citizens over age 12 about their experiences with reported and unreported violent crimes. Homicides are not included because the victims cannot be interviewed.

Source

U.S. Department of Justice, Bureau of Justice Statistics. *Criminal Victimization in the United States, 1992* (Washington, DC: U.S. Government Printing Office, 1994), p. 148.

U.S. Department of Justice, Bureau of Justice Statistics, "The Costs of Crime to Victims" (Washington, DC: U.S. Government Printing Office, February 1994).

Contact

U.S. Department of Justice, Bureau of Justice Statistics Clearinghouse, Box 6000, Rockville, MD 20850. (800) 732-3277.

Violence

How Old Are Victims of Violent Crime?

Violent victimization rate, by age of victim, 1973–92.
Number of rapes, robberies, or assaults per 1,000 persons age 12 and older in the U.S.

Year	12–15	16–19	20–24	25–34	35–49	50–64	65+
1973	55.6	61.4	64.3	34.6	21.6	13.1	8.5
1974	52.7	68.0	61.3	38.7	20.9	11.8	9.0
1975	54.6	64.4	59.4	39.3	20.5	13.5	7.8
1976	52.0	66.7	58.5	40.6	20.0	12.2	7.6
1977	56.5	67.7	63.3	41.9	19.9	12.8	7.5
1978	57.0	68.9	66.9	39.9	19.9	11.4	7.9
1979	53.4	70.2	72.2	43.8	21.3	10.3	5.9
1980	49.5	68.7	68.7	39.8	21.1	11.8	6.8
1981	58.9	67.8	68.3	43.7	23.3	13.2	7.8
1982	52.0	71.2	68.6	46.0	21.5	10.5	5.7
1983	51.3	64.8	60.1	41.1	20.4	9.0	5.5
1984	53.2	67.9	65.4	38.0	21.4	10.1	4.9
1985	54.1	67.2	60.2	37.4	19.9	9.9	4.5
1986	52.4	60.7	58.8	34.3	20.0	8.2	4.5
1987	59.3	69.4	62.8	34.3	19.3	8.6	4.9
1988	56.9	72.0	58.9	35.2	21.8	10.2	4.1
1989	62.9	73.8	57.8	34.9	20.8	7.9	3.9
1990	68.8	74.4	63.1	36.4	19.2	7.5	3.5
1991	64.3	92.1	76.0	35.9	20.8	9.5	3.7
1992	75.7	77.9	70.1	37.6	21.2	10.0	4.8

Comments

The possibility of violent crime makes the ages between 16 and 24 dangerous times, according to the National Crime Victimization Survey (NCVS). Figures compiled from 1973 through 1992 showed the 16–19 and 20–24 age groups most often reported the highest rates of violent crime victims.

At the opposite extreme, ages 65 and older showed the least risk of people becoming victims of violent crimes.

From 1973 to 1992, the 12–15, 16–19, and 25–34 age groups all showed increasing chances of becoming violent crime victims. There were year-to-year rises and falls, so none of the age groups showed steadily increasing risk. The increases in 1992 risk levels over those for 1973 were greater at the lower end of the age range. The 12–15 age group went from 55.6 violent crimes per 1,000 persons in 1973 to 75.7 per 1,000 in 1992. At 16-19, the rise was from 61.4 in 1973 to 77.9 per 1,000 in 1992. The margin of increase continued to shrink at 20–24 and 25–34.

That trend translated into decreasing risks for the older age groups. For those aged 35–49, the risk of violent crime went from 21.6 per 1,000 in 1973 to 21.2 per 1,000 in 1992. The risk fall-off became wider with the 50–64 and then 65-plus age groups.

NCVS annually polls over 100,000 U.S. resident citizens over age 12 about their experiences with reported and unreported violent crimes. Homicides are not included because the victims cannot be interviewed.

Source

U.S. Department of Justice, Bureau of Justice Statistics, "Violent Crime" (Washington, DC: U.S. Government Printing Office, April 1994).

Contact

U.S. Department of Justice, Bureau of Justice Statistics Clearinghouse, Box 6000, Rockville, MD 20850. (800) 732-3277.

National Victim Center, 2111 Wilson Blvd., Suite 300, Arlington, VA 22201. (703) 276-2880.

Violence

Where Do the Injured Victims of Violent Crime Go for Help?

Percent distribution of where victims received medical care in the U.S., by type of crime and where care was received in 1992.

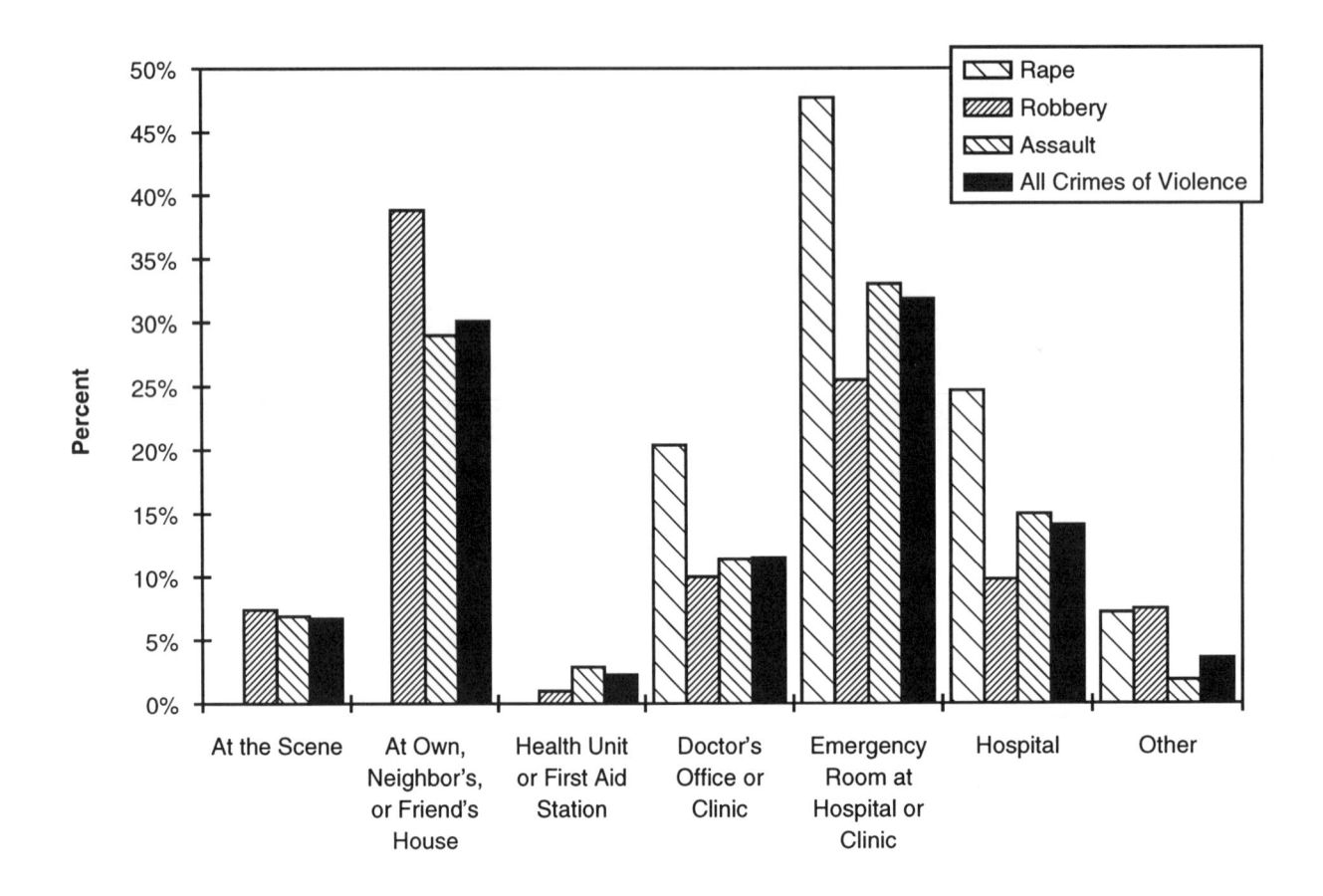

Location	Rape	Robbery	Assault	Crimes of Violence Total
At the scene	0.0%*	7.4%*	6.9%	6.7%
At own, neighbor's, or friend's house	0.0%*	38.8%	29.0%	30.1%
Health unit or first aid station	0.0%*	1.0%*	2.9%*	2.3%*
Doctor's office or clinic	20.4%	10.0%*	11.4%*	11.5%
Emergency room at hospital or clinic	47.7%*	25.5%	33.0%	31.8%
Hospital	24.7%	9.8%*	15.0%*	14.1%
Other	7.2%	7.5%*	1.9%*	3.6%*
Number of victims receiving medical care	68,070	355,570	996,290	1,419,940

* Estimate based on 10 or fewer sample cases.

Violence

Comments In 1992, about 31% of all victims of robbery and assault sustained some physical injury (rape itself is treated as physical injury), according to the National Crime Victimization Survey (NCVS). Over 100,000 U.S. residents annually respond to the NCVS, which inquires about both reported and unreported experiences with crime. There were 1,419,940 people injured during violent crimes.

NCVS said injured victims of violent crime received most medical treatment in private homes (30.1% of the cases) or at hospital emergency rooms (31.8%).

This concentration of treatment at these two specific locations partly may be due to how bad the injuries were. Medical treatment at the victim's own home or at a friend's or neighbor's home may be enough for those with minor injuries. Serious and life-threatening injuries, however, require immediate access to advanced medical care facilities such as emergency rooms. Rape victims often are treated at emergency rooms and hospitals because of the high level of skill needed to treat injuries and gather evidence.

NCVS said about 69% of the injured victims in 1992 had health insurance or were eligible for public medical services. For violent crimes, cost of treating injuries was $250 or more in 65% of the cases for which this information was available. NCVS found access to and costs of medical care were similar for black and white victims.

Source U.S. Department of Justice, Bureau of Justice Statistics. *Criminal Victimization in the United States, 1992* (Washington, DC: U.S. Government Printing Office, 1994), p. 88.

U.S. Department of Justice, Bureau of Justice Statistics, "The Costs of Crime to Victims" (Washington, DC: U.S. Government Printing Office, February 1994).

Contact U.S. Department of Justice, Bureau of Justice Statistics Clearinghouse, Box 6000, Rockville, MD 20850. (800) 732-3277.

Violence

How Old Are Murderers and the People They Kill?

Murder victims and offenders in the U.S. by age, 1993.

Age (years)	Murder Victims	Percent of All Murder Victims *	Murder Offenders	Percent of All Murder Offenders *
< 1	272	1.19	0	0.00
1–4	459	2.00	0	0.00
5–9	173	0.75	2	0.01
10–14	387	1.69	319	1.87
15–19	3,084	13.44	4,650	27.30
20–24	4,355	18.98	4,233	24.85
25–29	3,466	15.10	2,459	14.44
30–34	3,083	13.44	1,763	10.35
35–39	2,318	10.10	1,246	7.31
40–44	1,620	7.06	832	4.88
45–49	1,077	4.69	541	3.18
50–54	717	3.12	349	2.05
55–59	465	2.03	218	1.28
60–64	393	1.71	162	0.95
65–69	319	1.39	100	0.59
70–74	292	1.27	67	0.39
75+	467	2.04	94	0.55
Unknown	324	—	9,204	—
Total	23,271	100.00	26,239	100.00

* Does not include unknown ages. Percents may not add to total because of rounding.

Violence

Comments

The age groups between 15 and 34 had the greatest numbers of murder victims during 1993, the Federal Bureau of Investigation reports. Those groups accounted for 16,306 of 23,271 murder victims. The 20–24 age group had the most victims: 4,355, or 18.98% of the total. Ages 5–9 accounted for the fewest victims: 173, or 0.75%.

Those same age groups also accounted for the greatest numbers of murderers—when ages were available. They accounted for 14,351 of 26,239 offenders. However, ages were not available for 9,204 murderers. The 15–19 age group had the most offenders: 4,650, or 27.30%. The 5–9 group had two offenders, or 0.01%. There were none in the under 1 and 1–4 age groups.

The 15–19 and 20–24 age groups are the only ones in which the percentages of offenders exceed the percentages of victims. There are some possible explanations. First, this group, those aged 15–24, may have murdered a disproportionately high amount of persons from other age groups. Second, persons from other age groups may have murdered a disproportionately low number of those aged 15–24. It is also possible that, to some extent, both conditions existed.

Another possibility is that the large number of unknown cases may have affected the outcome of the age distributions. The murderer's age was unknown 28 times more often than the victim's age was not known. This lopsided difference in the reliability of the data can make comparisons between the two categories difficult.

In 1993, the number of murder victims for whom age was unknown amounted to just 1.4%. However, the number of murderers whose ages were unknown came to 36.1%.

Source

U.S. Department of Justice, Federal Bureau of Investigation, *Crime in the United States, 1993* (Washington, DC: U.S. Government Printing Office, 1994), p. 16.

Contact

U.S. Department of Justice, Federal Bureau of Investigation, Uniform Crime Reports, Criminal Justice Information Services Division, Washington, DC 20535. Information Dissemination: (202) 324-5015.

Violence

Murder Circumstances in 1993 by Relationship of Victim to the Offender

The conditions or reasons surrounding murders in the U.S. in 1993 and the relationships between the murder victims and the murderers.

Murder Circumstance	Family	Acquaintance	Friend	Boyfriend or Girlfriend	Neighbor	Stranger	Unknown Relationship	Total
Total murder victims	2,725	6,217	859	859	207	3,259	9,145	23,271
Felony type total	140	1,097	90	23	52	1,333	1,716	4,451
Rape	7	34	6	0	7	32	30	116
Robbery	29	412	39	5	27	959	830	2,301
Burglary	9	42	3	0	5	54	66	179
Larceny-theft	2	6	1	0	0	15	8	32
Motor vehicle theft	0	8	0	3	0	32	18	61
Arson	13	28	2	2	3	29	74	151
Prostitution and commercialized vice	0	3	0	0	0	5	9	17
Other sex offenses	3	5	1	1	3	3	9	25
Narcotic drug laws	13	479	32	1	1	151	610	1,287
Gambling	0	8	0	0	0	1	1	10
Other, not specified	64	72	6	11	6	52	61	272
Suspected felony type	6	22	0	1	2	19	94	144
Other than felony type	2,331	4,542	698	768	136	1,558	2,202	12,235
Romantic triangle	95	178	27	43	2	33	24	439
Child killed by baby-sitter	3	30	0	0	0	0	0	33
Brawl due to influence of alcohol	54	154	53	17	10	62	31	381
Brawl due to influence of narcotics	11	114	11	2	2	34	88	262
Argument over money or property	47	265	40	12	15	35	31	445
Other arguments	1,337	2,308	447	548	78	759	815	6,292
Gangland killings	1	61	5	0	0	29	51	147
Juvenile gangland killings	0	627	9	0	0	205	306	1,147
Institutional killings	0	10	0	0	0	2	3	15
Sniper attack	0	0	0	0	0	3	4	7
Other, not specified	783	795	106	109	29	396	849	3,067
Unknown	248	556	71	67	17	349	5,133	6,441

Violence

Comments Of the 23,271 murders counted in a 1993 Federal Bureau of Investigation study, 46.7%, or 10,867, were committed by someone the victim knew. This could be a family member, an acquaintance, a boyfriend or girlfriend, or neighbor.

Acquaintances committed 26.7%, or 6,217, of all murders in 1993. Murders by strangers accounted for 14%, or 3,259. About 11.7%, or 2,725, were committed by family members.

There were 9,145 cases (39%) in which the relationship between victim and murderer was unknown. If those cases were solved and added to the categories in which they belong, the rankings could be changed significantly.

Each year, the FBI tabulates the number of murders occurring within the United States according to certain characteristics. One of those involves the relationship between the victim and the murderer.

Random, senseless, and malicious killings often receive the most public attention. However, the murdered victim is just as often a friend, family member, neighbor, or acquaintance of the murderer.

Source U.S. Department of Justice, Federal Bureau of Investigation, *Crime in the United States, 1993* (Washington, DC: U.S. Government Printing Office, 1994), p. 20.

Contact U.S. Department of Justice, Federal Bureau of Investigation, Uniform Crime Reports, Criminal Justice Information Services Division, Washington, DC 20535. Information Dissemination: (202) 324-5015.

Violence

Why a Murder?

Murder circumstances in the U.S., 1989–93. Conditions under which a murder occurred. The information presented provides details from supplemental homicide reports about murder victims.

Murder Circumstance	1989	1990	1991	1992	1993
Total murder victims	18,954	20,273	21,676	22,716	23,271
Felony type total	4,049	4,209	4,636	4,917	4,451
Rape	131	152	132	138	116
Robbery	1,728	1,871	2,226	2,266	2,301
Larceny-theft	18	28	32	41	32
Motor vehicle theft	37	55	53	66	61
Arson	165	152	138	148	151
Prostitution and commercialized vice	12	27	20	32	17
Other sex offenses	58	50	47	34	25
Narcotic drug laws	1,402	1,367	1,353	1,302	1,287
Gambling	23	11	33	20	10
Other, not specified	263	294	405	658	272
Suspected felony type	150	148	210	280	144
Other than felony type	10,270	10,889	11,220	11,244	12,235
Romantic triangle	385	407	314	334	439
Child killed by baby-sitter	24	34	32	36	33
Brawl due to influence of alcohol	432	533	500	429	381
Brawl due to influence of narcotics	306	242	254	253	262
Argument over money or property	551	514	520	483	445
Other arguments	5,736	6,044	6,108	6,066	6,292
Gangland killings	56	104	206	137	147
Juvenile gangland killings	542	679	840	813	1,147
Institutional killings	22	16	19	18	15
Sniper attack	49	41	12	33	7
Other, not specified	2,167	2,275	2,415	2,642	3,067
Unknown	4,485	5,027	5,610	6,275	6,441

Violence

Comments Arguments over things other than money provided the basis for more murders than any other defined cause in Federal Bureau of Investigation figures for 1989–93. They accounted for between 5,736 and 6,292 of the 18,954–23,271 murders recorded during the period. Unknown causes were involved in 4,485–6,441 murders; unknowns topped the arguments group in three of the five years.

The FBI annually tabulates the reasons why murders happen when such details are available. During 1989–93, each year most murders were not related to felonies. Felony cases accounted for only 19–21% of all murders. Non-felony cases accounted for 49–53% of all murders. Murders that happened under unknown circumstances made up 24–28% of all cases.

Most of the murders related to felonies were committed during robberies or drug law violations. During 1989–93, robbery was the circumstance under which 9–10% of all murders took place. Drug law offenses accounted for 6–7%. Murders resulting from rape or arson each usually accounted for less than 1%.

The rest of the murders were committed as a result of other circumstances. Many of these situations involved intense, typically spur-of-the-moment emotional outbursts. Also, there were cases involving gangs and organized crime. About 3–4% of all murders were due to alcohol- or drug-influenced brawls. Of recent concern also are juvenile gang killings, which more than doubled from 1989 to 1993. In 1989, there were 542 juvenile gang killings. By 1993, that had risen to 1,147.

Source U.S. Department of Justice, Federal Bureau of Investigation, *Crime in the United States, 1993* (Washington, DC: U.S. Government Printing Office, 1994), p. 21.

Contact U.S. Department of Justice, Federal Bureau of Investigation, Uniform Crime Reports, Criminal Justice Information Services Division, Washington, DC 20535. Information Dissemination: (202) 324-5015.

Violence

Murders and Murder Rates by State/Territory, 1993

State	Estimated 1993 Population (1,000s)	Total Murders	Murders per 100,000 Inhabitants
Alabama	4,187	484	11.6
Alaska	599	54	9.0
Arizona	3,936	339	8.6
Arkansas	2,424	247	10.2
California	31,211	4,096	13.1
Colorado	3,566	206	5.8
Connecticut	3,277	206	6.3
Delaware	700	35	5.0
District of Columbia	578	454	78.5
Florida	13,679	1,224	8.9
Georgia	6,917	789	11.4
Hawaii	1,172	45	3.8
Idaho	1,099	32	2.9
Illinois	11,697	1,332	11.4
Indiana	5,713	430	7.5
Iowa	2,814	66	2.3
Kansas	2,531	161	6.4
Kentucky	3,789	249	6.6
Louisiana	4,295	874	20.3
Maine	1,239	20	1.6
Maryland	4,965	632	12.7
Massachusetts	6,012	233	3.9
Michigan	9,478	933	9.8
Minnesota	4,517	155	3.4
Mississippi	2,643	357	13.5
Missouri	5,234	590	11.3
Montana	839	25	3.0
Nebraska	1,607	63	3.9
Nevada	1,389	144	10.9
New Hampshire	1,125	23	2.0
New Jersey	7,879	418	5.3
New Mexico	1,616	130	8.0
New York	18,197	2,420	13.3
North Carolina	6,945	785	11.3
North Dakota	635	11	1.7
Ohio	11,091	667	6.0
Oklahoma	3,231	273	8.4
Oregon	3,032	140	4.6
Pennsylvania	12,048	823	6.8
Puerto Rico	3,622	948	26.2

[Continued]

Violence

Murders and Murder Rates by State/Territory, 1993

[Continued]

State	Estimated 1993 Population (1,000s)	Total Murders	Murders per 100,000 Inhabitants
Rhode Island	1,000	39	3.9
South Carolina	3,643	377	10.3
South Dakota	715	24	3.4
Tennessee	5,099	521	10.2
Texas	18,031	2,147	11.9
Utah	1,860	58	3.1
Vermont	576	21	3.6
Virginia	6,491	539	8.3
Washington	5,255	271	5.2
West Virginia	1,820	126	6.9
Wisconsin	5,038	222	4.4
Wyoming	470	16	3.4

Comments People living in the District of Columbia faced the greatest risk of being murdered, a Federal Bureau of Investigation report for 1993 shows. The study of murder cases in the United States and Puerto Rico showed the safest location was Maine.

The three most dangerous places were DC, with 78.5 murders for every 100,000 residents; Puerto Rico, 26.2; and Louisiana, 20.3. Least likely places for murders to happen were Maine, with 1.6 per 100,000 residents; North Dakota, 1.7; and New Hampshire, 2.0.

Although some states had many murders in 1993 (such as California, 4,096; New York, 2,420; and Texas, 2,147), these states also had large populations. As a result, their murder rates were California, 13.1 per 100,000 residents; New York, 13.3; and Texas, 11.9. To accurately compare murder rates in states of widely varying sizes, the report looks at how many cases occurred for every 100,000 residents.

A state's murder rate can vary from year to year. This may happen because the number of murders changes or the population varies. For example, a state's murder rate would drop if there were fewer killings or if the number of killings did not change but the total population grew.

Source Federal Bureau of Investigation, *Crime in the United States, 1993* (Washington, DC: U.S. Government Printing Office, 1994), pp. 68–78, 189. Corresponding 1993 population estimate for Puerto Rico provided by Bureau of the Census staff.

Contact U.S. Department of Justice, Federal Bureau of Investigation, Uniform Crime Reports, Criminal Justice Information Services Division, Washington, DC 20535. Information Dissemination: (202) 324-5015.

Violence

Number and Rate of Reported Forcible Rapes, 1993

The number of reported rapes occurring in the 50 states, the District of Columbia, and Puerto Rico in 1993, and the rate per 100,000 inhabitants.

State	Number of Reported Forcible Rapes	Rate per 100,000 Inhabitants
Alabama	1,471	35.1
Alaska	502	83.8
Arizona	1,488	37.8
Arkansas	1,028	42.4
California	11,766	37.7
Colorado	1,633	45.8
Connecticut	800	24.4
Delaware	539	77.0
District of Columbia	324	56.1
Florida	7,359	53.8
Georgia	2,448	35.4
Hawaii	394	33.6
Idaho	388	35.3
Illinois	4,046	34.6
Indiana	2,234	39.1
Iowa	686	24.4
Kansas	1,016	40.1
Kentucky	1,301	34.3
Louisiana	1,817	42.3
Maine	329	26.6
Maryland	2,185	44.0
Massachusetts	2,006	33.4
Michigan	6,740	71.1
Minnesota	1,588	35.2
Mississippi	1,125	42.6
Missouri	1,894	36.2
Montana	234	27.9
Nebraska	447	27.8
Nevada	846	60.9
New Hampshire	499	44.4
New Jersey	2,215	28.1
New Mexico	842	52.1
New York	5,008	27.5
North Carolina	2,379	34.3
North Dakota	149	23.5
Ohio	5,444	49.1
Oklahoma	1,592	49.3
Oregon	1,554	51.3

[Continued]

Number and Rate of Reported Forcible Rapes, 1993

[Continued]

State	Number of Reported Forcible Rapes	Rate per 100,000 Inhabitants
Pennsylvania	3,195	26.5
Puerto Rico	401	11.1
Rhode Island	286	28.6
South Carolina	1,905	52.3
South Dakota	318	44.5
Tennessee	2,544	49.9
Texas	9,922	55.0
Utah	829	44.6
Vermont	229	39.8
Virginia	2,083	32.1
Washington	3,384	64.4
West Virginia	365	20.1
Wisconsin	1,269	25.2
Wyoming	161	34.3

Comments Alaska (83.8 cases per 100,000 residents), Delaware (77.0), and Michigan (71.1) were the states where the risk of rape was greatest during 1993. Figures gathered by the Federal Bureau of Investigation included all 50 states, the District of Columbia, and Puerto Rico.

Risk was smallest in Puerto Rico (11.1 cases reported per 100,000 residents), West Virginia (20.1), and North Dakota (23.5).

California (11,766), Texas (9,922), and New York (5,008) had the highest numbers of reported rapes. However, when those numbers are compared to the large populations of those states, the risk rates fall into the middle ground. The fewest rapes were reported by North Dakota (149), Wyoming (161) and Vermont (229).

It is important to remember that these numbers only measure rapes of females reported in 1993, and that those numbers can vary from year to year. Furthermore, the willingness of females to report rapes may vary from state to state.

Source U.S. Department of Justice, Federal Bureau of Investigation, *Crime in the United States, 1993* (Washington, DC: U.S. Government Printing Office, 1994), pp. 68–78.

Contact U.S. Department of Justice, Federal Bureau of Investigation, Uniform Crime Reports, Criminal Justice Information Services Division, Washington, DC 20535. Information Dissemination: (202) 324-5015.

National Victim Center, 2111 Wilson Blvd., Suite 300, Arlington, VA 22201. (703) 276-2880.

Violence

When Is a Rape Reported to the Police?

Rape victimizations in the U.S. in 1992. Details are given according to type of crime and whether or not it was reported to the police. Includes both heterosexual and homosexual rape.

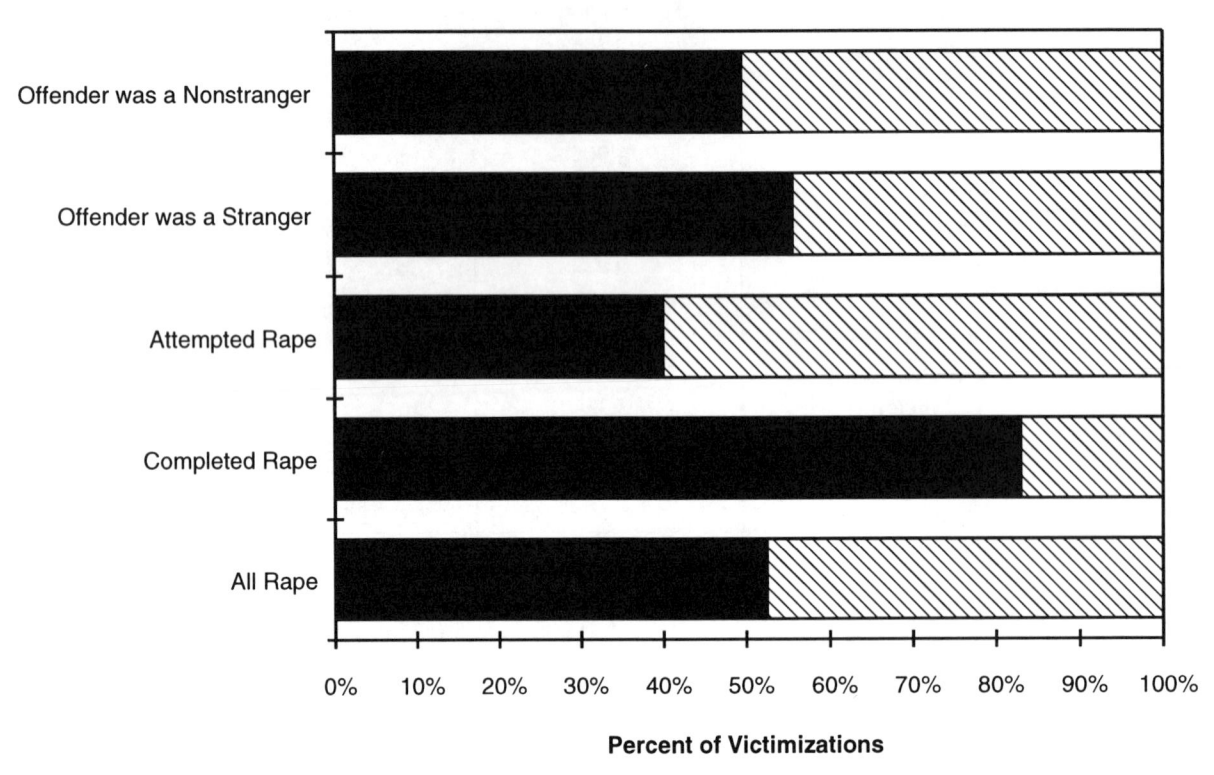

Percent of Victimizations

■ Reported to police   ▨ Not reported to police

Type of Victimization	Number of Victimizations	Reported to Police	Not Reported to Police
All rape	140,930	52.5	47.5
Completed rape	40,730	83.0	17.0
Attempted rape	100,200	40.0	60.0
Offender was a stranger	68,140	55.6	44.4
Offender was a nonstranger	72,790	49.5	50.5

Violence

Comments

Only 52.5% of all rapes in 1992 were reported to the police, according to the National Crime Victimization Survey (NCVS). Each year NCVS questions over 100,000 U.S. resident citizens age 12 and older about reported and unreported crimes. It uses the responses to estimate the frequency of crime for the entire United States.

In 140,930 cases described to NCVS, there were 40,730 completed rapes.

Only 40% of all attempted rapes were reported, but police were usually informed about completed rapes (83%). When the rapist was a stranger, victims informed police 55.6% of the time in 1992. However, 49.5% of all rapes were reported to police when the offender was a friend, relative, or acquaintance of the victim.

Rape is a malicious crime that primarily affects women, although some men are victimized as well. Since rape is a sexual violation, psychological trauma often occurs. This type of trauma can linger long after the incident and usually calls for professional counseling.

Completed rapes often involve more immediate physical injury and trauma than attempted rapes, and are treated as a more serious crime. Completed rapes also may have other physical consequences (such as sexually transmitted diseases and pregnancy) that extend far beyond the original crime.

Source

U.S. Department of Justice, Bureau of Justice Statistics. *Criminal Victimization in the United States, 1992* (Washington, DC: U.S. Government Printing Office, 1994), pp. 55, 102.

Contact

U.S. Department of Justice, Bureau of Justice Statistics Clearinghouse, Box 6000, Rockville, MD 20850. (800) 732-3277.

National Victim Center, 2111 Wilson Blvd., Suite 300, Arlington, VA 22201. (703) 276-2880.

Violence

How Often Does a Rape Victim Know the Offender?

Percent distribution showing relationship between rape victim and offender. The victim's age is also shown. Survey of rape victims in three states in 1991.

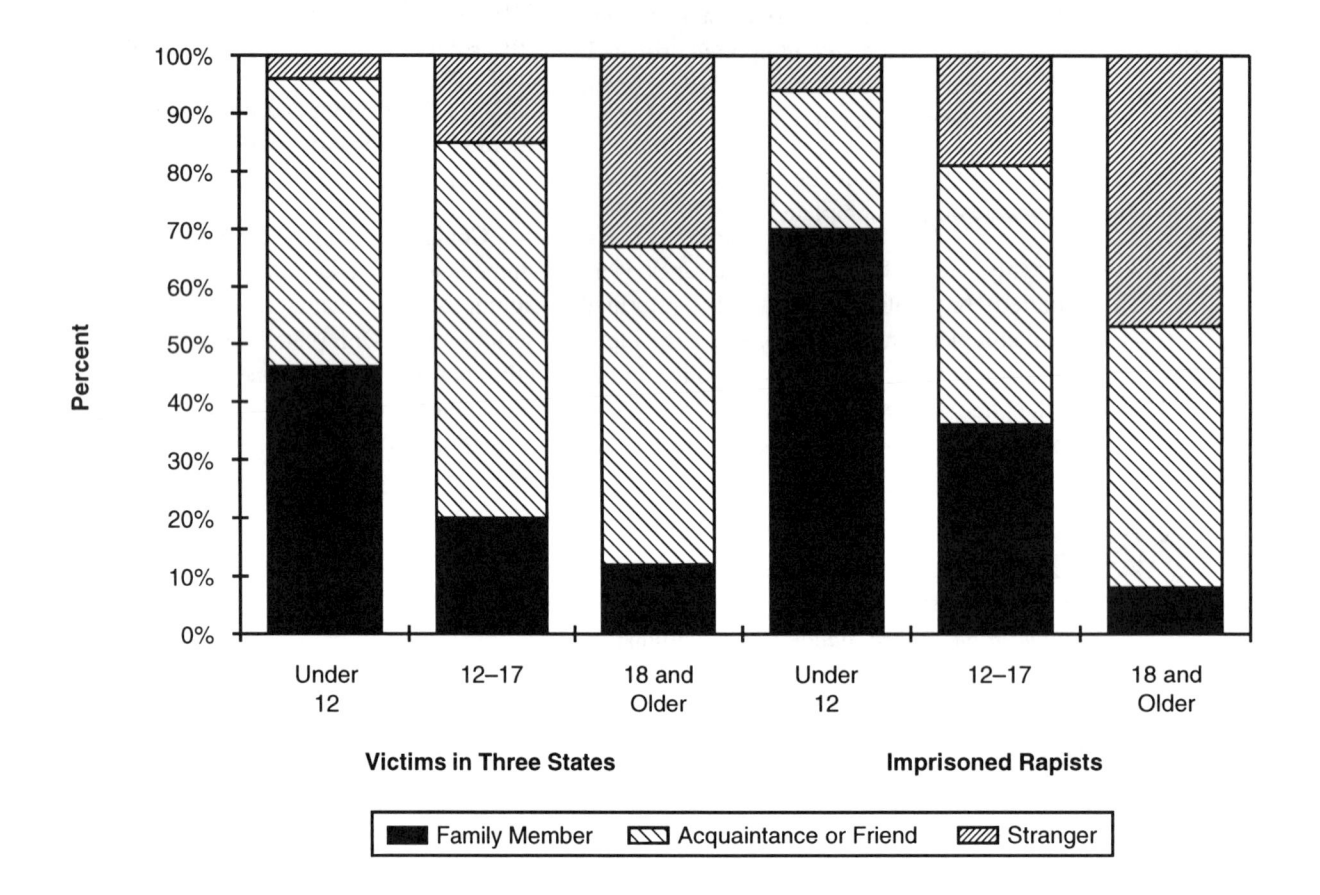

Legend: Family Member | Acquaintance or Friend | Stranger

Age	Family Member	Acquaintance or Friend	Stranger
Source: Victims in three states			
Under 12	46%	50%	4%
12–17	20%	65%	15%
18 and older	12%	55%	33%
Source: Imprisoned rapists			
Under 12	70%	24%	6%
12–17	36%	45%	19%
18 and older	8%	45%	47%

Violence

Comments

The federal Bureau of Justice Statistics reports the likelihood of rape by a family member is greatest when the victim is under age 12. It eases as the person grows.

The FBI's Uniform Crime Reporting (UCR) program and the Bureau of Justice Statistics' National Crime Victimization Survey (NCVS) provided some of the data.

A survey of rape victims in three states found the offenders were family members 46% of the time when the child was under age 12. Between ages 12 and 17, the offender was a family member 20% of the time. And 12% of the offenders consisted of family members when the victims were 18 or older. A survey of imprisoned rapists found a similar pattern: Family members were the offenders in 70% of the cases where victims were under age 12. This dropped to 36% when the victim was between ages 12 and 17, and to 8% if the victim was over 18.

However, the survey of victims found friends or acquaintances were more likely to be the offenders regardless of the victims' ages. In both surveys, chances of a stranger being the offender grew markedly when the victim was 18 or older.

Although the NCVS statistics provide details on victims' ages, they do not include children under 12. The UCR numbers do include children under 12, but there are no age details. In order to acquire more information regarding the problem of child rape, a 1991 Bureau of Justice Statistics' survey collected data on victims' ages in several states. In three of those states (Alabama, North Dakota, and South Carolina), two sources provided information on rapists. One source was from interviews with rape victims reported to law enforcement agencies. The other was from interviews with rapists confined in state prisons.

Source

U.S. Department of Justice, Bureau of Justice Statistics, "Child Rape Victims, 1992" (Washington, DC: U.S. Government Printing Office, June 1994).

Contact

U.S. Department of Justice, Bureau of Justice Statistics Clearinghouse, Box 6000, Rockville, MD 20850. (800) 732-3277.

Children's Defense Fund, 25 E St. NW, Washington, DC 20001. (202) 628-8787.

Violence

Number and Rate of Reported Robberies, 1993

Ranking of the states according to number of reported robberies and rate per 100,000 inhabitants.

Rank	Ranked by Number of Reported Robberies		Ranked by Rate per 100,000 Inhabitants	
1.	California	126,436	District of Columbia	1,229.6
2.	New York	102,122	Florida	785.7
3.	Florida	48,913	New York	561.2
4.	Illinois	44,584	Puerto Rico	502.0
5.	Texas	40,469	Maryland	434.7
6.	New Jersey	23,319	Delaware	417.1
7.	Michigan	22,601	California	405.1
8.	Maryland	21,582	Illinois	381.2
9.	Pennsylvania	21,563	Nevada	340.1
10.	Ohio	21,373	New Jersey	296.0
11.	Puerto Rico	18,181	Louisiana	283.6
12.	Georgia	17,154	Georgia	248.0
13.	North Carolina	13,364	Missouri	241.8
14.	Missouri	12,654	Michigan	238.5
15.	Louisiana	12,182	Texas	224.4
16.	Tennessee	11,224	Tennessee	220.1
17.	Massachusetts	10,563	Connecticut	196.7
18.	Virginia	9,216	Ohio	192.7
19.	Washington	7,204	North Carolina	192.4
20.	District of Columbia	7,107	South Carolina	187.3
21.	Indiana	6,845	Pennsylvania	179.0
22.	South Carolina	6,825	Massachusetts	175.7
23.	Alabama	6,677	Arizona	162.9
24.	Connecticut	6,447	Alabama	159.5
25.	Arizona	6,412	Virginia	142.0
26.	Wisconsin	5,714	Mississippi	139.3
27.	Minnesota	5,092	New Mexico	138.4
28.	Nevada	4,724	Washington	137.1
29.	Colorado	4,160	Oregon	129.6
30.	Oklahoma	3,935	Arkansas	124.9
31.	Oregon	3,930	Kansas	123.6
32.	Mississippi	3,683	Alaska	122.4
33.	Kentucky	3,425	Oklahoma	121.8
34.	Kansas	3,128	Indiana	119.8
35.	Arkansas	3,027	Colorado	116.7
36.	New Mexico	2,237	Wisconsin	113.4
37.	Iowa	1,517	Minnesota	112.7
38.	Delaware	1,307	Hawaii	103.6
39.	Hawaii	1,214	Rhode Island	101.1
40.	Utah	1,090	Kentucky	90.4
41.	Rhode Island	1,011	Utah	58.6

[Continued]

Number and Rate of Reported Robberies, 1993

[Continued]

Rank	Ranked by Number of Reported Robberies		Ranked by Rate per 100,000 Inhabitants	
42.	Nebraska	890	Nebraska	55.4
43.	West Virginia	782	Iowa	53.9
44.	Alaska	733	West Virginia	43.0
45.	New Hampshire	307	Montana	32.4
46.	Montana	272	New Hampshire	27.3
47.	Maine	264	Maine	21.3
48.	Idaho	186	Wyoming	17.2
49.	South Dakota	107	Idaho	16.9
50.	Wyoming	81	South Dakota	15.0
51.	North Dakota	53	Vermont	9.0
52.	Vermont	52	North Dakota	8.3

Comments Florida and New York ranked among the top three in numbers of robberies and the rate at which robberies occurred during 1993, Federal Bureau of Investigation figures show. North Dakota and Vermont fell among the bottom three in both categories. The FBI looked at robberies in the 50 states, the District of Columbia, and Puerto Rico.

The risk of robbery was greatest in DC, with 1,229.6 cases per 100,000 residents. Florida (785.7) and New York (561.2) followed. California had the most robberies, with 126,436, followed by New York (102,122), and Florida (48,913).

The least risky locations for robberies were North Dakota (8.3 per 100,000 residents), Vermont (9.0), and South Dakota (15.0). In terms of numbers, the bottom three were Vermont (52), North Dakota (53), and Wyoming (81).

There were over 659,700 robberies reported in the United States in 1993. The national robbery rate that year was 255.8 reported cases per 100,000 residents.

It is important to remember that these numbers only measure reported robberies in 1993, and that the totals can vary from year to year.

Source U.S. Department of Justice, Federal Bureau of Investigation, *Crime in the United States, 1993* (Washington, DC: U.S. Government Printing Office, 1994), pp. 68–78.

Contact U.S. Department of Justice, Federal Bureau of Investigation, Uniform Crime Reports, Criminal Justice Information Services Division, Washington, DC 20535. Information Dissemination: (202) 324-5015.

National Victim Center, 2111 Wilson Blvd., Suite 300, Arlington, VA 22201. (703) 276-2880.

Violence

When Is a Robbery Reported to the Police?

Robbery victimizations throughout the U.S. in 1992.
Percentages are given according to type of crime and whether or not it was reported to the police.

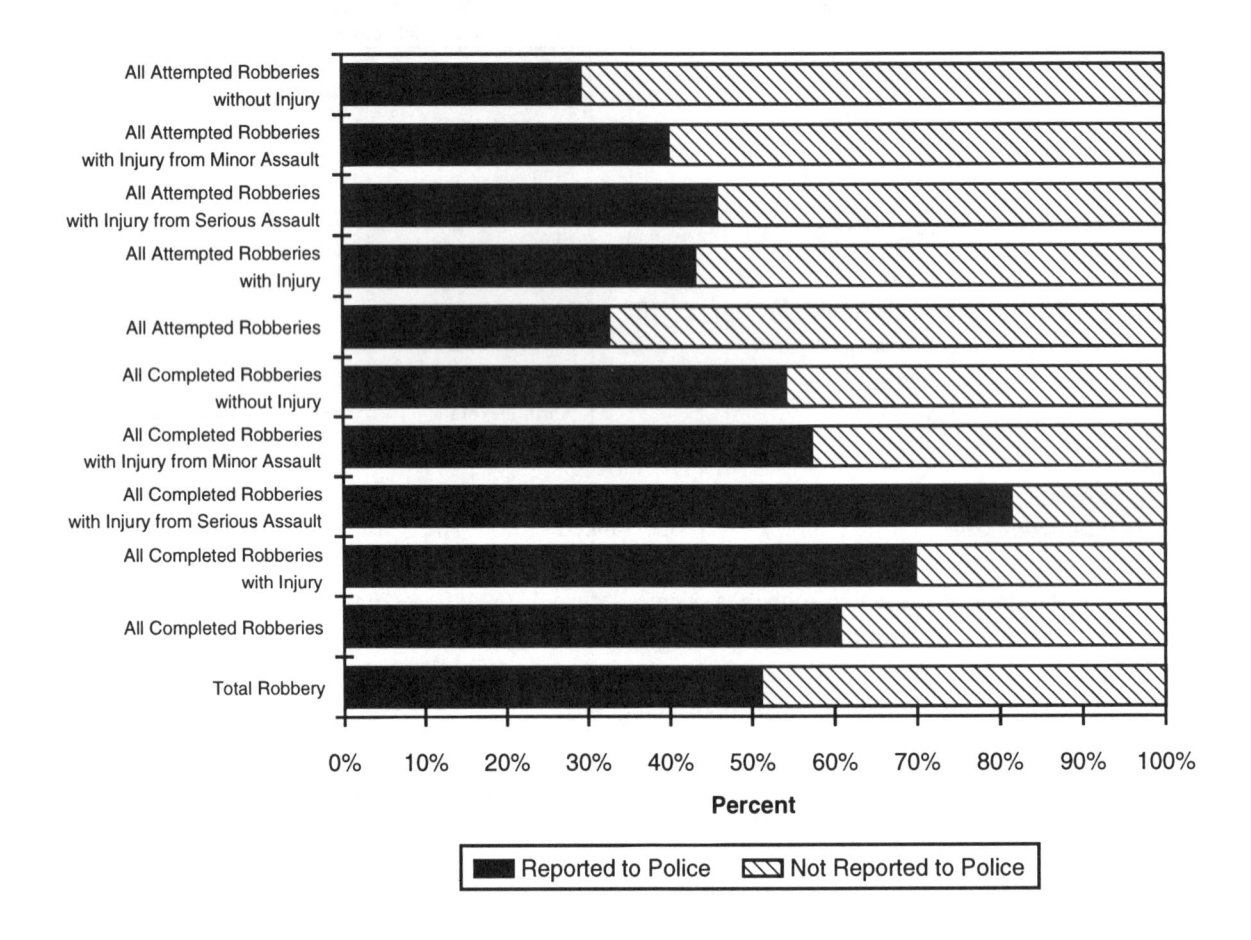

■ Reported to Police   ▨ Not Reported to Police

Type of Victimization	Number of Victimizations	Reported to Police	Not Reported to Police
Total robbery	1,225,510	51.1	48.9
Completed	806,460	60.7	39.3
With injury	334,040	69.8	30.2
From serious assault	173,480	81.4	18.6
From minor assault	160,550	57.3	42.7
Without injury	472,420	54.2	45.8
Attempted	419,040	32.7	67.3
With injury	103,320	43.2	56.8
From serious assault	55,570	45.9	54.1
From minor assault	47,560	40.0	60.0
Without injury	315,720	29.3	70.7

Violence

Comments A study of 1992 robberies shows only 51.1% of such cases were reported to police. The information comes from the National Crime Victimization Survey. Each year, the survey questions more than 100,000 U.S. resident citizens age 12 and older about reported and unreported crimes.

Completed robberies were much more likely to be reported (60.7% of the time) than attempted robberies. The most frequently reported case was a completed robbery that resulted in a serious injury to the victim; 81.4% of these were reported.

Serious injuries involve the victim being shot, stabbed, or beaten. When injuries were less serious, cases were reported 57.3% of the time. If there was no injury, the robbery was reported in 54.2% of the cases.

Attempted robberies were reported to police only 32.7% of the time in 1992. Even when an attempted robbery included a serious assault injury, the victim only notified police 45.9% of the time. Attempts involving minor injuries were reported in 40% of the cases. Victims informed police only 29.3% of the time when an attempted robbery caused no injury. This was probably because the victim suffered little property loss and so was less inclined to call police.

The survey looked at 1,225,510 robbery cases. Of these, 806,460 were completed robberies and 419,040 were attempts.

Source U.S. Department of Justice, Bureau of Justice Statistics. *Criminal Victimization in the United States, 1992* (Washington, DC: U.S. Government Printing Office, 1994), p. 102.

Contact U.S. Department of Justice, Bureau of Justice Statistics Clearinghouse, Box 6000, Rockville, MD 20850. (800) 732-3277.

National Victim Center, 2111 Wilson Blvd., Suite 300, Arlington, VA 22201. (703) 276-2880.

Violence

Where Are Robberies Happening?

Robberies in the U.S. by site of offense, 1989–93.

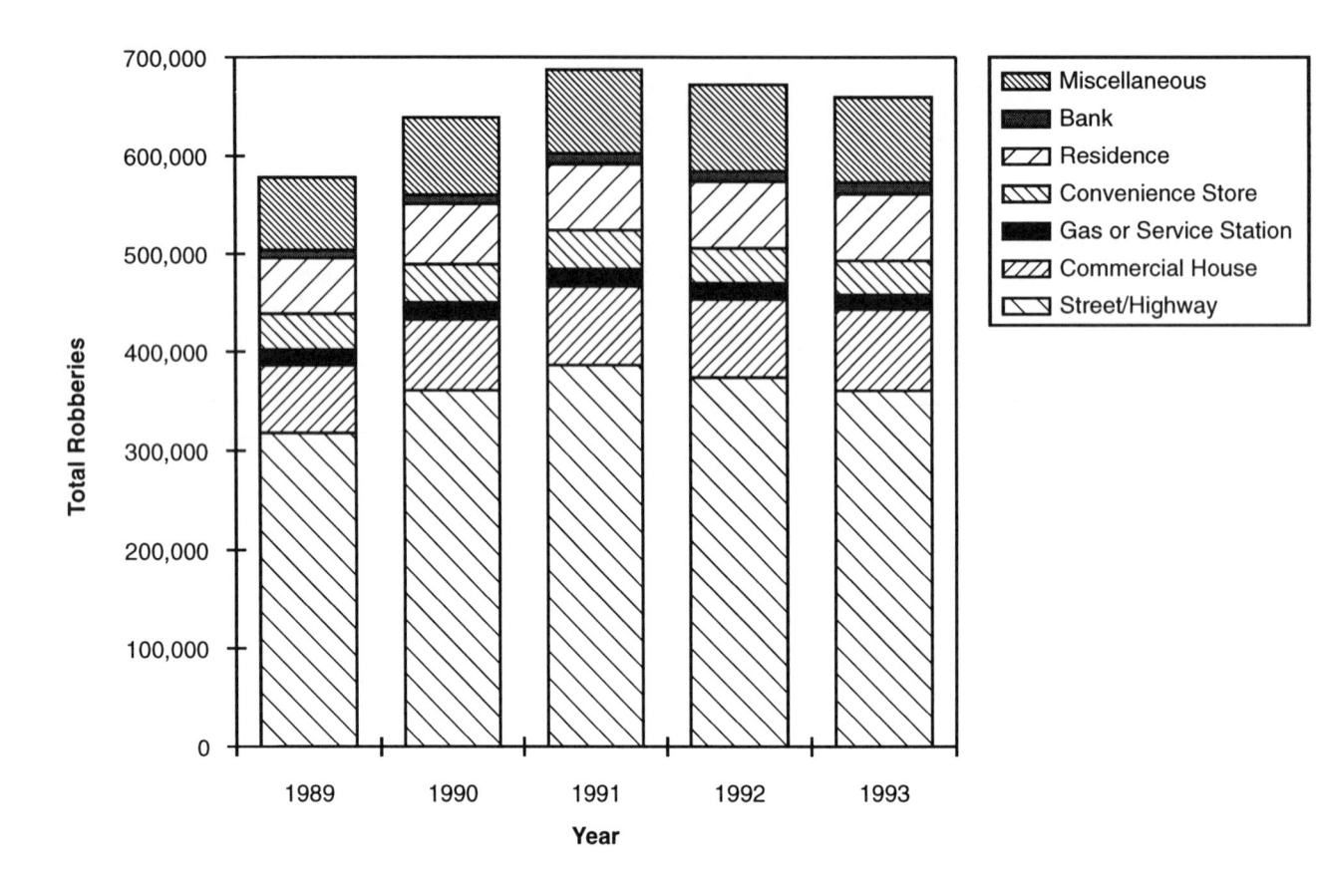

Site of Offense	1989	1990	1991	1992	1993
Street/highway	318,017	360,861	386,552	374,157	360,739
Commercial establishment	68,173	72,589	80,448	79,717	82,371
Gas or service station	16,355	17,394	17,829	16,752	15,389
Convenience store	36,381	38,643	39,429	35,312	34,811
Residence	56,928	61,733	67,592	67,619	67,902
Bank	7,932	9,345	11,019	11,121	11,854
Miscellaneous	74,544	78,705	84,863	87,802	86,693
Total	578,330	639,270	687,730	672,480	659,760

Comments

Over half of all reported robberies occur on the street or highway, according to FBI Uniform Crime Reports figures. Such robberies often involve just one victim and one offender. Whether victims are robbed randomly or are chosen because they look wealthy, the chance for the robber to steal a lot of money is hit-or-miss.

The total robbery cases studied varied between 578,330 and 687,730 per year between 1989 and 1993. Robberies on streets or highways ran between 318,017 and 386,552.

Chances for success in robberies at homes (not to be confused with burglaries) often are hit-or-miss. Besides the chance of a small criminal reward, robbery attempts at homes may result in violent incidents with trapped residents.

Robberies at businesses, however, often involve multiple victims because several employees and customers may be present. Commercial robbery requires the offender to quickly grab cash while controlling and intimidating employees and customers. Robbers of businesses often work in teams of two or more. In these cases, different individuals usually have defined roles within the robberies. Such roles can include getting the cash or valuables, controlling employees and customers, watching for police, and handling the escape.

Robberies of different types of businesses carry different risks and criminal rewards. For example, robberies of convenience stores and gas and service stations often are successful. The cash taken in such robberies, however, is often very little compared to the risk of arrest, prosecution, and punishment.

On the other hand, bank robberies are riskier because of increased security. However, success brings more loot. Among the robbery site categories listed, banks came in last, with 7,932–11,854 cases per year.

Source

U.S. Department of Justice, Federal Bureau of Investigation, *Crime in the United States, 1993* (Washington, DC: U.S. Government Printing Office, 1994), p. 108.

Contact

U.S. Department of Justice, Federal Bureau of Investigation, Uniform Crime Reports, Criminal Justice Information Services Division, Washington, DC 20535. Information Dissemination: (202) 324-5015.

Violence

Aggravated and Simple Assault Rate in 1993

The frequency of aggravated and simple assault in the U.S. (per 1,000 persons age 12 and older), by selected characteristics.

Selected Characteristics of Victim	Aggravated Assault Rate	Simple Assault Rate	Total Assault Rate
Total	12.2	30.8	43.0
Sex			
Male	16.3	35.8	52.1
Female	8.3	26.2	34.5
Age			
12–15	23.3	79.3	102.6
16–19	30.0	68.1	98.1
20–24	27.1	50.3	77.4
25–34	15.0	34.1	49.1
35–49	8.8	27.5	36.2
50–64	4.0	10.0	13.9
65 and older	1.1	3.0	4.1
Race			
White	11.4	31.1	42.4
Black	19.0	32.3	51.3
Other	8.8	20.8	29.5
Hispanic status			
Hispanic	17.2	29.0	46.2
Non-Hispanic	11.8	31.0	42.8

Violence

Comments Certain individuals were more prone than others to be assault victims in 1993, according to the National Crime Victimization Survey (NCVS). Characteristics such as gender, age, race, and Hispanic status helped classify which individuals were most frequently the victims of aggravated or simple assault.

Aggravated assaults involve severe injuries and often weapons. In simple assaults, the injuries are less severe.

NCVS said males, young persons, blacks, and Hispanics were victims more often than people in other groups. For example, men (16.3 per 1,000 of population) were almost twice as likely as women (8.3 per 1,000) to experience aggravated assault. Men also were more prone than women to be the victims of simple assault.

The chance of someone becoming a victim of assault generally declined with age. Persons under age 25 were victims most often (77.4–102.6 per 1,000), while those 65 or older had the lowest assault rate (4.1 per 1,000).

Blacks were more likely than whites or persons of other races (such as Asians and Native Americans) to be victims of assault. For instance, in 1993 there were 19.0 aggravated assaults per 1,000 black persons, 11.4 per 1,000 whites, and 8.8 per 1,000 persons in other racial categories. Blacks were slightly more at risk for simple assault than whites; again, other races ranked third.

Hispanics also were more likely to be victims of assault. Their rates were 17.2 per 1,000 for aggravated assaults, versus 11.8 for other groups, and 46.2 per 1,000 for total assaults, compared to 42.8. However, the non-Hispanic group had slightly more simple assaults. NCVS annually polls over 100,000 U.S. resident citizens over age 12 about their experiences with reported and unreported violent crimes. Homicides are not included because the victims cannot be interviewed.

Source U.S. Department of Justice, Bureau of Justice Statistics, "Criminal Victimization 1993" (Washington, DC: U.S. Government Printing Office, May 1995).

Contact U.S. Department of Justice, Bureau of Justice Statistics Clearinghouse, Box 6000, Rockville, MD 20850. (800) 732-3277.

Violence

Aggravated Assaults in the States Ranked by Number and by Rate, 1993

Ranking of the states according to number of reported aggravated assaults and rate per 100,000 inhabitants.

Rank	Ranked by Number of Reported Aggravated Assaults		Ranked by Rate per 100,000 Residents	
1.	California	194,083	District of Columbia	1,557.6
2.	Florida	107,479	Florida	785.7
3.	New York	85,802	South Carolina	773.4
4.	Texas	84,881	New Mexico	731.1
5.	Illinois	62,298	Louisiana	715.4
6.	Michigan	44,747	California	621.8
7.	Massachusetts	35,591	Massachusetts	592.0
8.	Louisiana	30,727	Alabama	574.3
9.	North Carolina	30,650	Alaska	545.6
10.	Georgia	29,628	Illinois	532.6
11.	Ohio	28,431	Maryland	506.4
12.	South Carolina	28,174	Arizona	505.7
13.	Maryland	25,141	Tennessee	485.5
14.	Tennessee	24,758	Michigan	472.1
15.	Pennsylvania	24,714	New York	471.5
16.	Alabama	24,044	Texas	470.8
17.	Missouri	23,825	Nevada	463.9
18.	New Jersey	23,438	Oklahoma	455.3
19.	Arizona	19,903	Missouri	455.2
20.	Indiana	18,432	North Carolina	441.3
21.	Washington	16,181	Georgia	428.3
22.	Oklahoma	14,712	Delaware	417.1
23.	Colorado	14,230	Arkansas	415.8
24.	Kentucky	12,555	Colorado	399.0
25.	Virginia	12,322	Kentucky	331.4
26.	New Mexico	11,815	Kansas	326.3
27.	Arkansas	10,079	Indiana	322.6
28.	Oregon	9,630	Oregon	317.6
29.	District of Columbia	9,003	Washington	307.9
30.	Kansas	8,259	New Jersey	297.5
31.	Minnesota	7,943	Rhode Island	268.1
32.	Connecticut	7,496	Ohio	256.3
33.	Iowa	6,890	Nebraska	252.0
34.	Puerto Rico	6,806	Iowa	244.8
35.	Nevada	6,443	Mississippi	238.4
36.	Mississippi	6,302	Wyoming	231.3
37.	Wisconsin	6,116	Connecticut	228.7
38.	Nebraska	4,050	Idaho	226.7

[Continued]

Violence

Aggravated Assaults in the States Ranked by Number and by Rate, 1993

[Continued]

Rank	Ranked by Number of Reported Aggravated Assaults		Ranked by Rate per 100,000 Residents	
39.	Utah	3,622	Pennsylvania	205.1
40.	Alaska	3,268	Utah	194.7
41.	Delaware	2,920	Virginia	189.8
42.	Rhode Island	2,681	Puerto Rico	187.9
43.	West Virginia	2,520	Minnesota	175.8
44.	Idaho	2,491	South Dakota	145.6
45.	Hawaii	1,408	West Virginia	138.5
46.	Wyoming	1,087	Wisconsin	121.4
47.	South Dakota	1,041	Hawaii	120.1
48.	Montana	958	Montana	114.2
49.	Maine	945	Maine	76.3
50.	New Hampshire	721	New Hampshire	64.1
51.	Vermont	356	Vermont	61.8
52.	North Dakota	309	North Dakota	48.7
	United States Total *	1,135,099	United States Rate *	440.1

* Puerto Rico not included in national totals.

Comments

People in the District of Columbia, Florida, and South Carolina were more likely to be aggravated assault victims in 1993 than people in any other state or Puerto Rico. Federal Bureau of Investigation figures showed 1,557.6 aggravated assaults reported per 100,000 residents in DC, 785.7 in Florida, and 773.4 in South Carolina.

The greatest numbers of aggravated assaults occurred in California (194,083), Florida (107,479), and New York (85,802).

The bottom three states, and their order, were the same for both categories of data. North Dakota had the lowest aggravated assault rate, with 48.7 per 100,000 residents, and a total of 309 incidents. Following were Vermont (61.8 per 100,000 and 356 total) and New Hampshire (64.1 per 100,000 and 721 total).

There were 1,135,099 aggravated assaults reported in the United States during 1993. The rate was 440.1 per 100,000 residents.

Source

U.S. Department of Justice, Federal Bureau of Investigation, *Crime in the United States, 1993* (Washington, DC: U.S. Government Printing Office, 1994), pp. 68–78. Population estimate for Puerto Rico provided by Bureau of the Census staff.

Contact

U.S. Department of Justice, Federal Bureau of Investigation, Uniform Crime Reports, Criminal Justice Information Services Division, Washington, DC 20535. Information Dissemination: (202) 324-5015.

National Victim Center, 2111 Wilson Blvd., Suite 300, Arlington, VA 22201. (703) 276-2880.

Violence

When Is an Assault Reported to the Police?

Assault victimizations in the U.S. in 1992. Percentages are given according to type of crime and whether or not it was reported to the police.

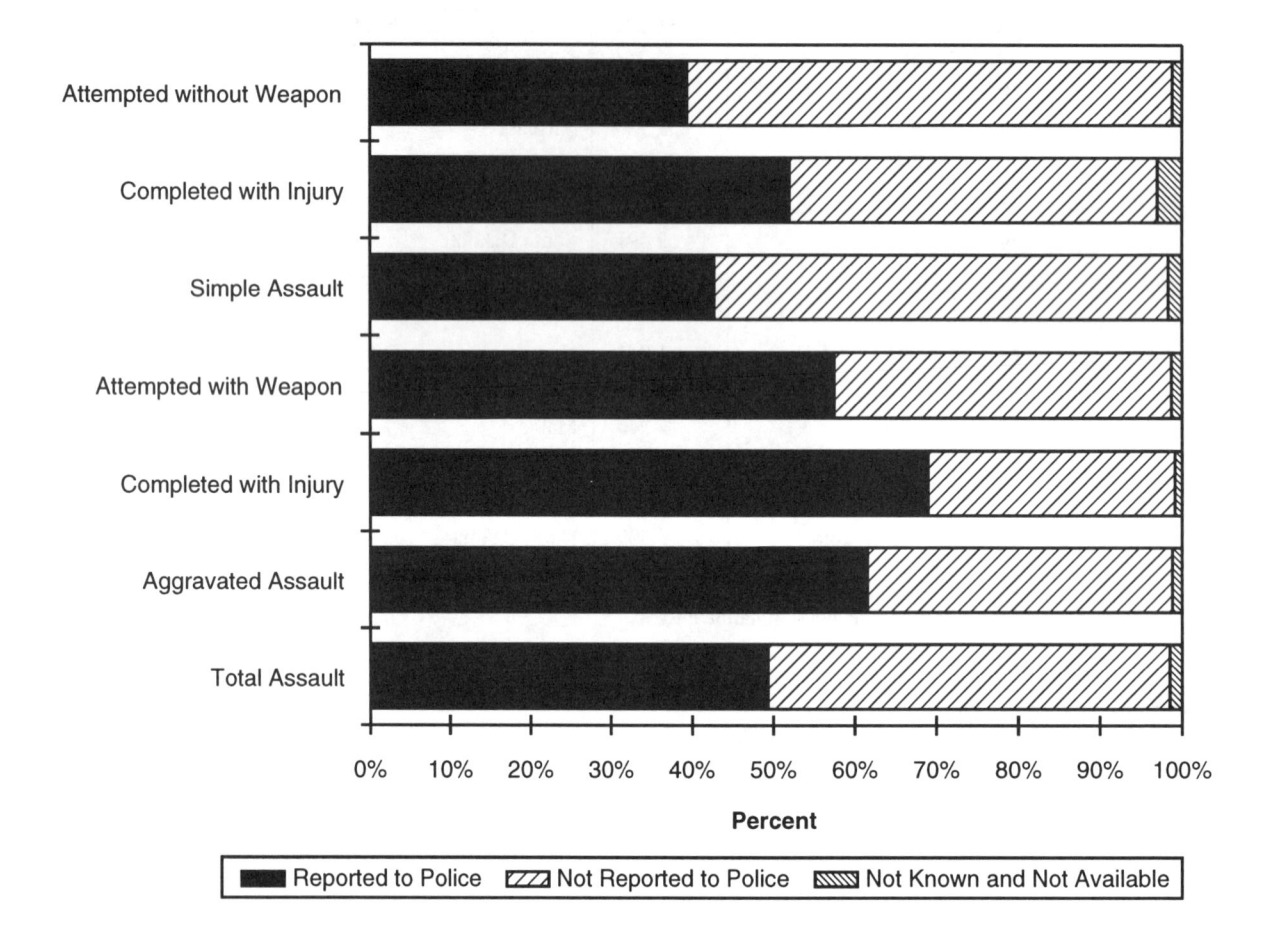

Legend: ■ Reported to Police ▨ Not Reported to Police ▧ Not Known and Not Available

Type of Victimization	Number of Victimizations	Reported to Police	Not Reported to Police	Not Known and Not Available
Total assault	5,254,690	49.4%	49.1%	1.5%
Aggravated assault	1,848,530	61.6%	37.3%	1.2%
Completed with injury	657,550	69.0%	30.1%	0.9%
Attempted with weapon	1,190,970	57.5%	41.2%	1.3%
Simple assault	3,406,160	42.8%	55.6%	1.7%
Completed with injury	904,770	51.9%	45.1%	3.0%
Attempted without weapon	2,501,390	39.4%	59.4%	1.2%

Violence

Comments

Severity of the case and use of a weapon appear to affect whether an assault is reported to police. The federal Bureau of Justice Statistics says completed aggravated assaults were reported to police 69.0% of the time in 1992 when the victim was injured. Attempted aggravated assaults were reported in 57.5% of cases. Aggravated assaults are those in which weapons are used and which involve injuries requiring two or more days in the hospital.

Simple assaults were reported 51.9% of the time when they were completed and there were injuries. Failed attempts were reported in 39.4% of the cases. Simple assaults are those in which weapons are not used.

Every year, the bureau polls over 100,000 U.S. resident citizens through the National Crime Victimization Survey (NCVS). The NCVS gathers information on both reported and unreported incidents of crime from persons 12 and older. Its figures show 49.4% out of a total of 5,254,690 assaults in the survey were reported to police.

The type of case reported the least often is an attempted simple assault. This type of case probably is reported so infrequently because no physical injury occurs and there is no deadly weapon present. This type of crime is less serious than any of the other categories listed.

Source

U.S. Department of Justice, Bureau of Justice Statistics. *Criminal Victimization in the United States, 1992* (Washington, DC: U.S. Government Printing Office, 1994), p. 102.

Contact

U.S. Department of Justice, Bureau of Justice Statistics Clearinghouse, Box 6000, Rockville, MD 20850. (800) 732-3277.

National Victim Center, 2111 Wilson Blvd., Suite 300, Arlington, VA 22201. (703) 276-2880.

Violence

Violent Crime within the Family

Estimated percentage of nonfatal violent crime incidents in the U.S. in 1992 where the victim was related to the offender.

Type of Crime	Total Number of Victimizations	Total Victimizations Committed by a Relative	Total	Spouse	Ex-Spouse	Parent	Own Child	Other Relatives
Crimes of violence	6,621,140	489,460	7.4%	2.6%	1.3%	0.3%	0.7%	2.5%
Completed	2,409,520	227,140	9.4%	3.6%	1.1%	0.5%	1.0%	3.2%
Attempted	4,211,610	262,310	6.2%	2.0%	1.4%	0.2%	0.6%	2.0%
Rape	140,930	3,550	2.5%	0.0%	0.0%	0.0%	0.0%	2.5%
Robbery	1,225,510	64,960	5.3%	2.8%	1.2%	0.0%	0.0%	1.4%
Completed	806,460	39,110	4.8%	1.9%	1.2%	0.0%	0.0%	1.8%
Attempted	419,040	25,850	6.2%	4.4%	1.2%	0.0%	0.0%	0.6%
Assault	5,254,690	420,930	8.0%	2.6%	1.4%	0.4%	0.9%	2.7%
Completed	1,848,530	131,670	7.1%	1.5%	1.2%	0.2%	0.8%	3.4%
Attempted	3,406,160	289,250	8.5%	3.2%	1.5%	0.5%	0.9%	2.4%

Victimizations Committed by a Relative (percent)

Violence

Comments A National Crime Victimization Survey (NCVS) study found that relatives of victims committed about 7.4% of all violent crimes in 1992. About 9.4% of all completed violent crimes such as rapes, robberies, and assaults and 6.2% of all attempted violent crimes were committed by victims' relatives.

Spouses were the family members most frequently involved in violent crimes within families, accounting for 2.6% of all violent offenses. Other relatives (such as cousins, in-laws, and extended family members) ranked second among violent offenders within families at 2.5%.

Assault was the most common violent offense occurring between family members. The victims' own relatives committed about 8.0% of all assaults in 1992. Family members committed a greater percentage of simple assaults (8.5%) than aggravated assaults (7.1%) against each other. Simple assaults involve minor injuries; aggravated assaults involve more serious injuries and often weapons.

NCVS annually polls over 100,000 U.S. resident citizens over age 12 about their experiences with reported and unreported violent crimes. Homicides are not included because the victims cannot be interviewed.

It is important to remember that the NCVS numbers are estimates. In this situation, the number of incidents committed by victims' relatives made up a small portion of all cases. Therefore, in many of the categories shown, estimates were based on small numbers of sample cases and may not reliably represent actual conditions.

Source U.S. Department of Justice, Bureau of Justice Statistics. *Criminal Victimization in the United States, 1992* (Washington, DC: U.S. Government Printing Office, 1994) p. 150–51.

Contact U.S. Department of Justice, Bureau of Justice Statistics Clearinghouse, Box 6000, Rockville, MD 20850. (800) 732-3277.

National Resource Center on Domestic Violence, 6400 Flank Dr. Suite 1300, Harrisburg PA 17112-2778. (800) 537-2238.

National Victim Center, 2111 Wilson Blvd., Suite 300, Arlington, VA 22201. (703) 276-2880.

Violence

Murders within the Family

Murder victims and defendants among family members in 1988. Numbers shown are percentages of family murder victims and defendants according to family relationship and sex, race, and age. Percentages show the relationships of victim to assailant for murders within the family in the 75 largest urban counties of the U.S. *

Charac-teristic	Spouse Victims	Spouse Defendants	Offspring Victims	Offspring Defendants	Parent Victims	Parent Defendants	Sibling Victims	Sibling Defendants	Other Victims	Other Defendants	All Family Victims	All Family Defendants
Male	40.2	59.3	55.8	45.4	57.2	81.6	73.0	84.9	74.9	83.5	55.5	65.5
Female	59.8	40.7	44.2	54.6	42.8	18.4	27.0	15.1	25.1	16.5	44.5	34.5
White	41.2	41.8	32.6	34.5	54.8	49.8	33.5	32.2	34.1	38.1	39.0	39.7
Black	56.4	56.1	65.6	64.5	45.2	50.2	64.5	65.8	61.0	56.1	58.6	58.0
Other	2.4	2.2	1.8	1.0	0.0	0.0	2.0	2.0	4.9	5.9	2.4	2.3
Under 12	0.0	0.0	78.5	0.0	0.0	0.0	8.7	0.0	4.6	0.0	18.8	0.0
12–19	0.0	0.9	10.9	17.2	0.0	38.2	2.0	16.9	8.2	18.0	3.9	13.0
20–29	27.9	21.9	7.7	36.4	0.9	30.7	43.3	36.7	19.1	35.9	20.3	29.7
30–59	65.0	66.1	3.0	40.3	56.7	29.4	42.6	46.4	47.5	41.3	45.3	50.5
60 or older	7.1	11.1	0.0	6.0	42.4	1.7	3.3	0.0	20.6	4.9	11.6	6.8
Total Number	528	531	285	258	154	150	123	121	218	224	1,308	1,284

* "Spouse" includes common-law spouse. "Offspring" includes grandchild and step-child. "Parent" includes grandparent and step-parent. "Sibling" includes step-sibling. "Other" includes cousin, in-law, extended family members, and other family members.

Comments

Murderers found victims within their own families in 13.4%, or 1,284, of 9,576 cases that were solved during 1988. The U.S. Justice Department studied murder cases within the family in the 75 largest urban counties. Most often, the victims and their killers were spouses; least frequently, the victims and defendants were siblings.

Spouses were defendants about 40.4% of the time (531 cases) and victims in 528 cases. Overall, husbands were the killers 59.3% of the time. The frequency of husbands as defendants, however, varied by race. In murders among blacks, wives were about as likely as husbands to be charged with murder.

The second most common type of murder within a family involved parents killing their offspring. This accounted for 21.8% of all family murder cases, or 285. Cases of offspring murdering parents made up 11.7%, or 154, of the cases.

About 65.5% of the defendants in family murder cases were male. But females killed their own offspring more often than did males. Mothers were the defendants in 54.6% of these cases.

Source

U.S. Department of Justice, Bureau of Justice Statistics, "Murder in Families" (Washington, DC: U.S. Government Printing Office, July 1995).

Contact

U.S. Department of Justice, Bureau of Justice Statistics Clearinghouse, Box 6000, Rockville, MD 20850. (800) 732-3277.

Violence

Victim and Defendant Characteristics for Murder within the Family

Status regarding alcohol use at the time of murder, history of mental illness, unemployment, and homelessness for victims and defendants of family murder in 1988 in the 75 largest U.S. counties.

Relationship	Alcohol Use at Time of Murder - Defendants	Alcohol Use at Time of Murder - Victims	History of Mental Illness - Defendants	History of Mental Illness - Victims	Unemployed - Defendants	Unemployed - Victims	Homeless - Defendants	Homeless - Victims
Within family	47.6%	32.7%	14.3%	0.9%	29.1%	7.4%	1.2%	0.2%
Spouse	54.4%	49.6%	12.3%	1.5%	25.0%	12.8%	1.6%	0.5%
Offspring	29.8%	5.7%	15.8%	1.3%	28.9%	0.0%	0.0%	0.0%
Parent	28.4%	25.4%	25.1%	0.0%	33.6%	4.4%	2.3%	0.0%
Sibling	53.9%	34.9%	17.3%	0.0%	34.9%	17.7%	3.3%	0.0%

Violence

Comments A survey of 1988 murder cases revealed that many of the defendants and victims in cases of family murder were in situations that strained emotional stability. The federal Bureau of Justice Statistics survey included about 10,000 defendants in the nation's 75 most populous counties. Their cases accounted for over 8,000 victims.

Alcohol usage at the time of the murder was common for both killers (47.6%) and victims (32.7%) of murder within the family. Spouses especially were likely to have been drinking alcohol at the times of the murders. This was true in 54.4% of spouse murders.

Also, about 49.6% of those mates who were killed had been drinking at the time. Alcohol consumption also was common for persons who killed their brothers or sisters (53.9%).

A history of mental illness was much more common among persons charged with killing family members than it was for the murdered relatives. About 14.3% of those charged with killing family members had histories of mental illness. A parent who murdered his or her own child had the greatest frequency of mental illness (25.4%).

Unemployment and (to a lesser degree) homelessness also were evident in persons charged with murdering kin. Some 29.1% of those who had killed relatives were unemployed. Persons who murdered brothers or sisters were unemployed 34.9% of the time. About 17.7% of the murdered siblings were themselves unemployed.

Source U.S. Department of Justice, Bureau of Justice Statistics, "Murder in Families" (Washington, DC: U.S. Government Printing Office, July 1994).

Contact U.S. Department of Justice, Bureau of Justice Statistics Clearinghouse, Box 6000, Rockville, MD 20850. (800) 732-3277.

National Resource Center on Domestic Violence, 6400 Flank Dr. Suite 1300, Harrisburg, PA 17112-2778. (800) 537-2238.

Violence

Violent Victimizations among Intimates, 1987–92

Number, rate, and percent of single offender victimizations in the U.S. committed by intimate partners. The number of victimizations is given according to the gender of the victim.

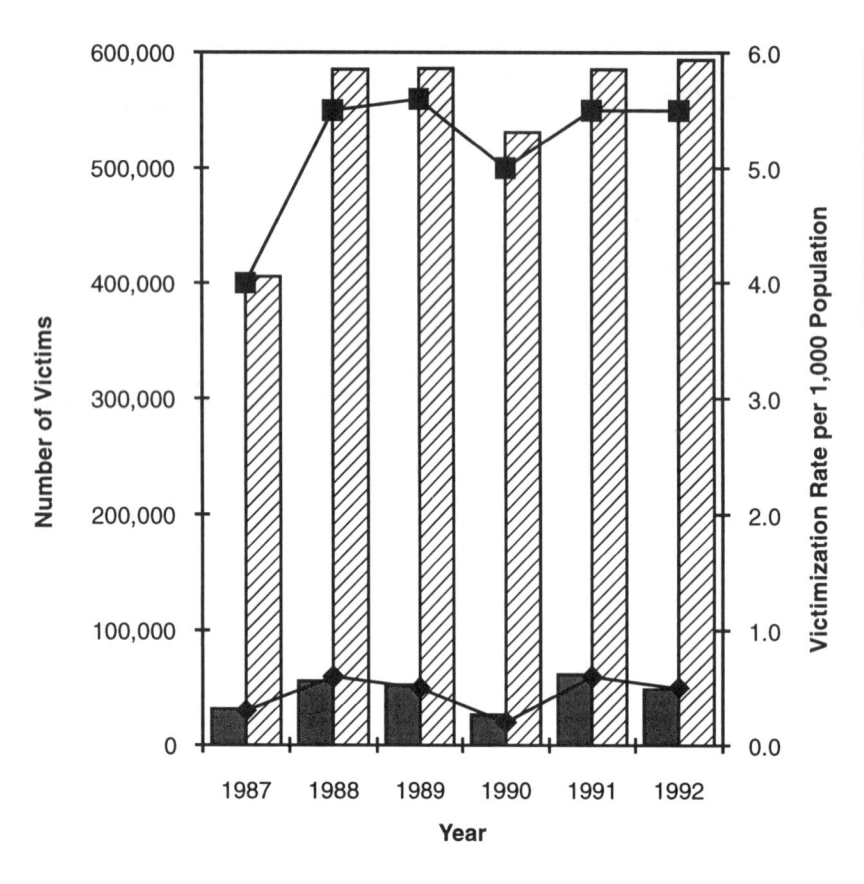

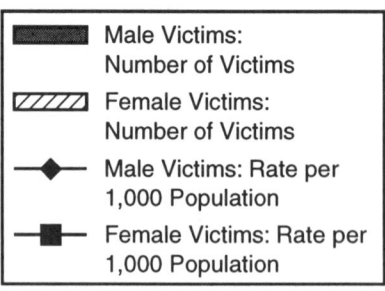

Year	Male Victims: Number of Victims	Male Victims: Rate per 1,000 Population	Male Victims: Percent of All Intimate Victimizations	Female Victims: Number of Victims	Female Victims: Rate per 1,000 Population	Female Victims: Percent of All Intimate Victimizations
1987	31,685	0.3	1.6	405,640	4.0	27.0
1988	55,877	0.6	2.1	585,261	5.5	26.6
1989	52,816	0.5	2.0	586,137	5.6	28.1
1990	26,737	0.2	1.1	531,179	5.0	26.9
1991	62,004	0.6	2.2	585,385	5.5	27.4
1992	49,038	0.5	2.2	593,546	5.5	27.4

Violence

Comments

Acts of violence rose from 1987 to 1992 among victims who knew their attackers. The National Crime Victimization Survey (NCVS) defines these acts as murders, rapes, robberies, or assaults committed by spouses, ex-spouses, boyfriends, or girlfriends.

Women are much less likely than men to become victims of violent crime in general, but they are more likely than men to be victimized by people such as husbands or boyfriends. Violent acts against women rose from 405,640 in 1987 to 593,546 in 1992. About 4 women per 1,000 in the United States were victims in 1987. By 1992, that rate had risen to 5.5 per 1,000. Mates or former mates committed 27.0% of violent acts against women in 1987; the rate rose to 27.4% in 1992.

Men suffered 31,685 of these violent actions in 1987; by 1992, the number was 49,038. Chances of such violence against men also rose from 1987 to 1992. In 1987, .3 men per 1,000 living in the United States were victims; that climbed to .5 per 1,000 in 1992. Mates or former mates committed 1.6% of violent acts against men in 1987; by 1992, the rate had risen to 2.2%.

About 20% of the females victimized by their spouses or ex-spouses told NCVS they had been victims of a series of three or more assaults in the previous six months. These women also said the incidents were so similar or there had been so many that specific acts could not be recalled.

Source

U.S. Department of Justice, Bureau of Justice Statistics, "Violence between Intimates" (Washington, DC: U.S. Government Printing Office, November 1994).

Contact

U.S. Department of Justice, Bureau of Justice Statistics Clearinghouse, Box 6000, Rockville, MD 20850. (800) 732-3277.

National Resource Center on Domestic Violence, 6400 Flank Dr. Suite 1300, Harrisburg, PA 17112-2778. (800) 537-2238.

Violence

Homicide Committed among Intimate Partners, 1977–92

Estimated number of homicide victims in the U.S. that were an intimate partner of the offender. Rates shown are per 100,000 population age 16 and older.

Year	Total Intimate Homicide Victims	Wife or Girlfriend *	Husband or Boyfriend *	Wife or Girlfriend Rate	Husband or Boyfriend Rate
1977	2,581	1,396	1,185	1.6	1.5
1978	2,523	1,428	1,095	1.7	1.4
1979	2,575	1,438	1,137	1.6	1.4
1980	2,627	1,498	1,129	1.7	1.4
1981	2,635	1,486	1,149	1.6	1.4
1982	2,416	1,408	1,008	1.5	1.2
1983	2,530	1,487	1,043	1.6	1.2
1984	2,317	1,420	897	1.5	1.0
1985	2,315	1,480	835	1.6	1.0
1986	2,391	1,525	866	1.6	1.0
1987	2,332	1,508	824	1.6	0.9
1988	2,357	1,592	765	1.6	0.9
1989	2,258	1,441	817	1.5	0.9
1990	2,321	1,524	797	1.5	0.9
1991	2,242	1,528	714	1.5	0.8
1992	2,167	1,510	657	1.5	0.7

* Includes ex-spouses.

Violence

Comments The estimated annual number of homicide victims killed by their intimate partners fell between 1977 and 1992, according to Federal Bureau of Investigation statistics. The FBI tabulates murders according to the relationship between the victim and the offender.

The drop in the total number of intimate homicide victims was due almost entirely to the decline in male victims (husbands and boyfriends). The number of wives and girlfriends killed by their partners has climbed at an unsteady rate since the late 1970s.

Although the number of women killed by their partners has grown, the rate has remained stable. The rate of men killed by their intimate partners fell significantly. The rate of 0.7 per 100,000 of population in 1992 was less than half of the 1977 rate (1.5).

Growth in the overall population can affect the homicide rates listed. For example, if the number of people killed remains the same from one year to the next but the overall population grows, the rate per 100,000 will fall.

Source U.S. Department of Justice, Federal Bureau of Investigation, *Crime in the United States* (Washington, DC: U.S. Government Printing Office), 1977–92 annual. Estimates for the population age 16 and older were provided by U.S. Bureau of the Census.

U.S. Department of Justice, Bureau of Justice Statistics, "Violence between Intimates" (Washington, DC: U.S. Government Printing Office, November 1994).

Contact U.S. Department of Justice, Federal Bureau of Investigation, Uniform Crime Reports, Criminal Justice Information Services Division, Washington, DC 20535. Information Dissemination: (202) 324-5015.

U.S. Department of Justice, Bureau of Justice Statistics Clearinghouse, Box 6000, Rockville, MD 20850. (800) 732-3277.

National Resource Center on Domestic Violence, 6400 Flank Dr. Suite 1300, Harrisburg, PA 17112-2778. (800) 537-2238.

National Coalition Against Domestic Violence, P.O. Box 18749, Denver, CO 80218-0749. (303) 839-1852.

National Clearinghouse for the Defense of Battered Women, 125 S. 9th St. Suite 302, Philadelphia, PA 19107. (215) 351-0100.

Violence

Trends in Reporting Child Abuse, 1976–93

The frequency of reported child abuse (per 1,000 children) in the U.S.

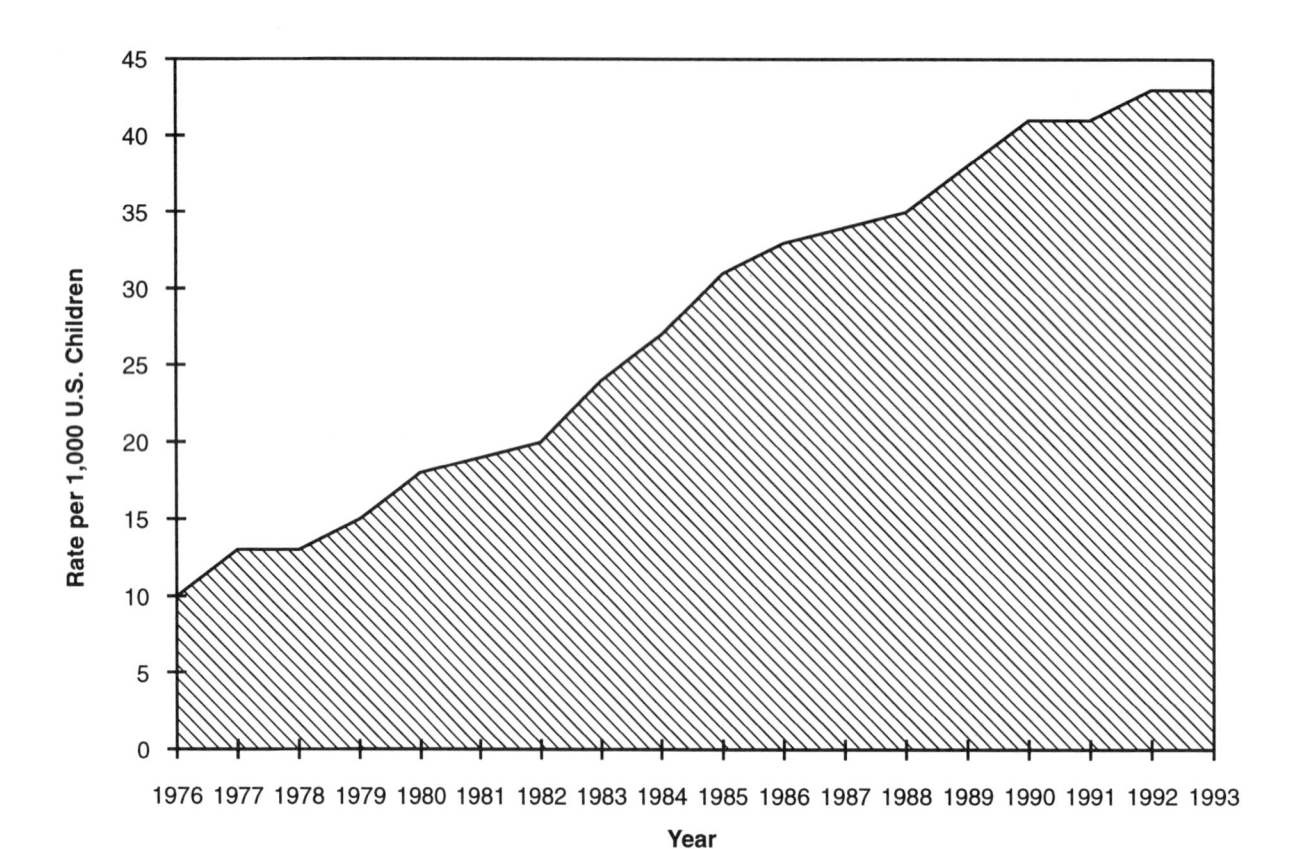

Year	Rate per 1,000 U.S. Children	Year	Rate per 1,000 U.S. Children
1976	10	1985	31
1977	13	1986	33
1978	13	1987	34
1979	15	1988	35
1980	18	1989	38
1981	19	1990	41
1982	20	1991	41
1983	24	1992	43
1984	27	1993	43

Violence

Comments Reports of child abuse have grown from 10 per 1,000 children in the United States in 1976 to 43 per 1,000 in 1993. The rate of abuse had risen every year from 1976 to 1992. The National Center on Child Abuse and Neglect, which reported these figures, defines a child as being under age 18.

Since 1976, reports of child abuse had risen about 9% each year. During 1984–88, the rate of increase was 7%. From 1989 to 1993, however, abuse reports rose about 3% per year.

The growth in reported child abuse during these years may have several causes. First, child abuse itself may be growing. Also, people now may be more able to spot signs of abuse and/or are more willing to report suspected child abuse. Until recently, many people saw child abuse as a very private family matter, and they avoided action to stop it from outside the family. About one in five reports of child abuse comes from within the victim's family. If this same condition were true years ago, then much child abuse in the past may have gone unreported.

Source U.S. Department Of Health and Human Services, National Center on Child Abuse and Neglect, *Child Maltreatment 1993: Reports From the States to the National Center on Child Abuse and Neglect* (Washington, DC: U.S. Government Printing Office, 1995), p. 2-1.

Contact National Clearinghouse on Child Abuse and Neglect Information, P.O. Box 1182, Washington, DC 20013-1182. (800) 394-3366.

Children's Defense Fund, 25 E St. NW, Washington, DC 20001. (202) 628-8787.

Violence

Sources of Child Maltreatment Reports, 1993

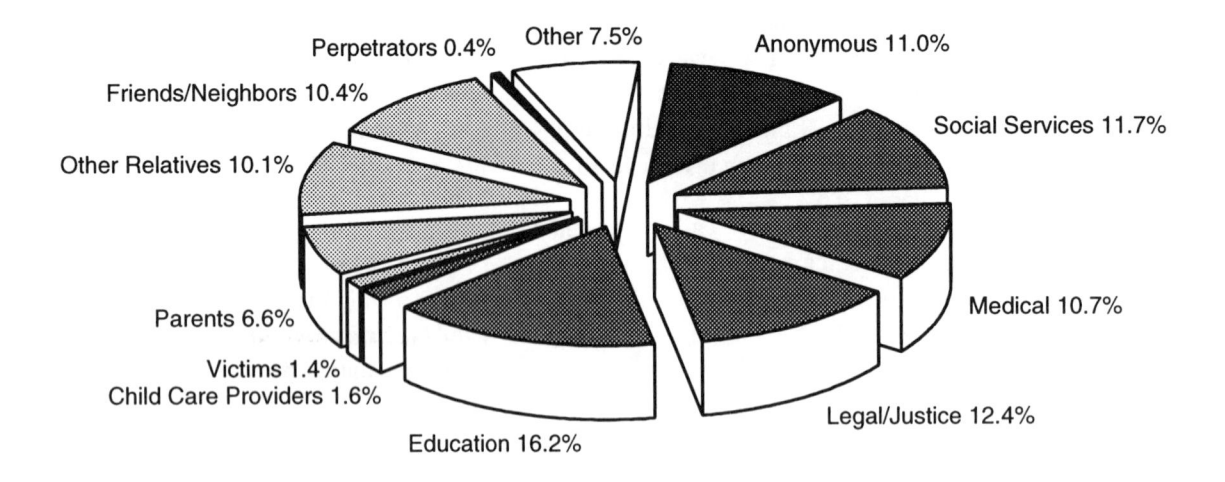

Source	Number of Reports	Percent
Professionals	**787,538**	**52.6**
Social services	174,754	11.7
Medical	159,616	10.7
Legal/justice	185,615	12.4
Education	243,431	16.2
Child care providers	24,122	1.6
Family members	**270,315**	**18.1**
Victims	20,464	1.4
Parents	99,343	6.6
Other relatives	150,508	10.1
Friends/neighbors	**155,369**	**10.4**
Perpetrators	**6,698**	**0.4**
Other	**111,918**	**7.5**
Anonymous	**164,002**	**11.0**
Total	**1,495,840**	**100.0**

Violence

Comments More than half of all child abuse reports came from professionals in 1993, said the National Center on Child Abuse and Neglect (NCCAN). NCCAN gathers information on child abuse reports in order to understand how common the problem is.

Educational, legal, social services, medical, and child care professionals accounted for 52.6% of all child abuse reports in 1993. Nationally, educators have been the most frequent source of child abuse reports each year since 1990.

NCCAN reported that in 1993 educators were the most frequent source of reports in 20 states and the second most frequent source in 14 states.

Those within the family of the victim (victims, parents, and other relatives) accounted for 18.1% of the reports. The children who were abused themselves were the source of child abuse reports only 1.4% of the time. Other reports came from friends or neighbors (10.4%), people who refused to identify themselves (11.0%), and the people committing the abuse (0.4%). Other sources accounted for 7.5% of the child abuse reports.

NCCAN said these percentages have remained consistent since this type of data collection method began in 1990.

Source U.S. Department Of Health and Human Services, National Center on Child Abuse and Neglect, *Child Maltreatment 1993: Reports From the States to the National Center on Child Abuse and Neglect* (Washington, DC: U.S. Government Printing Office, 1995), pp. 2-2, 2-3, 3-3, 3-4.

Contact National Clearinghouse on Child Abuse and Neglect Information, P.O. Box 1182, Washington, DC 20013-1182. (800) 394-3366.

Children's Defense Fund, 25 E St. NW, Washington, DC 20001. (202) 628-8787.

National Maternal and Child Health Clearinghouse, 8201 Greensboro Dr. Suite 600, McLean, VA 22102. (703) 821-8955, ext. 254/255.

Violence

Number of Child Abuse Victims by Type of Maltreatment, 1993

Percent distribution of reported child abuse cases in the U.S. in 1993 by case type, and the percentage of child abuse victims by case type.

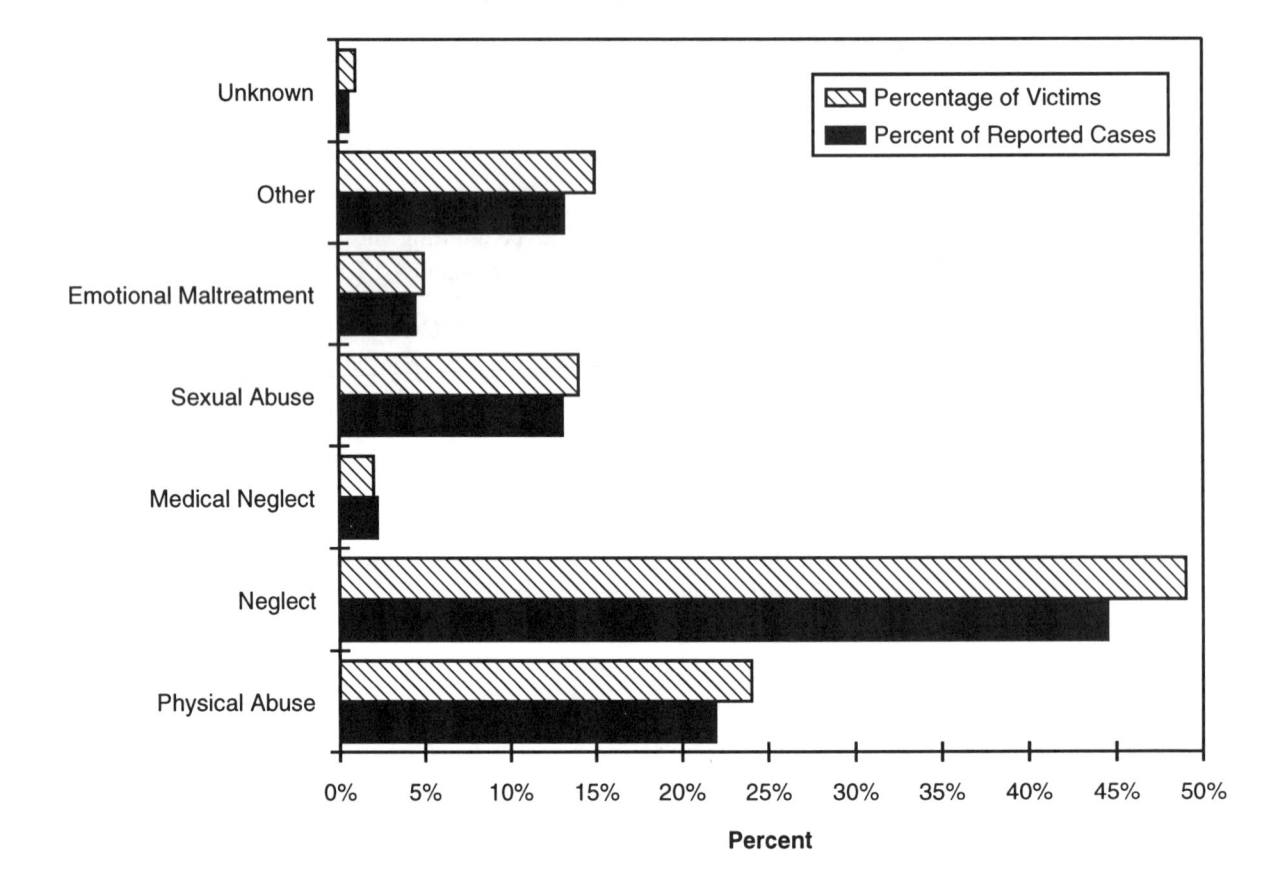

Type of Abuse	Number	Percent of Reported Cases	Percentage of Victims *
Physical abuse	233,487	21.9	24
Neglect	475,153	44.5	49
Medical neglect	23,009	2.2	2
Sexual abuse	139,817	13.1	14
Emotional maltreatment	48,288	4.5	5
Other	140,618	13.2	15
Unknown	6,859	0.6	1
Total	1,067,231	100.0	

* Because some states reported more than one kind of abuse per victim, the total does not add to 100%.

Violence

Comments Almost 45%, or 475,153, of all child abuse victims suffered from neglect in 1993. This is more than double the number of those who suffered from physical abuse, which was the next-leading cause at 21.9%, or 233,487 cases.

The third-leading cause was sexual abuse at 13.1%, or 139,817 cases. Emotional abuse was involved in 4.5% of the cases and medical neglect in 2.2% of them. Other causes, such as abandonment, congenital drug addiction, and threats, accounted for 13.2% of the cases. No cause was reported 0.6% of the time.

Although nearly every state reported information regarding physical abuse, neglect, and sexual abuse, only 42 gave emotional abuse figures. Just 30 reported on medical neglect.

The figures come from the National Center on Child Abuse and Neglect. It reported 1,067,231 maltreatment cases in 1993. Reporting methods did not account for an individual child receiving multiple forms of abuse. As a result, the estimate for the total number of victims was 966,163 in 1993.

Source U.S. Department Of Health and Human Services, National Center on Child Abuse and Neglect, *Child Maltreatment 1993: Reports From the States to the National Center on Child Abuse and Neglect* (Washington, DC: U.S. Government Printing Office, 1995), pp. 2-6, 2-8, 3-7.

Contact National Clearinghouse on Child Abuse and Neglect Information, P.O. Box 1182, Washington, DC 20013-1182. (800) 394-3366.

Children's Defense Fund, 25 E St. NW, Washington, DC 20001. (202) 628-8787.

National Maternal and Child Health Clearinghouse, 8201 Greensboro Dr. Suite 600, McLean, VA 22102. (703) 821-8955, ext. 254/255.

Violence

How Old Are Abused Children?

Age distribution of U.S. child abuse victims in 1993.

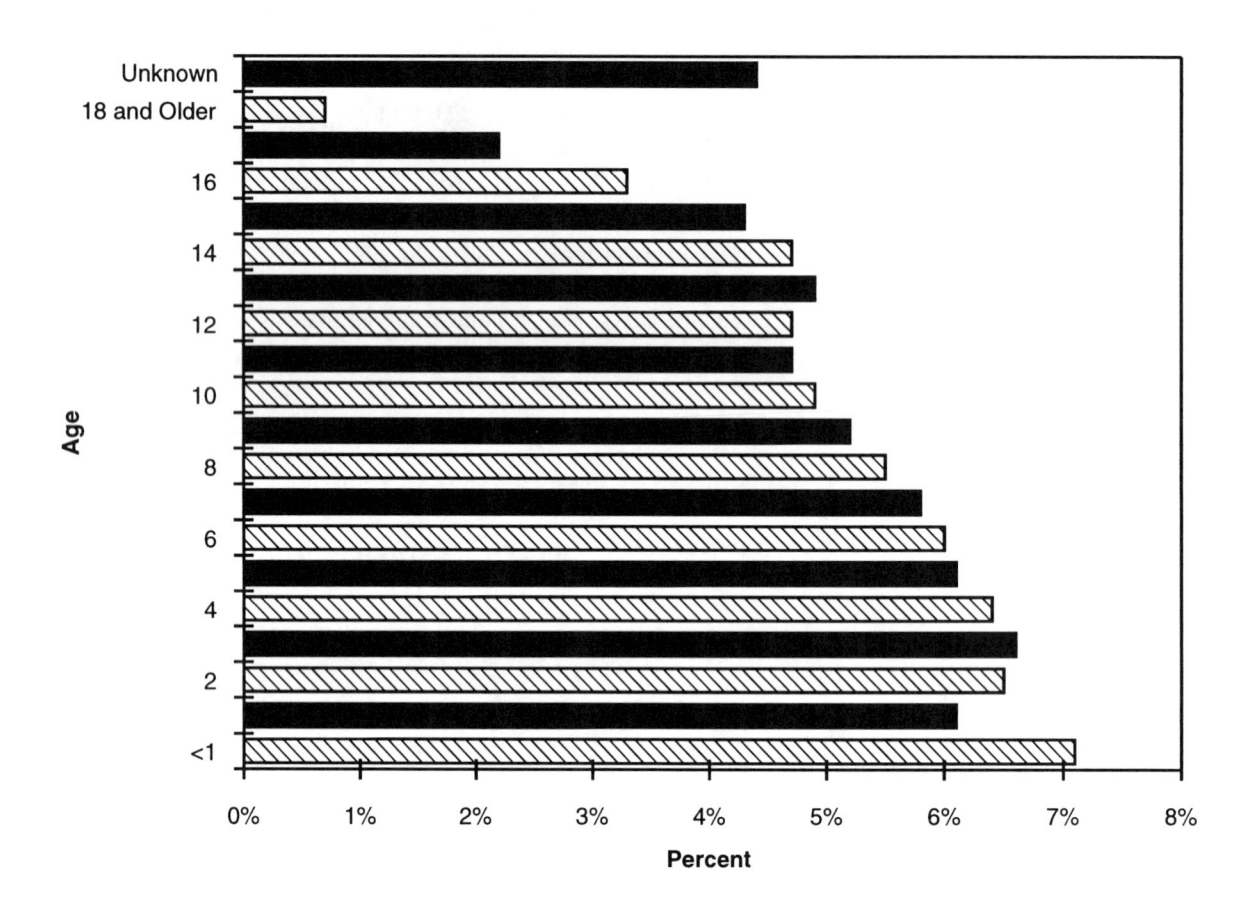

Age of Victim (years)	Number of Victims	Percent *
<1	65,602	7.1
1	56,098	6.1
2	60,253	6.5
3	61,289	6.6
4	58,879	6.4
5	56,576	6.1
6	55,488	6.0
7	54,209	5.8
8	51,271	5.5
9	48,324	5.2
10	45,195	4.9

Age of Victim (years)	Number of Victims	Percent *
11	43,586	4.7
12	43,830	4.7
13	44,970	4.9
14	43,532	4.7
15	39,557	4.3
16	30,695	3.3
17	20,082	2.2
18 and older	6,799	0.7
Unknown	40,439	4.4
Total	926,674	100.0

* Does not add to total because of rounding.

Violence

Comments National Center on Child Abuse and Neglect figures for 1993 show younger children are more likely to be abused than older ones.

Victims who had not yet reached their first birthdays accounted for 7.1%, or 65,602, of the 926,674 cases reported. Eighteen-year-olds were involved in only 0.7%, or 6,799, of the reports. From birth to age 18, child abuse cases generally declined as age increased. A few age groups strayed from the pattern, but not by much. The largest declines were for 16-, 17-, and 18-year-olds.

Older children are more able than younger ones to elude abusers. Also, they are more capable of successfully resisting physical abuse. These factors may affect the decrease in abuse reports as children get older.

Ages were not available for 40,439, or 4.4% of the reports.

Source U.S. Department Of Health and Human Services, National Center on Child Abuse and Neglect, *Child Maltreatment 1993: Reports From the States to the National Center on Child Abuse and Neglect* (Washington, DC: U.S. Government Printing Office, 1995), pp. 2-8, 3-8, 3-9.

Contact National Clearinghouse on Child Abuse and Neglect Information, P.O. Box 1182, Washington, DC 20013-1182. (800) 394-3366.

Children's Defense Fund, 25 E St. NW, Washington, DC 20001. (202) 628-8787.

National Maternal and Child Health Clearinghouse, 8201 Greensboro Dr. Suite 600, McLean, VA 22102. (703) 821-8955, ext. 254/255.

Violence

Relationship of Perpetrator to Child Abuse Victim, 1993

The relationship between the child and the child abuser in reported cases of child abuse occurring in the U.S. during 1993.

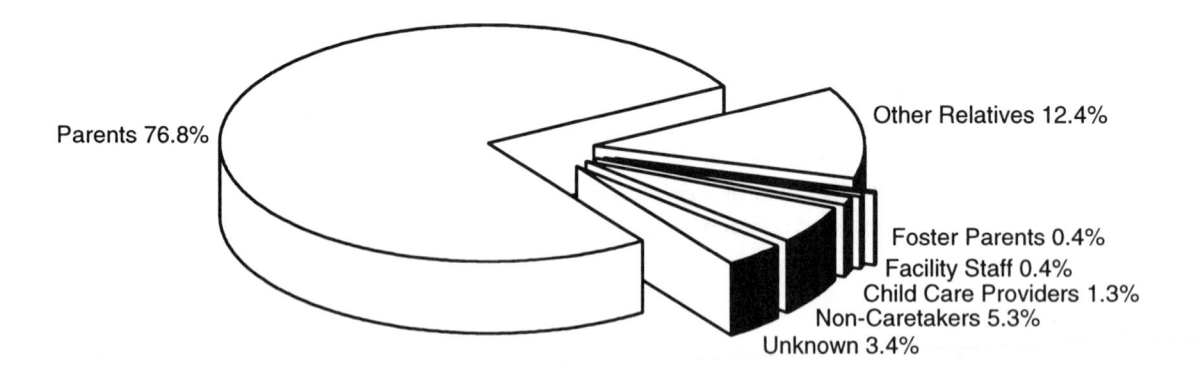

- Parents 76.8%
- Other Relatives 12.4%
- Foster Parents 0.4%
- Facility Staff 0.4%
- Child Care Providers 1.3%
- Non-Caretakers 5.3%
- Unknown 3.4%

Relationship	Number of Victims	Percent
Parents	437,386	76.8
Other relatives	70,620	12.4
Foster parents	2,402	0.4
Facility staff	2,118	0.4
Child care providers	7,163	1.3
Non-caretakers	30,428	5.3
Unknown	19,482	3.4
Total	569,599	100.0

Violence

Comments

Parents and other relatives were the people most likely to abuse children, a National Center on Child Abuse and Neglect (NCCAN) report for 1993 shows. The data came from child protective services agencies in 40 states.

Parents were named as abusers in 76.8%, or 437,386, of the reports; other relatives were named 12.8% of the time (70,620 cases). Only 5.3% of reported child abusers were people who don't usually supervise children. They accounted for 30,428 cases. Identities of the abusers were not available in 3.4%, or 19,482, of the cases. There were 569,599 child abuse cases reported for 1993.

NCCAN says a large number of child abusers may be repeat offenders. It has gathered child abuse data each year since 1990 through its National Child Abuse and Neglect Data System. NCCAN reports abuse case percentages have remained stable since this type of data collection began in 1990.

Source

U.S. Department Of Health and Human Services, National Center on Child Abuse and Neglect, *Child Maltreatment 1993: Reports From the States to the National Center on Child Abuse and Neglect* (Washington, DC: U.S. Government Printing Office, 1995), pp. 2-12, 3-12.

Contact

National Clearinghouse on Child Abuse and Neglect Information, P.O. Box 1182, Washington, DC 20013-1182. (800) 394-3366.

Children's Defense Fund, 25 E St. NW, Washington, DC 20001. (202) 628-8787.

National Maternal and Child Health Clearinghouse, 8201 Greensboro Dr. Suite 600, McLean, VA 22102. (703) 821-8955, ext. 254/255.

Violence

How Much of the Crime Problem Is at School?

Victimizations at schools in 1992. Percentage of all nonfatal violent incidents that occurred at U.S. schools.

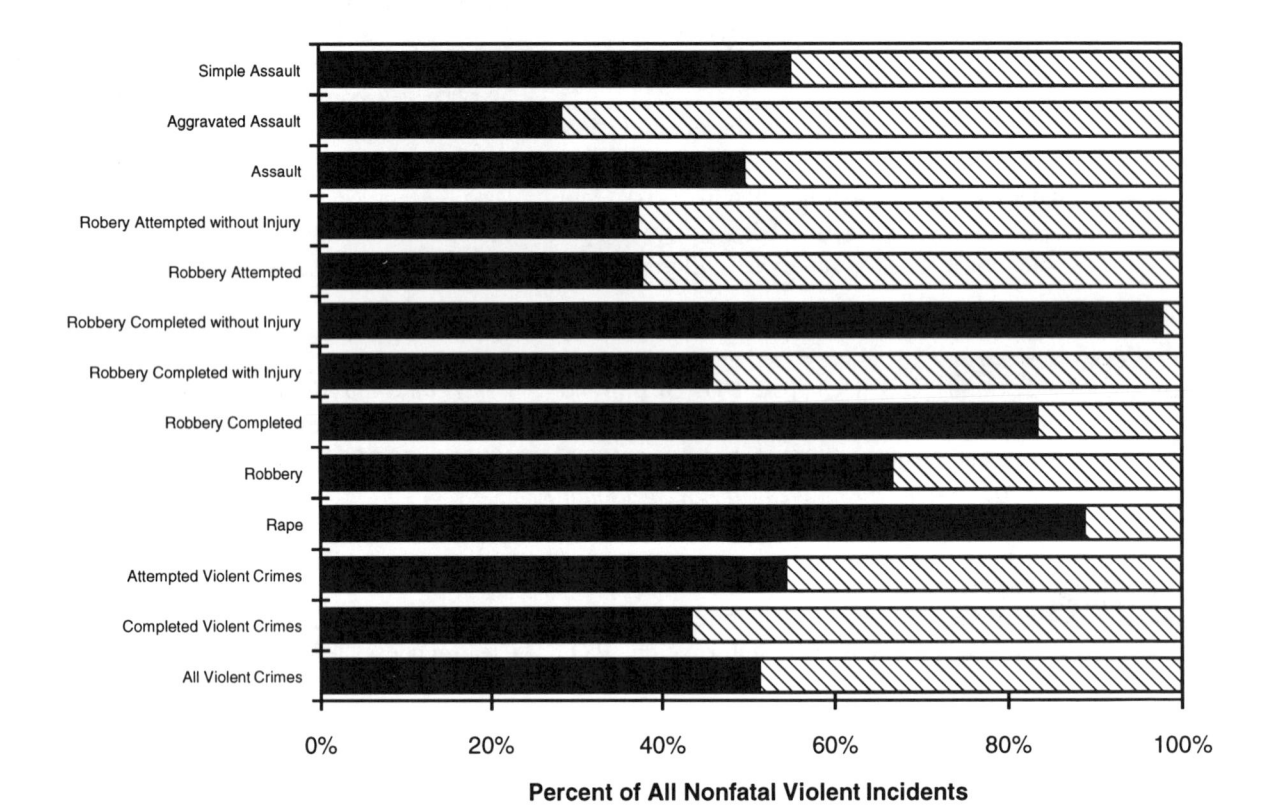

■ Inside School Building ▨ On School Property

Type of Crime	Inside School Building	On School Property
All violent crimes	6.2%	5.9%
Completed violent crimes	3.9%	5.1%
Attempted violent crimes	7.5%	6.3%
Rape	7.1%*	0.9%*
Robbery	2.6%*	1.3%*
Completed	3.0%*	0.6%*
With injury	1.1%*	1.3%*
Without injury	4.5%*	0.1%*
Attempted	1.7%*	2.8%*
With injury	0.0%*	0.0%*
Without injury	2.2%*	3.7%*
Assault	7.0%	7.1%
Aggravated	2.3%*	5.8%
Simple	9.4%	7.7%

* Estimate is based on about 10 or fewer sample cases.

Violence

Comments Violent incidents in schools or on school grounds accounted for 12.1% of all such crimes in 1992, according to the National Crime Victimization Survey. The survey annually questions over 100,000 U.S. residents 12 and older about their experiences with crime, regardless of whether the incidents were reported to police.

Simple assaults (not involving weapons) represented the most common violent crimes in schools (9.4% of cases) or on school property (7.7%). Incidents in junior and senior high schools or on such school property usually involve more youths than adults. However, these statistics include everyone over age 12. Also, these statistics include incidents at community colleges and universities. Violent acts at these kinds of institutions are likely to involve a greater proportion of adult victims and offenders.

It is important to remember that many of the percentages given for specific crimes are estimates based on only small numbers of cases. Such estimates probably are not very reliable in showing how often such incidents occur.

Source U.S. Department of Justice, Bureau of Justice Statistics. *Criminal Victimization in the United States, 1992* (Washington, DC: U.S. Government Printing Office, 1994), p. 75.

Contact U.S. Department of Justice, Bureau of Justice Statistics Clearinghouse, Box 6000, Rockville, MD 20850. (800) 732-3277.

Violence

Students in 6th–12th Grade Reporting a Violent Victimization at School

Estimates of nonfatal violent victimization occurring at school to students in grades 6–12. The estimates are based on a 1989 survey.

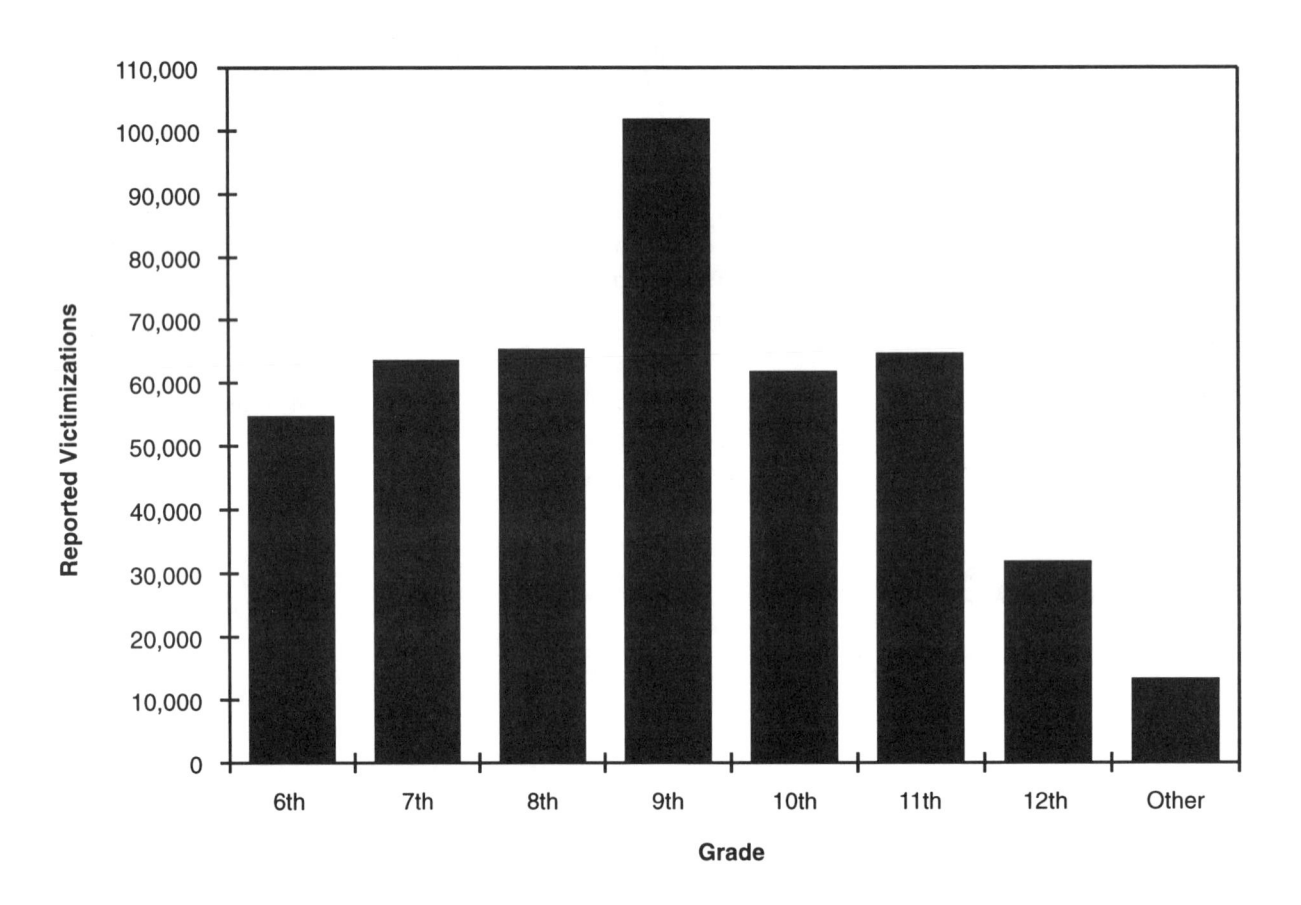

Grade	Total Number Of Students	Percent Surveyed Who Reported Violent Victimization at School	Estimated Number Reporting Victimization at School
6th	1,817,511	3%	54,500
7th	3,170,126	2%	63,400
8th	3,258,506	2%	65,200
9th	3,390,701	3%	101,700
10th	3,082,441	2%	61,600
11th	3,223,624	2%	64,500
12th	3,171,819	1%	31,700
Other	439,364	3%	13,200

Violence

Comments About 2% of students ages 12-19 were victims of violent crimes in or around their schools over a six-month period in 1989, according to the Bureau of Justice Statistics. The bureau conducted a survey in the nation's public and private schools to determine how frequently students are victims of violent crimes.

There were an estimated 455,800 violent acts committed against the 21,554,092 students in grades 6–12.

These crimes can involve attacks without weapons and may result in minor injury, such as cuts or bruises. They also include aggravated assaults (involving weapons), robberies, and rapes.

According to the survey, 6th and 9th graders had a greater risk (3%) of becoming violence victims than any other group analyzed. The 9th grade reported the greatest number of estimated victims: 3,390,701.

It is important to remember, however, that these are only estimates and that the numbers of victims can vary from year to year for the grades shown.

Source U.S. Department of Justice, Bureau of Justice Statistics, *School Crime: A National Crime Victimization Survey Report* (Washington, DC: U.S. Government Printing Office, 1991), p. 2.

Contact U.S. Department of Justice, Bureau of Justice Statistics Clearinghouse, Box 6000, Rockville, MD 20850. (800) 732-3277.

Violence

Fights at High Schools, 1993

Percentage of high school students who were involved or injured in a physical fight. The table also shows the gender and grade of students, and the estimated total number of fights (per 100 students) occurring within the past year.

Race/Ethnicity and Grade	In a Physical Fight (percent) Female	Male	Total	Injured in a Physical Fight (percent) Female	Male	Total	12-Month Incidence of Physical Fighting (episodes per 100 students) Female	Male	Total
White, non-Hispanic	29.5	50.0	40.3	2.2	4.2	3.2	88.0	161.8	126.3
Black, non-Hispanic	41.8	57.5	49.5	4.3	8.5	6.4	124.8	202.8	163.2
Hispanic	34.1	52.2	43.2	3.7	6.5	5.1	110.2	189.7	150.2
9th grade	41.3	58.9	50.4	3.6	4.7	4.1	130.8	208.8	170.9
10th grade	31.9	52.0	42.2	2.5	5.3	4.0	94.0	175.6	136.2
11th grade	28.0	51.8	40.5	2.6	5.3	4.0	84.0	177.3	132.6
12th grade	26.5	42.7	34.8	2.1	5.3	3.7	76.0	119.8	98.1
Total	31.7	51.2	41.8	2.7	5.2	4.0	96.9	173.2	136.8

Confidence intervals for table above

Race/Ethnicity and Grade	In a Physical Fight (percent) Female	Male	Total	Injured in a Physical Fight (percent) Female	Male	Total	12-Month Incidence of Physical Fighting (episodes per 100 students) Female	Male	Total
White, non-Hispanic	±2.7	±2.3	±2.2	±0.9	±1.3	±1.0	±16.7	±27.4	±17.4
Black, non-Hispanic	±4.0	±5.0	±3.6	±1.8	±2.6	±1.8	±37.5	±44.5	±38.1
Hispanic	±4.3	±4.2	±3.1	±1.1	±1.8	±1.1	±36.7	±63.3	±47.9
9th grade	±4.2	±2.9	±3.0	±1.8	±1.2	±1.0	±34.7	±25.5	±25.5
10th grade	±3.1	±3.4	±2.9	±0.9	±2.0	±1.1	±20.1	±35.6	±22.4
11th grade	±2.4	±5.0	±3.0	±1.2	±2.0	±1.4	±17.8	±41.0	±23.4
12th grade	±3.8	±3.2	±3.1	±1.0	±2.2	±1.3	±21.2	±29.9	±20.5
Total	±2.3	±2.1	±1.9	±0.8	±1.1	±0.9	±17.2	±25.3	±18.3

Violence

Comments A 1993 study suggests 16.2% of all U.S. high school students in 1993 were in fights at school during the 12 months preceding the survey.

The Youth Risk Behavior Surveillance System (YRBSS) conducted the survey. It monitors six prominent health risk factors among young people: tobacco use, alcohol and other drug use, sexual behaviors, dietary behaviors, physical activity, and behaviors leading to unintentional and intentional injuries (for example, physical fighting).

In general, fighting was more common among male students than among females. Black male and female students were more likely to have been in fights than white male and female students. Also, the tendency of any student to be involved in a fight steadily declined from 9th to 12th grade.

In 1993, YRBSS used an intricate sample design to produce a group of 9th through 12th graders who represented national trends. By matching characteristics of the sample group to the entire U.S. high school population, one can study behavioral trends without having to survey every student.

The table of confidence intervals gives the margin of error ranges for each statistic shown. Each confidence interval indicates the range into which 95% of all known cases fall. For example, fighting among 9th graders was reported at 50.4%, ±3.0%. This means that although the number for the sample group was 50.4%, it actually could have been as low as 47.4% or as high as 53.4% for all 9th graders.

Source U.S. Department Of Health and Human Services, Public Health Service, Centers for Disease Control and Prevention, *Morbidity and Mortality Weekly Report* 1995; 44 (no. SS-1), p. 26.

Contact U.S. Department of Health and Human Services, Public Health Service, Centers for Disease Control and Prevention, 1600 Clifton Rd. NE, Atlanta, GA 30333. (404) 332-4555. The CDC also maintains a World-Wide Web server at http://www.cdc.gov/.

Violence

A State-by-State Look at Fighting among High School Students

High school students who were in a physical fight or injured in one (percentage), and the 12-month incidence of physical fighting per 100 students for selected sites in 1993. Arranged by state/territory. Unweighted data (in italics) applies only to the surveyed students. It is not possible to make any state-to-state comparisons using unweighted data.

State/Territory [Note: Italics indicate unweighted data.]	In a Physical Fight (percent)	Injured in a Physical Fight (percent)	12-Month Incidence of Physical Fighting (episodes per 100 students) †
Alabama	35.0	4.0	107.9
American Samoa	60.8	12.2	261.8
Arkansas	44.9	5.1	163.1
California	—	—	—
San Diego	39.8	5.0	146.8
San Francisco	35.2	5.3	121.9
Delaware	42.3	7.0	139.5
District of Columbia	45.6	8.2	139.9
Florida	—	—	—
Fort Lauderdale	38.5	5.2	132.7
Miami	38.7	5.7	137.1
Georgia	40.8	3.9	126.7
Hawaii	37.0	4.3	122.7
Idaho	39.7	4.3	142.8
Illinois	42.7	5.0	149.2
Chicago	43.7	6.6	144.7
Kentucky	36.9	2.4	116.6
Louisiana *	44.6	5.1	142.5
New Orleans	45.6	7.4	133.6
Maine	39.6	2.4	143.2
Massachusetts	41.6	4.3	143.1
Boston	43.0	7.8	160.8
Mississippi	39.3	3.1	115.7
Montana	41.9	3.1	134.6
Nebraska	34.5	3.4	119.3
Nevada	42.1	4.1	134.6
New Hampshire	36.9	4.7	122.0
New Jersey	40.4	5.2	138.5
Jersey City	46.9	9.3	155.6
New Mexico	42.6	4.8	154.8
New York *	42.0	4.9	143.0
New York City	42.9	5.9	149.6
North Carolina	37.8	3.7	128.1
Ohio	44.4	5.0	145.8
Oregon	38.9	4.9	138.5
Pennsylvania	—	—	—
Philadelphia	51.4	7.9	183.0

[Continued]

A State-by-State Look at Fighting among High School Students

[Continued]

State/Territory [Note: Italics indicate unweighted data.]	In a Physical Fight (percent)	Injured in a Physical Fight (percent)	12-Month Incidence of Physical Fighting (episodes per 100 students) †
South Carolina	36.9	4.1	118.2
South Dakota	39.8	4.0	151.0
Tennessee	39.9	3.7	122.7
Texas	—	—	—
Dallas	42.8	4.5	147.1
Utah	36.3	3.8	136.7
Vermont	41.8	4.8	143.5
Virgin Islands	29.8	5.3	93.3
Washington	—	—	—
Seattle	37.5	NA	129.9
West Virginia	41.7	4.4	140.8
Wisconsin	39.4	4.7	144.2
Wyoming	40.1	4.0	139.1

* Survey did not include students from the state's largest city.

† Students who reported fighting two or three times were assigned a fighting frequency of 2.5; four or five times, 4.5; six or seven times, 6.5; eight or nine times, 8.5; 10 or 11 times, 10.5; and ≥12 times, 12.0.

Comments

School violence has become an area of concern across the United States. The frequency of violence occurring at school has many factors.

These include school location, student population characteristics and density, and the level of strictness and enforcement of discipline.

This 1993 survey was part of the Youth Risk Behavior Surveillance System, which sampled twenty-four state and nine local school systems.

The frequency of fighting among an area's high school students is shown by the "incidence of physical fighting" statistic. This number estimates how many fights occurred within a year. The frequency rate is per 100 students. This frequency number can rise quickly if just a small percentage of students regularly are in fights.

Source

U.S. Department Of Health and Human Services, Public Health Service, Centers for Disease Control and Prevention, *Morbidity and Mortality Weekly Report* 1995; 44 (no. SS-1), pp. 27, 28.

Contact

U.S. Department of Health and Human Services, Public Health Service, Centers for Disease Control and Prevention, 1600 Clifton Rd. NE, Atlanta, GA 30333. (404) 332-4555. The CDC also maintains a World-Wide Web server at http://www.cdc.gov/.

Violence

Violence at Schools

Percentage of high school students who reported engaging in violence-related behaviors on school property. The survey is from 1993 and details the student's grade and race/ethnicity.

Race/Ethnicity and Grade	Felt too unsafe to go to school (on 1 or more of the 30 days preceding the survey)	Carried a weapon on school property (e.g., gun, knife, club)	Threatened or injured with a weapon on school property*	In a physical fight on school property*	Property stolen or deliberately damaged on school property*
White, non-Hispanic	3.0	10.9	6.3	15.0	32.0
Black, non-Hispanic	7.1	15.0	11.2	22.0	35.5
Hispanic	10.1	13.3	8.6	17.9	32.2
9th grade	6.1	12.6	9.4	23.1	37.2
10th grade	5.2	11.5	7.3	17.2	32.8
11th grade	3.3	11.9	7.3	3.8	32.3
12th grade	3.0	10.8	5.5	11.4	28.9
All 9th–12th graders	4.4	11.8	7.3	16.2	32.7

* One or more times during the 12 months preceding the survey.

Confidence intervals for table above

Race/Ethnicity and Grade	Felt too unsafe to go to school	Carried a weapon on school property	Threatened or injured with a weapon on school property	In a physical fight on school property	Property stolen or deliberately damaged on school property
White, non-Hispanic	±0.7	±1.7	±1.1	±1.3	±2.2
Black, non-Hispanic	±1.6	±1.7	±1.9	±2.7	±2.0
Hispanic	±1.9	±2.1	±1.6	±3.4	±4.2
9th grade	±0.9	±1.4	±1.8	±3.0	±2.5
10th grade	±1.4	±1.9	±1.2	±2.1	±2.8
11th grade	±0.9	±2.8	±1.3	±2.5	±2.4
12th grade	±1.0	±1.6	±1.2	±1.3	±2.5
All 9th–12th graders	±0.7	±1.4	±0.9	±1.2	±1.8

Violence

Comments

About 4.4% of 9th–12th graders reported feeling too unsafe to go to school during 1993.

The national school-based Youth Risk Behavior Survey collected the data and reported that with an adjustment factor of ±0.7%, the figure could range from 3.7% to 5.1%.

The survey is a component of the Youth Risk Behavior Surveillance System (YRBSS). It examines major health risk behaviors among youth and young adults, including behaviors leading to unintentional and intentional injuries. Intentional injuries include fighting. The YRBSS sampling design aims to produce a sample group of students in grades 9–12 that accurately represents the entire nation.

If the sample group represented all U.S. high school students in 1993, then 11.8% of them carried weapons to school at some time in the month before the survey. Also, 16.2% had been in fights and 7.3% had been threatened or injured with weapons at school during the previous year.

The most common violence-related behavior was property being stolen or deliberately damaged on school grounds. Some people consider this action more malicious than violent, but it can prompt violence through retaliation.

It is possible to learn about general behavioral trends without having to question every student in the country. This is done by carefully matching the qualities of a sample group to the whole U.S. high school population. The table of confidence intervals gives the margin of error ranges for each statistic shown. Each confidence interval indicates that 95% of all known cases fall within that particular range.

Researchers frequently use the 95% confidence level to study behavioral trends and other aspects of social science. In business, market research often requires the use of confidence intervals. Medical research often uses a 99% confidence level, particularly when test results are a matter of life or death.

Source

U.S. Department Of Health and Human Services, Public Health Service, Centers for Disease Control and Prevention, *Morbidity and Mortality Weekly Report* 1995; 44 (no. SS-1), p. 29.

Contact

U.S. Department of Health and Human Services, Public Health Service, Centers for Disease Control and Prevention, 1600 Clifton Rd. NE, Atlanta, GA 30333. (404) 332-4555. The CDC also maintains a World-Wide Web server at http://www.cdc.gov/.

Campus Violence

Violent offenses* on U.S university and college campuses that were known to police in 1993.

State†	Number of Institutions Analyzed	Student Enrollment‡	Violent Crime Offenses	Rate per 1,000 Students
Alabama	10	75,352	57	0.8
Alaska	1	8,116	22	2.7
Arizona	7	142,195	103	0.7
Arkansas	5	41,846	40	1.0
California	43	695,027	410	0.6
Colorado	9	77,992	15	0.2
Connecticut	5	47,359	21	0.4
Florida	7	141,104	84	0.6
Georgia	29	173,200	110	0.6
Indiana	5	135,664	99	0.7
Iowa	1	25,695	15	0.6
Kentucky	9	121,744	75	0.6
Louisiana	6	61,054	77	1.3
Maine	3	24,657	5	0.2
Maryland	11	93,049	108	1.2
Massachusetts	11	123,700	116	0.9
Mississippi	5	36,728	71	1.9
Missouri	5	65,569	22	0.3
Montana	2	21,149	12	0.6
Nebraska	2	32,944	6	0.2
Nevada	2	30,588	15	0.5
New Hampshire	1	13,872	10	0.7
New Jersey	15	158,377	101	0.6
New Mexico	3	22,216	29	1.3
New York	25	186,589	108	0.6
North Carolina	22	186,985	217	1.2
North Dakota	1	12,289	2	0.2
Ohio	12	251,899	142	0.6
Oklahoma	11	106,627	32	0.3
Pennsylvania	15	122,282	63	0.5
Rhode Island	2	23,042	14	0.6
South Carolina	10	79,827	63	0.8
South Dakota	1	9,260	2	0.2
Tennessee	6	70,540	39	0.6
Texas	56	486,698	223	0.5
Utah	8	123,766	34	0.3
Vermont	1	10,885	4	0.4

[Continued]

Campus Violence

[Continued]

State†	Number of Institutions Analyzed	Student Enrollment‡	Violent Crime Offenses	Rate per 1,000 Students
Virginia	20	226,462	128	0.6
Washington	5	78,654	44	0.6
West Virginia	7	51,332	18	0.4
Wisconsin	11	134,692	39	0.3
Wyoming	1	12,044	11	0.9

* Violent crimes are offenses of murder, forcible rape, robbery, and aggravated assault.
† Data for Delaware, the District of Columbia, Hawaii, Idaho, Illinois, Kansas, Michigan, Minnesota, and Oregon were either unavailable or incompatible.
‡ Student enrollment figures are for 1992 and include full-time and part-time students.

Comments

Violent crimes (murder, forcible rape, robbery, and aggravated assault) on university and college campuses occur much less frequently than do property crimes (burglary, larceny-theft, motor vehicle theft, and arson). Colleges and universities are frequently targets of violent criminals, because there often are many people living near campus.

Easy public access to a college or university also can make it difficult to maintain security. Most campuses have open areas between buildings that robbers and rapists often use to trap victims who walk alone. Many of these campuses discourage students from walking alone at night and may even offer security escort services.

The statistics compiled for the states shown do not necessarily include all public and private colleges and universities. Usually the figures only include the large public colleges and universities. It is unfair to make detailed state-to-state comparisons. Data for Delaware, the District of Columbia, Hawaii, Idaho, Illinois, Kansas, Michigan, Minnesota, and Oregon were unavailable or incompatible.

These statistics treat murder, rape, robbery, and aggravated assault equally in seriousness. A murder is counted as a single violent crime, given equal attention with an aggravated assault. However, rates for a more serious violent crime like murder may widely vary between campuses. Also, states with mostly urban campuses experience more violent crime than states with mostly rural or suburban campuses, since violent crime is more common in larger urban areas.

These statistics can only provide a general idea on the frequency of violent crime at selected colleges and universities. Most violent crimes committed on campuses are aggravated assaults (involving weapons). Forcible rapes and robberies are in the minority; murder is very rare.

Source

Federal Bureau of Investigation, *Crime in the United States 1993* (Washington, DC: U.S. Government Printing Office) pp. 158–167.

Contact

U.S. Department of Justice, Federal Bureau of Investigation, Uniform Crime Reports, Criminal Justice Information Services Division, Washington, DC 20535. Information Dissemination: (202) 324-5015.

Violence

Percentage of Students Reporting Victimization and Fear of Attack, by Gang Presence at School

Percentage of students over age 12 who experienced or feared a crime victimization at school in 1989.

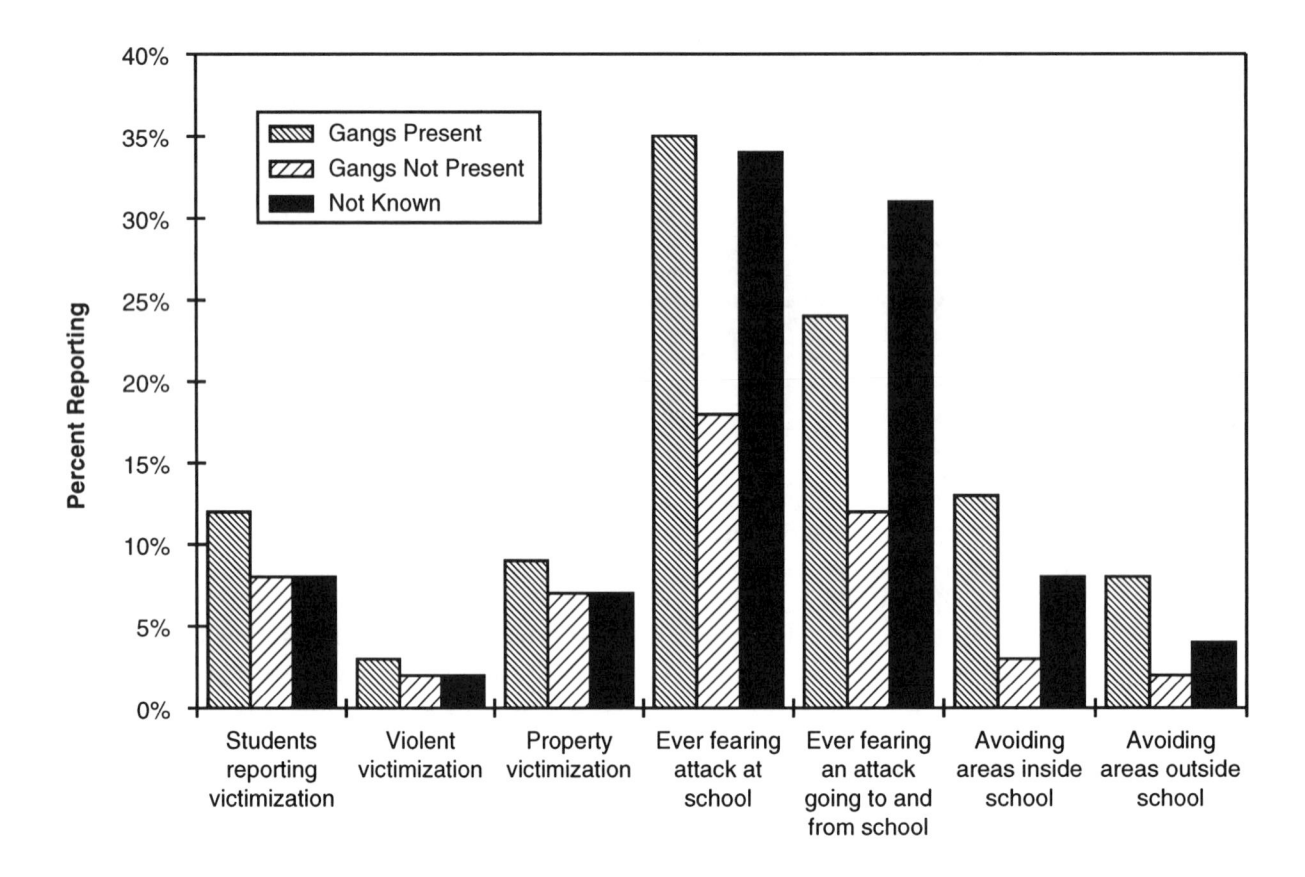

Type of Victimization or Fear	Gangs Present	Gangs Not Present	Not Known
Students reporting victimization	12%	8%	8%
Violent victimization	3%	2%	2%
Property victimization	9%	7%	7%
Ever fearing attack at school	35%	18%	34%
Ever fearing an attack going to and from school	24%	12%	31%
Avoiding areas inside school	13%	3%	8%
Avoiding areas outside school	8%	2%	4%

Violence

Comments Students' fear of being attacked at school or while going to and from school is about twice as great when gangs are present.

In 1989, the Bureau of Justice Statistics' annual National Crime Victimization Survey included a special School Crime Supplement. It questioned more than 10,000 youths 12 and older about crimes that had occurred within the previous six months.

When gangs were present, students feared attack 34% of the time, compared to 18% when there was no gang activity. Fear of attack while going to or from school was mentioned by 24% where gangs were present and 12% where they were not.

Increased violence at schools has long been a topic of public discussion and has received even more prominent attention since the mid-1980s. The survey found the percentage of victimized students was larger in schools where gangs were active. Most of this difference, however, was from an increase in property crimes and not violent crimes.

If the survey results accurately represented the whole U.S. population, then it is possible to estimate gang activity in schools across the nation. The survey estimated that in 1989 there were over 3.3 million students in schools were gangs were present. The number of students at schools where no gangs were active exceeded 17 million. There were 1.2 million students at schools where it was not known if there was gang activity.

Results of the survey consistently show that school crime goes up when gangs are present.

Source U.S. Department of Justice, Bureau of Justice Statistics, *School Crime: A National Crime Victimization Survey Report* (Washington, DC: U.S. Government Printing Office, 1991).

Contact U.S. Department of Justice, Bureau of Justice Statistics Clearinghouse, Box 6000, Rockville, MD 20850. (800) 732-3277.

Violence

Types of Gangs and Their Crimes

The presence and violent crime and drug trafficking activities of different types of gangs. Reports were provided by state prosecutors' offices in 192 U.S. counties during 1991–92.

Type of Gang	Counties with 250,000 or more Residents - Operate Here	Commit Violent Crimes	Engage in Drug Trafficking	Counties with 50,000 to 250,000 Residents - Operate Here	Commit Violent Crimes	Engage in Drug Trafficking
Locally based African-American gangs	83.1%	93.9%	93.9%	60.3%	84.1%	84.1%
Motorcycle gangs	61.9%	71.2%	90.4%	49.3%	61.6%	86.1%
Hispanic gangs	63.6%	97.3%	88.0%	42.5%	83.9%	80.6%
Hate gangs *	52.5%	74.2%	9.7%	23.3%	58.8%	29.4%
Asian gangs	51.7%	91.8%	45.9%	13.7%	90.0%	40.0%
Los Angeles based gangs †	50.0%	89.8%	91.5%	41.1%	76.7%	96.7%
Gangs, from the Caribbean	43.2%	78.4%	100.0%	16.4%	66.7%	100.0%
Other	28.8%	76.5%	41.0%	34.2%	72.0%	36.0%

* Includes gangs advocating racist behaviors (e.g., skinheads, KKK, Aryan Nation).
† Includes the Crips and the Bloods.

Violence

Comments

Historically, most street gangs have formed along racial or ethnic lines. Gangs most frequently present in larger urban areas are local African-American gangs, followed by Hispanic and motorcycle gangs. Locally based African-American gangs are also the most prevalent type of gang in the smaller urban areas, followed by motorcycle and Hispanic gangs.

This information comes from a 1991–92 study by the National Institute of Justice (NIJ). It looked at gang activities such as member migration patterns, drug sales, criminal behavior, and gang presence in prisons. The survey used the responses of state prosecutors' offices in 118 large urban counties and 74 smaller urban counties.

The category called "operate here" shows the presence of particular types of gangs as indicated by the prosecutors' offices. The other categories show the illegal activity of the gangs present in those communities. Prosecutors regarded street gangs as distinct from more sophisticated organized crime groups.

In the larger urban areas, Hispanic gangs most frequently were known to commit violent crimes, followed by local African-American and Asian gangs. In the smaller urban counties, the types of gangs known to commit violent crimes most often were Asian, followed by local African-American and Hispanic gangs. Drug trafficking in the larger urban counties was most common among Caribbean gangs, followed by local African-American and Los Angeles-based gangs. In the smaller urban counties, Caribbean and Los Angeles-based gangs were the most frequent drug traffickers.

Asian and hate gangs were involved more often with violent crime than drug trafficking. Gangs with Caribbean origins were more well-known for their drug trafficking than for violence crimes.

Street gangs have existed throughout the history of the United States. Researchers have studied gangs since the 1920s. Most of the problems associated with gangs of that era were in delinquent acts, minor crimes, and fights with other gangs. Gang activities since then have become increasingly violent and serious. Today's gangs typically traffic in drugs, terrorize neighborhoods, and commit shootings, assaults, robbery, extortion, and other felonies. The most ambitious urban gangs have begun "colonizing" in other cities by building drug trafficking networks.

Source

U.S. Department of Justice, National Institute of Justice, Office of Justice Programs, "Prosecuting Gangs: A National Assessment" (Washington, DC: U.S. Government Printing Office, February 1995).

Contact

U.S. Department of Justice, National Institute of Justice, National Criminal Justice Reference Service, Box 6000, Rockville, MD 20849. (800) 851-3420. Inquiries can also be sent by e-mail to askncjrs@aspensys.com.

Violence

Gang-Related Crime by Gender

The types of crimes committed by gangs in 1992, according to the sex of the gang member.

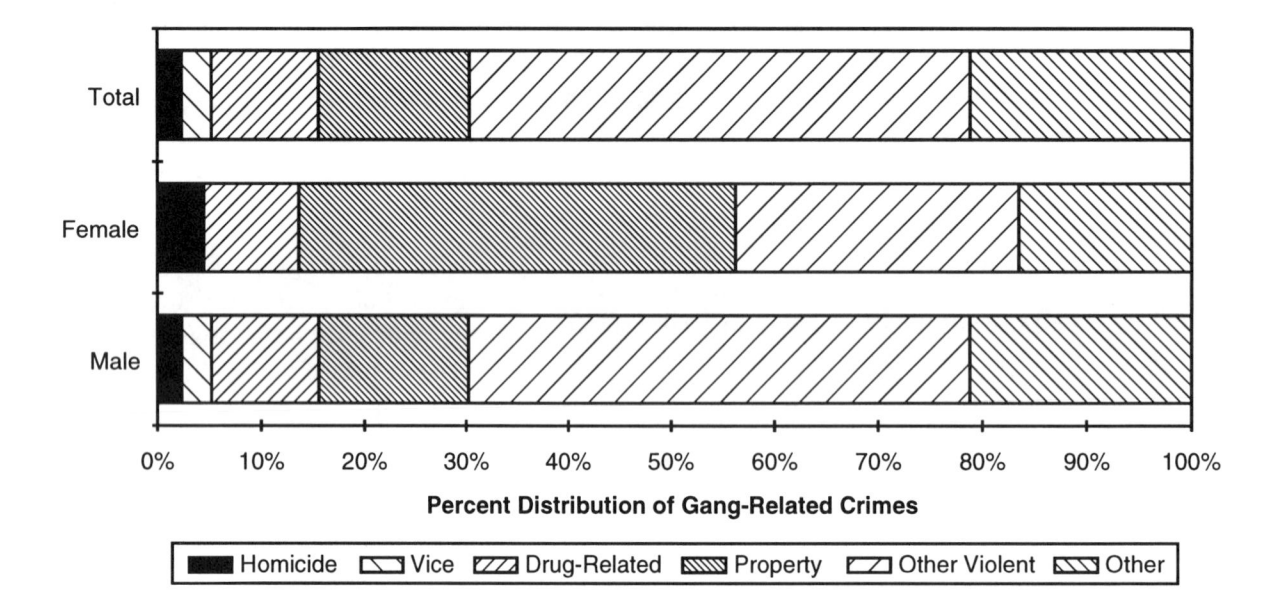

Percent Distribution of Gang-Related Crimes

Legend: Homicide, Vice, Drug-Related, Property, Other Violent, Other

Crime	Male	Female	Total
Homicide	2.3%	4.5%	2.3%
Vice *	2.9%	0.0%	2.9%
Drug-related	10.3%	9.1%	10.3%
Property	14.7%	42.6%	14.8%
Other violent	48.5%	27.3%	48.5%
Other	21.2%	16.5%	21.2%

*Includes crimes related to prostitution.

Violence

Comments

A 1992 study the National Institute of Justice (NIJ) found violence to be the major crime problem related to gang activity. Violent crimes, including homicides, accounted for 50.8% of gang-related crime.

During the year preceding the survey, gang members committed 46,359 crimes, including 1,072 gang-related homicides.

NIJ looked at the 79 largest U.S. cities with populations exceeding 200,000 and 43 cities with populations over 100,000. Seventy-two of the large cities and 38 of the smaller ones reported gang activity. These 110 cities counted 4,881 gangs with 249,324 members.

Males were 94.3% of all gang members; 5.7% were female. Males committed over 99% of all gang-related crimes. Only about 2% of the 4,881 known gangs were independent female gangs. Although females made up only a small fraction of gang members, they were almost twice as likely to commit homicide as male members (4.5% for females, compared with 2.3% for males). In terms of actual numbers, however, females committed only eight of the 1,072 gang-related homicides.

Among males, the largest crime category was violence other than homicides: 48.5%. For females, property crimes came out on top with 42.6%.

Source

U.S. Department of Justice, National Institute of Justice, Office of Justice Programs, "Gang Crime and Law Enforcement Recordkeeping" (Washington, DC: U.S. Government Printing Office, August 1995).

Contact

U.S. Department of Justice, National Institute of Justice, National Criminal Justice Reference Service, Box 6000, Rockville, MD 20849. (800) 851-3420. Inquiries can also be sent by e-mail to askncjrs@aspensys.com.

Violence

How Much Violence Is Involved in Juvenile Delinquency?

Juvenile delinquency cases in the U.S. by type of offense in 1992.

Type of Offense	Number of Cases	Percent of Total*	Percent of Violent Offense Cases*	Percent Change, 1991–92	Percent Change, 1988–92
Total Delinquency	1,471,200	100.0%	—	+7%	+26%
Violent offense cases	301,000	20.5%	100.0%	+13%	+56%
Criminal homicide	2,500	0.2%	0.8%	−9%	+55%
Forcible rape	5,400	0.4%	1.8%	+10%	+27%
Robbery	32,900	2.2%	10.9%	+9%	+52%
Aggravated assault	77,900	5.3%	25.9%	+16%	+80%
Simple assault	152,800	10.4%	50.8%	+14%	+47%
Other violent sex offenses	9,900	0.7%	3.3%	+13%	+60%
Other personal offenses	19,800	1.4%	6.6%	+11%	+63%
Other delinquency cases	1,170,200	79.5%	—	—	—

* May not add to 100.0% because of rounding.

Violence

Comments Simple and aggravated assaults together comprised 76.6% of all violent offense cases tried in juvenile court in 1992, according to the federal Office of Juvenile Justice and Delinquency Prevention (OJJDP). They made up 15.7% of all juvenile court cases. Simple assaults (those not involving weapons) alone accounted for 50.7% of the violent offenses and 10.4% of all cases.

Delinquency cases are acts committed by juveniles (people 10–17 years old) that normally would result in criminal prosecution if committed by adults. OJJDP found violent offenses accounted for 20.5% of all juvenile court cases in 1992. The study covered 1,471,200 juvenile cases in 1992; 301,000 of them involved violence.

The number of delinquency cases handled by U.S. juvenile courts increased 26% between 1988 and 1992. Much of this overall rise was due to the 56% increase in violent offenses during these years. Large increases occurred in the numbers of cases involving aggravated assaults (80%), criminal homicide (55%), robbery (52%), and simple assault (47%).

It is important to remember that the cases listed here are only juvenile court cases and do not include adult criminal court cases. More and more, juveniles are being tried in adult criminal courts, particularly for serious offenses like criminal homicide. These statistics would not include such cases.

Source U.S. Department of Justice, Office of Juvenile Justice and Delinquency Prevention, "Offenders in Juvenile Court, 1992" (Washington, DC: U.S. Government Printing Office, October 1994).

Contact U.S. Department of Justice, Juvenile Justice Clearinghouse, P.O. Box 6000, Rockville, MD 20849. (800) 638-8736.

Violence

Who Is Most Likely to be Murdered at Work?

Number and percent distribution of homicides at work in the U.S. by selected characteristics in 1992.

Selected Characteristics of Victims	Number	Percent
Total	1,004	100
Employee status		
Wage and salaried workers	764	76
Self-employed *	240	24
Sex		
Men	832	83
Women	172	17
Age		
Under 20 years	33	3
20 to 24 years	100	10
25 to 34 years	258	26
35 to 44 years	264	26
45 to 54 years	178	18
55 to 64 years	114	11
65 years and older	57	6
Race		
White	688	69
Black	183	18
Asian or Pacific Islander	83	8
Other	50	5
Hispanic Origin †		
Hispanic	123	12

* Includes paid and unpaid family workers, and may include owners of incorporated businesses, or members of partnerships.
† Persons of Hispanic origin may be of any race.

Comments

Wage and salaried workers, men, people ages 25–44 and whites stood the greatest risk of being murdered on the job in 1992. Of 6,083 workplace fatalities in 1992, 17%, or 1,004, involved murder, according to the Census of Fatal Occupational Injuries.

Wage and salaried workers accounted for 764 of the 1,004. The remainder were self-employed. Men were murdered nearly five times more often than women—832 versus 172. The 25–34 and 35–44 age groups had nearly equal numbers of workplace murder cases and accounted for 52% of the total. And whites were much more likely murder victims, with 688 of the total. Blacks were the next most at-risk, with 183 murders.

These numbers show how many murdered workers came from each group. However, they do not show how often members of particular groups were murdered.

For example, the rates of workplace homicides among Asians and Pacific Islanders, and females, were higher than the sizes of these groups in the total worker population.

This proportion is affected by the types of jobs often held by these workers. Both groups have high proportions of retail employment. Retailing accounted for about half of all workplace homicides in 1992, mostly resulting from robberies.

Other workers with an unusually high share of fatalities due to homicide include the self-employed. They accounted for 24% of workplace homicides but only comprised about 10% of the labor force.

Source

U.S. Department of Labor, Bureau of Labor Statistics, Office of Safety, Health and Working Conditions, *Census of Fatal Occupational Injuries, 1992*.

Contact

U.S. Department of Labor, Bureau of Labor Statistics, Office of Safety, Health and Working Conditions, 2 Massachusetts Ave., NE, Washington, DC 20212-0001. Census of Fatal Occupational Injuries office: (202) 606-6175.

U.S. Department of Health and Human Services, Public Health Service, Centers for Disease Control and Prevention, National Institute for Occupational Safety and Health, 4676 Columbia Parkway, Cincinnati, OH 45226. (800) 356-4674.

Violence

Homicides at Work in the Ten Largest Metropolitan Areas, 1992

The number and percent of workplace homicides occurring in the 10 largest metropolitan areas in the U.S. during 1992, compared with the number and percent of employment in those places.

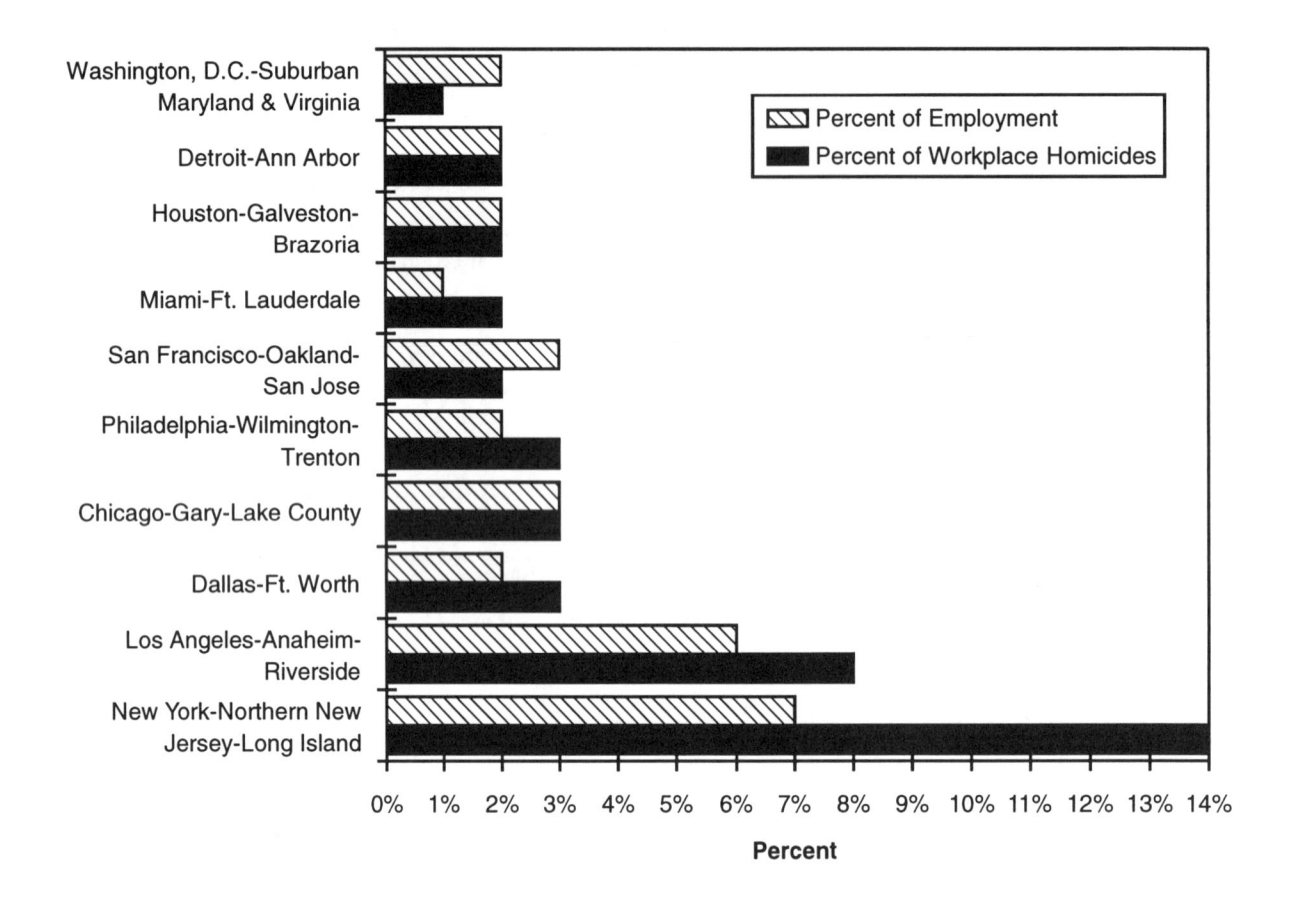

Metropolitan Area	Number of Workplace Homicides	Percent of Workplace Homicides	Number of Employment	Percent of Employment	Ratio of Workplace Homicides to Employment
Total U.S.	1,004	100	119,583,000	100	1 : 119,107
New York-Northern New Jersey-Long Island	138	14	8,140,000	7	1 : 58,986
Los Angeles-Anaheim-Riverside	80	8	6,753,000	6	1 : 84,413
Dallas-Ft. Worth	33	3	2,061,000	2	1 : 62,455
Chicago-Gary-Lake County	29	3	4,028,000	3	1 : 138,897
Philadelphia-Wilmington-Trenton	28	3	2,771,000	2	1 : 98,964
San Francisco-Oakland-San Jose	25	2	3,168,000	3	1 : 126,720
Miami-Ft. Lauderdale	21	2	1,514,000	1	1 : 72,095
Houston-Galveston-Brazoria	20	2	1,839,000	2	1 : 91,950
Detroit-Ann Arbor	18	2	2,106,000	2	1 : 117,000
Washington, DC-Suburban Maryland & Virginia	13	1	2,151,000	2	1 : 165,462

Violence

Comments

Workplace homicide is primarily an urban problem, according to the Census of Fatal Occupational Injuries. In 1992, about 80% of these homicides occurred in metropolitan areas, compared with 60% of total occupational fatal injuries. There were 1,004 workplace homicides in 1992

The New York metropolitan area, with about 7% of the nation's total employment, accounted for 14% of all workplace homicides. The area includes Long Island and northern New Jersey. The Los Angeles metropolitan area accounted for about 8% of the workplace homicides in 1992. Not all large urban areas have such disproportionately high rates of workplace murders. Some urban regions like Detroit, Houston, and Chicago had about the same share of workplace homicides as they had of national employment. Other places, like the Washington, DC, and San Francisco areas actually had smaller portions of workplace homicides, compared to employment.

This type of comparison is useful in learning about workplace homicide in the largest urban areas, but does not consider workplace murders in the more numerous smaller urban areas. Although 80% of workplace homicides occurred in urban areas, the metropolitan areas listed here only account for half of that total.

Source

U.S. Department of Labor, Bureau of Labor Statistics, Office of Safety, Health and Working Conditions, "Census of Fatal Occupational Injuries, 1992," and "Census of Fatal Occupational Injuries, 1993."

Contact

U.S. Department of Labor, Bureau of Labor Statistics, Office of Safety, Health and Working Conditions, 2 Massachusetts Ave., NE, Washington, DC 20212-0001. Census of Fatal Occupational Injuries office: (202) 606-6175.

U.S. Department of Health and Human Services, Public Health Service, Centers for Disease Control and Prevention, National Institute for Occupational Safety and Health, 4676 Columbia Parkway, Cincinnati, OH 45226. (800) 356-4674.

Violence

Circumstances of Workplace Homicides, 1992 and 1993

Number of homicides in the U.S. occurring at the workplace according to the circumstance.

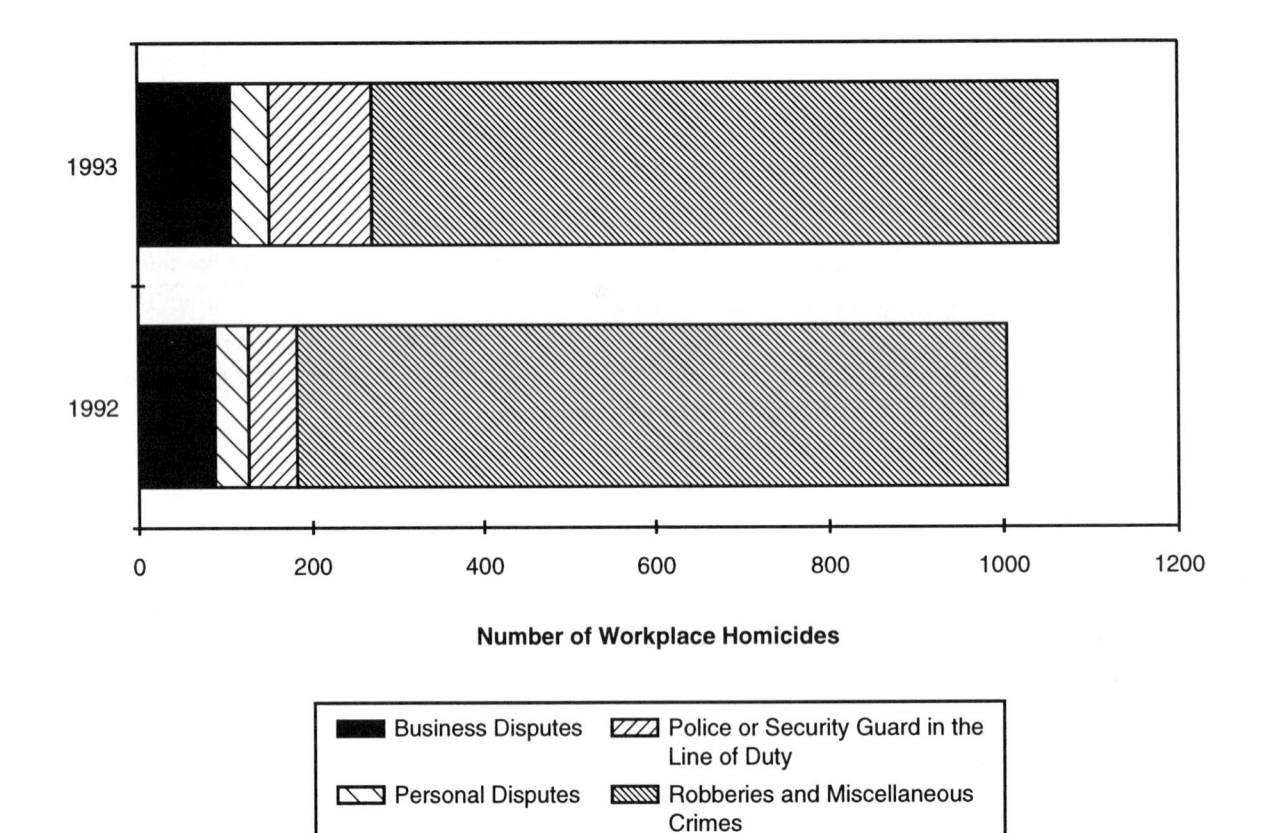

Number of Workplace Homicides

Legend:
- Business Disputes
- Police or Security Guard in the Line of Duty
- Personal Disputes
- Robberies and Miscellaneous Crimes

Circumstance	1992 Number	1992 Percent *	1993 Number	1993 Percent *
Business disputes	87	8.7	106	10.0
Co-worker, former co-worker	45	4.5	59	5.6
Customer and client	35	3.5	43	4.0
Other	7	0.7	4	0.4
Personal disputes	39	3.9	45	4.2
Relative of victim (primarily husband, ex-husband)	24	2.4	15	1.4
Boyfriend, ex-boyfriend	7	0.7	11	1.0
Other relative or acquaintance	8	0.8	17	1.6
Police or security guard in the line of duty	56	5.6	119	11.2
Robberies and miscellaneous crimes	822	81.9	793	74.6
Total	1,004	100.0	1,063	100.0

* May not add to total because of rounding.

Violence

Comments

Homicide was the second leading cause of fatal work injuries in 1992 and 1993 (after motor vehicle accidents), accounting for 17% of fatal injuries to workers in both years. Since robbery is the primary motive, work-related homicides are most common among retail stores, eating and drinking establishments, and other cash-oriented businesses with public access.

Workplace homicide has gained much publicity in recent years. It is often thought that such crimes typically are motivated by passion or by the anger of a "disgruntled employee."

The vast majority of workplace homicides, however, are the result of robberies, according to the Bureau of Labor Statistics' Census of Fatal Occupational Injuries (CFOI). The CFOI annually tabulates information regarding work-related homicides.

The victims of workplace homicide are usually male; in 1992 male workers comprised 83% of the victims of workplace homicide. Men, however, only make up 55% of the employed population of the United States. In 1992 and 1993, homicide was the leading cause of fatal workplace injury for females, accounting for about 40% of such deaths.

The victims of workplace homicide usually were between the ages of 25 and 54. However, about 30% of all deaths of 13- to 17-year-old workers were due to workplace homicide. Shootings accounted for 82% of all workplace homicides in 1993, and stabbings accounted for about 9%. Other victims were beaten, strangled, purposely run over by vehicles, or killed by fire.

Source

U.S. Department of Labor, Bureau of Labor Statistics, Office of Safety, Health and Working Conditions, "Census of Fatal Occupational Injuries, 1992" and "Census of Fatal Occupational Injuries, 1993."

Contact

U.S. Department of Labor, Bureau of Labor Statistics, Office of Safety, Health and Working Conditions, 2 Massachusetts Ave., NE, Washington, DC 20212-0001. Census of Fatal Occupational Injuries office: (202) 606-6175.

U.S. Department of Health and Human Services, Public Health Service, Centers for Disease Control and Prevention, National Institute for Occupational Safety and Health, 4676 Columbia Parkway, Cincinnati, OH 45226. (800) 356-4674.

Violence

Which Industries Have the Most Workplace Homicides?

Industries in the U.S. in which work-related homicides occurred during 1992 and 1993. Percent distribution of the 1,004 and 1,063 work-related homicides in 1992 and 1993, respectively.

Industry Type	1992 Percent	1993 Percent
Agriculture	1	1
Construction	2	2
Manufacturing	3	4
Transportation, communications, public utilities	11	12
Taxicabs	9	9
Other transportation, communications, public utilities	2	3
Wholesale trade	2	2
Retail trade	48	49
Eating and drinking places	14	14
Grocery stores	16	17
Gasoline stations	4	5
Other retail	14	13
Finance, insurance, real estate	4	3
Services	16	15
Business services	5	4
Other services	11	11
Government	10	12
Police protection	5	8
Other government	5	4

Violence

Comments

Retailers by far had the highest rates of workplace homicides during 1992 and 1993. With 48% of the nation's 1,004 on-the-job homicides in 1992 and 49% of the 1,063 total in 1993, the category had triple the rate found among service businesses. Retailing includes grocery and convenience stores, restaurants, bars, and gasoline service stations.

Homicides in service-related industries accounted for 16% of the total in 1992 and 15% in 1993. Service businesses include guard and armored car services, hotels and motels, and health and educational services.

Starting in 1992, the Bureau of Labor Statistics began annually collecting data regarding the nature of work-related fatalities, including homicides. The statistics analyze motive, primary work activity, and time of incident. Although the total number of workplace fatalities declined over the 1980s, intentional killings at the workplace have gained prominence.

Most homicides occurring in the workplace are the result of robberies. Therefore, many fatally injured workers in 1992 and 1993 had retail and service sector jobs. These occupations are in industries that typically involve contact with the public. These types of jobs also require frequent cash sales. The need for money to make these sales requires having on-site cash reserves, which tempt robbers.

Many of those intentionally killed at work were self-employed or working in family businesses. These types of employees accounted for 24% of worker homicides in 1992, but they only comprised 9% of total employment.

Source

U.S. Department of Labor, Bureau of Labor Statistics, Office of Safety, Health and Working Conditions, "Census of Fatal Occupational Injuries, 1992," and "Census of Fatal Occupational Injuries, 1993."

Contact

U.S. Department of Labor, Bureau of Labor Statistics, Office of Safety, Health and Working Conditions, 2 Massachusetts Ave., NE, Washington, DC 20212-0001. Census of Fatal Occupational Injuries office: (202) 606-6175.

U.S. Department of Health and Human Services, Public Health Service, Centers for Disease Control and Prevention, National Institute for Occupational Safety and Health, 4676 Columbia Parkway, Cincinnati, OH 45226. (800) 356-4674.

Violence

How Much of All Violent Crime Occurs at Work?

Percent distribution of violent incidents occurring at work, or on the way to or from work.
The percentages are based on approximately 5,964,090 nonfatal violent incidents occurring in the U.S. during 1992.

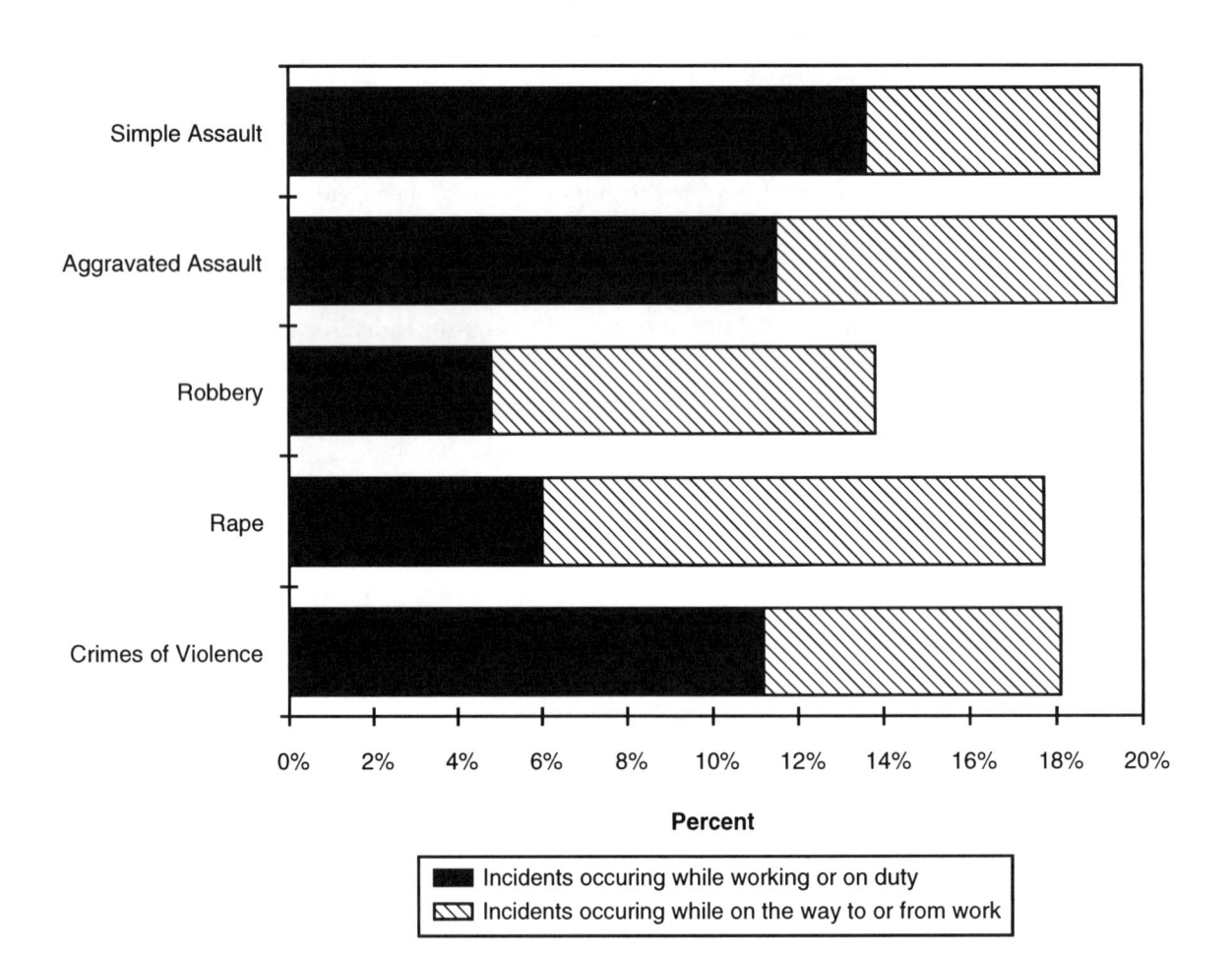

■ Incidents occuring while working or on duty
▨ Incidents occuring while on the way to or from work

Type of Incident	Total Number of Incidents	Incidents occuring while working or on duty Number*	Percent	Incidents occuring while on the way to or from work Number*	Percent
Crimes of violence	5,964,090	669,660	11.2%	410,280	6.9%
Rape	131,530	7,890	6.0%	15,390	11.7%
Robbery	1,113,300	53,440	4.8%	100,200	9.0%
Aggravated assault	1,594,210	183,330	11.5%	125,940	7.9%
Simple assault	3,125,030	425,000	13.6%	168,750	5.4%

* Estimated.

Violence

Comments

In 1992, 18.1% of all violent crimes occurred while the victim was traveling to or from work or was at work, according to the National Crime Victimization Survey (NCVS). The survey questions over 100,000 individuals each year about reported and unreported crimes. It excludes homicide victims and individuals under age 12.

NCVS said 11.2% of victims were at work when they became targets of crimes like rape, robbery, and assault. The total also includes workers whose jobs were mobile or otherwise did not have fixed job sites. There were 669,660 violent incidents at the workplace.

Simple assault was the most frequent type of violent crime occurring at work; 13.6% of all simple assaults in 1992 happened at the victim's workplace. Next came aggravated assault at 11.9%. Aggravated assaults involve weapons and serious injuries. Simple assaults do not involve weapons, and injuries are less severe.

Rape was the crime faced most often when the victim was in transit to or from work. It accounted for 11.7% of 410,280 violent incidents. Robbery followed at 9%.

It is important to remember that these numbers are based on survey responses. Some workers may have jobs that pose greater risks of violent crime than others. For example, those who work in retail businesses such as grocery and convenience stores, restaurants, bars, and gas stations are often at a higher risk of robbery. This is because these businesses usually must keep large amounts of cash available. In the same way, law enforcement personnel are more vulnerable to simple or aggravated assaults than many other working people.

Source

U.S. Department of Justice, Bureau of Justice Statistics. *Criminal Victimization in the United States, 1992* (Washington, DC: U.S. Government Printing Office, 1994), p. 79.

Contact

U.S. Department of Justice, Bureau of Justice Statistics Clearinghouse, Box 6000, Rockville, MD 20850. (800) 732-3277.

National Victim Center, 2111 Wilson Blvd., Suite 300, Arlington, VA 22201. (703) 276-2880.

Violence

Average Annual Number of Victimizations at Work, 1987–92

The average annual number of nonfatal violent victimizations occurring at the workplace in the U.S. during 1987–92, as well as the average annual number of injuries from such victimizations.

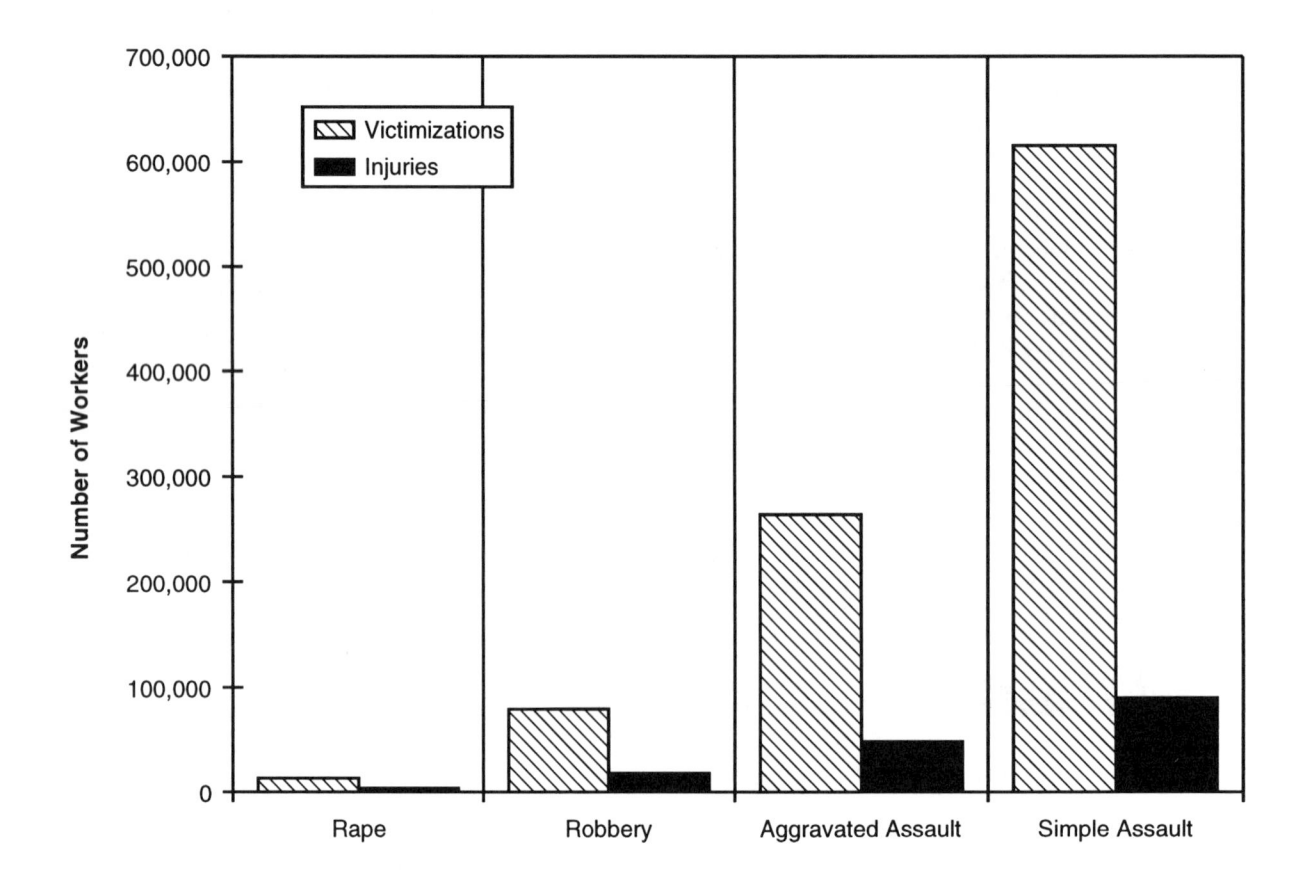

Type of Crime	Victimizations	Injuries	Percent of Victimizations Resulting in Injury
Crimes of violence	971,517	159,094	16.4%
Rape *	13,068	3,438	26.3%
Robbery	79,109	17,904	22.6%
Aggravated assault	264,174	48,180	18.2%
Simple assault	615,160	89,572	14.6%

* Injuries are those in addition to the rape.

Violence

Comments Simple assault was the most common violent crime committed at the workplace, with over 615,000 cases annually occurring during 1987–92. However, only 14.6% of these simple assaults resulted in injury, according to the National Crime Victimization Survey (NCVS). Simple assaults do not involve weapons.

NCVS annually asks over 100,000 resident U.S. citizens about experiences with violent crime, regardless of whether an incident was reported to police.

From 1987 to 1992, 971,517 people per year were victims of nonfatal violent acts in the workplace. Injuries resulted in 16.4% of the cases.

Aggravated assaults (involving weapons) ranked second in violent crimes at the workplace, averaging 264,174 annually. Aggravated assault occurred less often than simple assault but it resulted in injury more frequently; 18.2% of the cases produced injuries.

Rape and robbery are the violent acts most likely to injure employees. From 1987 to 1992, 26.3% of the rapes cited resulted in injuries in addition to the rapes themselves. Robberies produced injuries in 22.6% of the cases. Rapes averaged 13,068 per year; robberies, 79,109.

Source U.S. Department of Justice, Bureau of Justice Statistics, "Violence and Theft in the Workplace" (Washington, DC: U.S. Government Printing Office, July 1994).

Contact U.S. Department of Justice, Bureau of Justice Statistics Clearinghouse, Box 6000, Rockville, MD 20850. (800) 732-3277.

U.S. Department of Labor, Bureau of Labor Statistics, Office of Safety, Health and Working Conditions, 2 Massachusetts Ave., NE, Washington, DC 20212-0001. Census of Fatal Occupational Injuries office: (202) 606-6175.

Violence

How Much Time Does a Victim of Violent Crime Lose from Work?

Percent distribution of victimizations in the U.S. that resulted in loss of time from work in 1992. Details show how much time was usually lost from work according to the type of crime involved. *

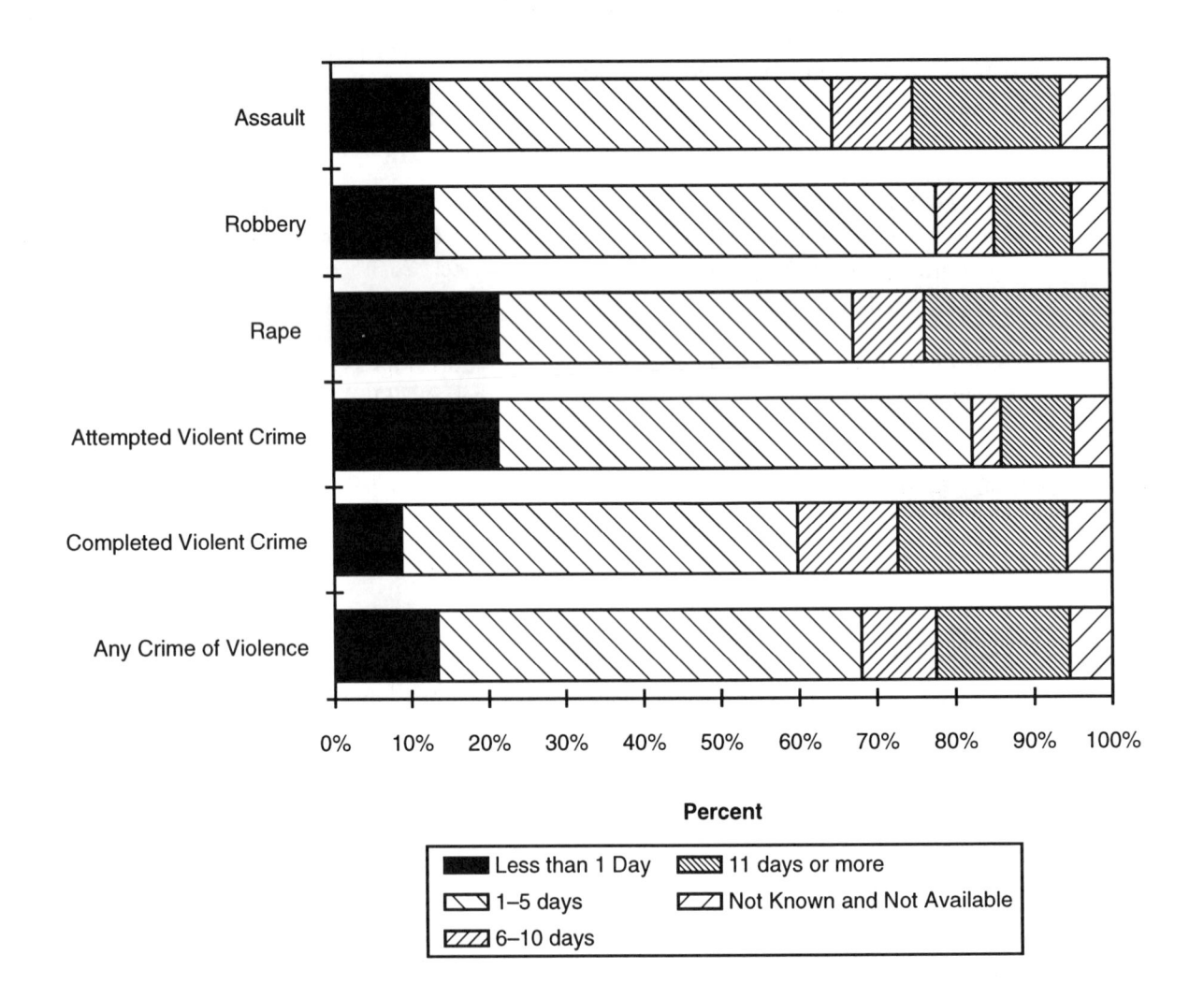

Legend:
- Less than 1 Day
- 1–5 days
- 6–10 days
- 11 days or more
- Not Known and Not Available

Type of Crime	Number of Victimizations	Less than 1 Day	1–5 Days	6–10 Days	11 Days or More	Not Known and Not Available
Crimes of violence	502,610	13.4%	54.6%	9.5%	17.0%	5.5%
Completed	318,850	8.8%	51.1%	12.8%	21.5%	5.8%
Attempted	183,760	21.4%	60.8%	3.7%	9.2%	4.9%
Rape	34,330	21.6%	45.6%	9.1%	23.8%	0.0%
Robbery	125,100	13.2%	64.6%	7.4%	9.9%	4.9%
Assault	343,170	12.7%	51.9%	10.3%	18.9%	6.2%

* Details may not add to 100% because of rounding. Many of the percentages shown here are based on 10 or fewer sample cases (the weighted estimates of less than 40,000 responses).

Violence

Comments

A violent crime often costs the victim one to five days of work time, according to the National Victimization Survey (NCVS). This happened in 54.6% of 502,610 cases that resulted in lost work time during 1992.

One to five days lost was the figure cited most often in the individual categories of violent crimes.

NCVS annually surveys over 100,000 resident U.S. citizens about their experiences with crime. The totals shown are estimates of all the reported and unreported incidents of violent crime. The total represents only incidents involving time lost from work. Completed violent crimes had a wide distribution of lost work time. Most resulted in one to five days of lost work time (51.1%), but 21.5% resulted in 11 or more days away from work.

The concentration in these two categories could be the result of different reasons. Many of those who lost eleven or more days from work most likely suffered serious injuries. Workers who were away from the job for one to five days may have been only slightly injured. Also, the one to five lost days of work may be the typical time required by police and the legal system if the crime is reported and the criminal caught.

Rapes and assaults resulted in a longer period away from work than did robberies. In 23.8% of rapes and 18.9% of assaults, victims lost eleven or more days of work. About 77.8% of all robberies resulted in five or fewer lost work days. This is because completed rapes and assaults result in physical injury. Not all completed robberies cause physical injury to victims.

Source

U.S. Department of Justice, Bureau of Justice Statistics. *Criminal Victimization in the United States, 1992* (Washington, DC: U.S. Government Printing Office, 1994), p. 98.

Contact

U.S. Department of Justice, Bureau of Justice Statistics Clearinghouse, Box 6000, Rockville, MD 20850. (800) 732-3277.

National Victim Center, 2111 Wilson Blvd., Suite 300, Arlington, VA 22201. (703) 276-2880.

U.S. Department of Health and Human Services, Public Health Service, Centers for Disease Control and Prevention, National Institute for Occupational Safety and Health, 4676 Columbia Parkway, Cincinnati, OH 45226. (800) 356-4674.

Violence

Violent Acts at the Workplace Resulting in Injuries

Number of people in the U.S. injured at work from violent acts in 1992.
Excludes homicides, self-inflicted injuries, and animal attacks.

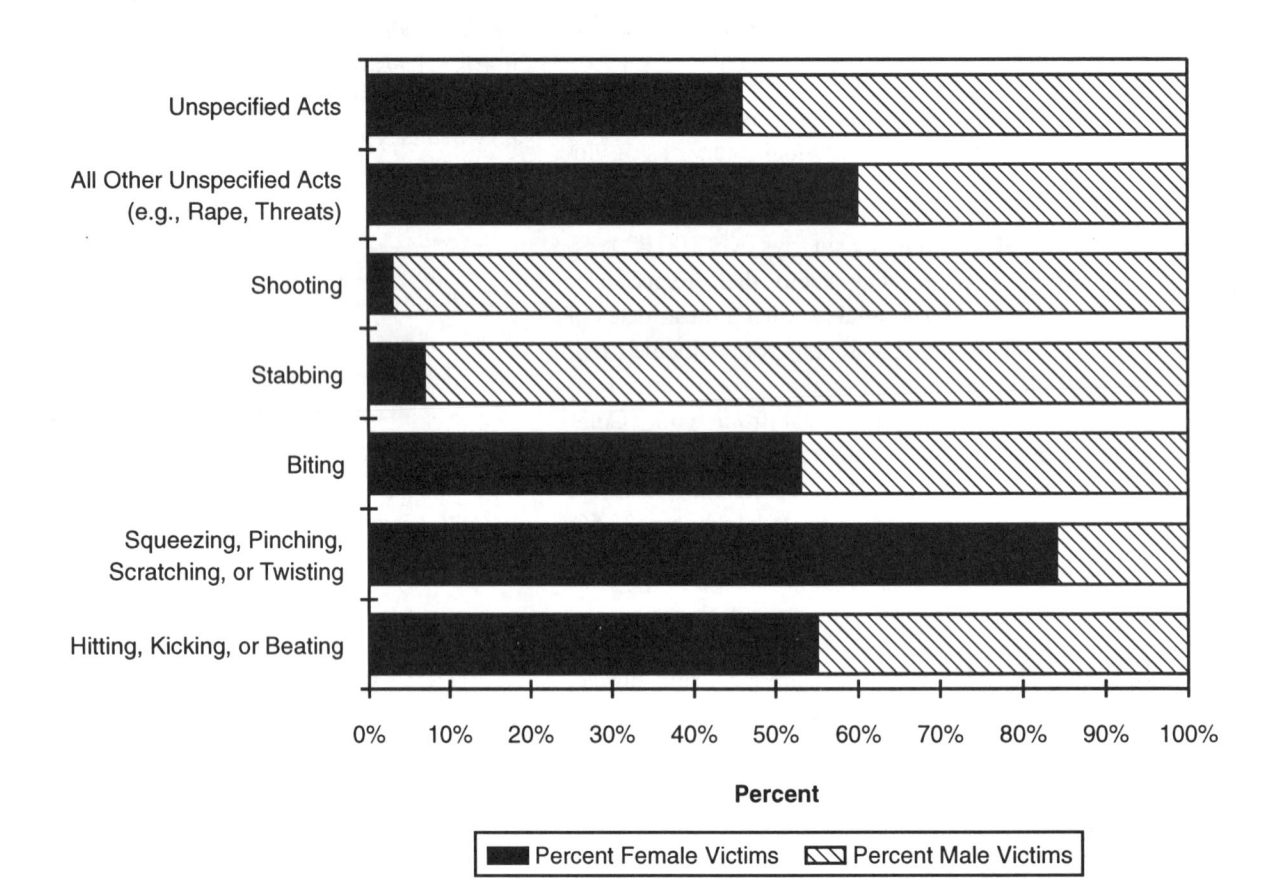

Violent Act	Total Cases	Percent Female Victims	Percent Male Victims	Median Days Away from Work
Hitting, kicking, or beating	10,425	55%	45%	5
Squeezing, pinching, scratching, or twisting	2,457	84%	16%	4
Biting	901	53%	47%	3
Stabbing	598	7%	93%	28
Shooting	560	3%	97%	30
All other unspecified acts (e.g., rape, threats)	5,157	60%	40%	5
Unspecified acts	2,301	46%	54%	6
Total	22,396	56%	44%	5

Violence

Comments

Hitting, kicking, or beating led all categories of injury-inflicting violence in the workplace during 1992. A survey by the federal Bureau of Labor Statistics (BLS) found 10,425 such cases among 22,396 nonfatal injuries due to violence on the job.

BLS began surveying the public in 1992 to measure the number of nonfatal assaults and other acts of violence at the workplace. Injuries from these causes often require employees to lose time from work due to injury, trauma, medical treatment, and legal procedures.

Although shootings and stabbings accounted for only 1,158 of the cases, their distribution among workers is interesting. Stabbing victims were male 93% of the time; 97% of the shooting victims were men. On the other hand, injuries due to squeezing, pinching, scratching, or twisting affected women 84% of the time.

In other defined categories, injuries were distributed more evenly between men and women. Overall, women were victims in 56% of the cases. They accounted for less than half of total employment.

Median time lost because of injuries was between three and six days for most categories. However, time lost rose to 28 days for stabbings and 30 for shootings.

"Median days lost from work" indicates that half of the victims missed more days from work and the other half missed fewer days.

Source

U.S. Department of Labor, Bureau of Labor Statistics, *Annual Survey, 1993* (Washington, DC: U.S. Government Printing Office, 1994).

Contact

U.S. Department of Labor, Bureau of Labor Statistics, Office of Safety, Health and Working Conditions, 2 Massachusetts Ave., NE, Washington, DC 20212-0001. Census of Fatal Occupational Injuries office: (202) 606-6175.

U.S. Department of Health and Human Services, Public Health Service, Centers for Disease Control and Prevention, National Institute for Occupational Safety and Health, 4676 Columbia Parkway, Cincinnati, OH 45226. (800) 356-4674.

Violence

Which Industries Are Most Affected by Violent Assaults at the Workplace?

Percent distribution of industries in the U.S. reporting workplace assaults and violent acts in 1992. These violent acts resulted in injuries and illnesses requiring time away from work. Excludes homicides, self-inflicted injuries, and animal attacks.

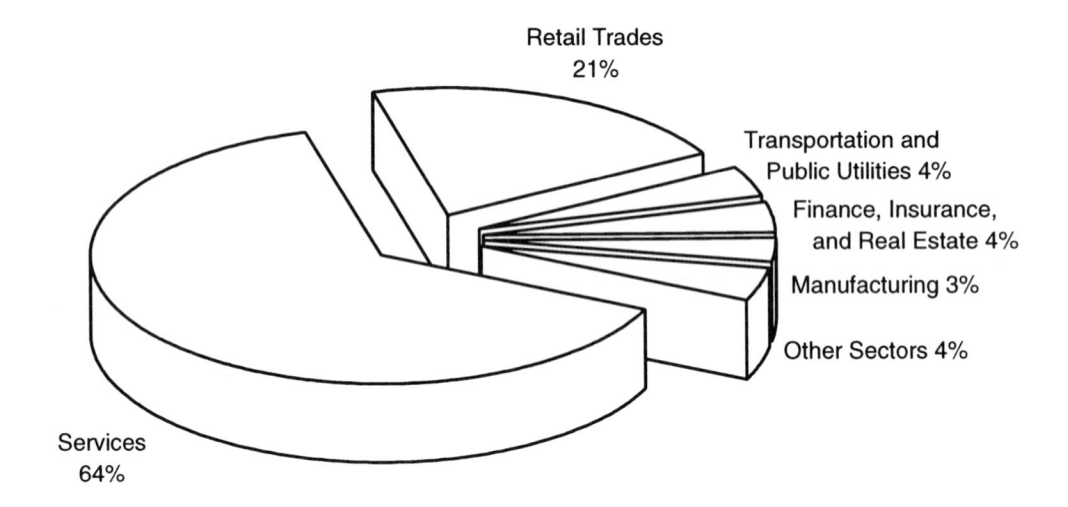

Industry	Percent
Services	**64%**
Nursing homes	27%
Social services	13%
Hospitals	11%
Other services	13%
Retail trades	**21%**
Grocery stores	6%
Eating & drinking places	5%
Other retail trades	10%
Transportation and public utilities	**4%**
Finance, insurance, and real estate	**4%**
Manufacturing	**3%**
Other sectors	**4%**

Violence

Comments

Services such as nursing homes, social services, and hospitals accounted for 64% of the nonfatal injuries due to violence on the job in 1992, according to the federal Bureau of Labor Statistics (BLS). The bureau annually measures the level of violence at the workplace.

BLS recorded 22,396 violent acts occurring at the workplace in 1992 (not including murders).

Many of the victims of nonfatal violence were caregivers in nursing homes (27%). Ironically, some of these injuries in the services sector occurred through contact with uncooperative patients who resisted assistance. Other victims were assaulted by patients mentally inclined to commit violence.

Retail trades accounted for 21% of the nonfatal violent acts. Many of these victims probably were injured during attempted or completed robberies.

Employment in services and retail trades has grown rapidly in recent years. With this in mind, it would not be surprising if the numbers of nonfatal violent incidents in these sectors rise as well.

Source

U.S. Department of Labor, Bureau of Labor Statistics, *Annual Survey, 1993* (Washington, DC: U.S. Government Printing Office, 1994).

Contact

U.S. Department of Labor, Bureau of Labor Statistics, Office of Safety, Health and Working Conditions, 2 Massachusetts Ave., NE, Washington, DC 20212-0001. Census of Fatal Occupational Injuries office: (202) 606-6175.

U.S. Department of Health and Human Services, Public Health Service, Centers for Disease Control and Prevention, National Institute for Occupational Safety and Health, 4676 Columbia Parkway, Cincinnati, OH 45226. (800) 356-4674.

Glossary

Accuracy: Ability to get the correct (or true) result.

Aggravated assault: An unlawful attack by one person upon another for the purpose of inflicting severe or serious bodily injury, regardless of whether an injury occurred. Serious injury includes broken bones, lost teeth, internal injuries, loss of consciousness, and any injury requiring two of more days of hospitalization. This type of assault usually is accompanied by the use of a weapon or by means likely to produce death or great bodily harm. It also includes conduct under these statutory names: aggravated assault and battery, assault with intent to kill, assault with intent to commit murder or manslaughter, atrocious assault, attempted murder, felonious assault, and assault with a deadly weapon. Simple assaults are excluded.

AIDS: A condition caused by a deadly virus that attacks the body's immune system. The disease is transmitted via body fluids, especially sexual secretions and blood. Intravenous drug users risk getting AIDS from infected needles.

Allegation of child maltreatment: A notification to the child protective agency of suspected maltreatment of a child.

American Indian/Alaskan Native: A person having origins in any of the original peoples of North America.

Arson: Any willful or malicious burning or attempt to burn, with or without intent to defraud, a dwelling house, public building, motor vehicle or aircraft, or any personal property of another. Also includes intentional destruction by means of explosion.

Assault: An unlawful physical attack or threat of attack. Assaults may be classified as simple or aggravated. Rape and attempted rape are excluded from this category, as well as robbery and attempted robbery. The severity of assaults ranges from minor threat to incidents that are nearly fatal.

Assault rifle: The original definition, as used by the military, differs from the definition typically used by the media. In the military, an assault rifle is a military-issue shoulder gun selectively capable of firing in either a fully automatic mode (like a machine gun) or in a semi-automatic mode (one bullet per squeeze of the trigger). A genuine military-issue assault rifle has a lever which enables the shooter to select between the automatic and semiautomatic modes. Some assault rifles in use by the military also are capable of firing in short bursts of three to five rounds.

There is no precise definition of the term in use by those outside the military. Among many journalists and politicians, the term usually refers to a civilian-issue rifle that can only fire in a semiautomatic mode (one bullet per squeeze of the trigger) but has a "military" look. This appearance can include the substitution of a black plastic stock in place of a wooden one, the use of nonreflective coatings, the capacity to operate with large magazines, and the presence of accessories such as a bayonet lug, flash supressor, or pistol grip. Aside from the cosmetic differences, these semiautomatic rifles function the same as common hunting and target rifles (which are also able to accept large magazines).

The terms "assault rifle" and "assault weapon" are fairly vague when used in public discourse. Since the emphasis of the non-military definition focuses on the appearance of the firearm rather than on its mechanical function, policy makers have had trouble in formulating an exact definition.

Assault weapon: A term typically used by persons in the media and politics to describe any semiautomatic rifle, shotgun, or semiautomatic pistol with a "military" appearance. See also *Assault rifle*.

Attempted forcible entry: A form of burglary in which force is used in an attempt to gain entry.

Average see mean.

Black, not of hispanic origin: A person having origins in any of the peoples of sub-Saharan Africa or Haiti who does not self-classify as Hispanic.

Burglary: *FBI Uniform Crime Reports definition:* The unlawful entry or attempted forcible entry of any fixed structure to commit a felony or theft. Attempted forcible entry is included. Vehicles and vessels used for regular

Glossary

residence, industry, or business are also included as fixed structures.

National Crime Victimization Survey definition: Unlawful or forcible entry or attempted entry of a residence. This crime usually, but not always, involves theft. The illegal entry may be by force, such as breaking a window or slashing a screen, or may be without force by entering through an unlocked door or an open window. As long as the person entering has no legal right to be present in the structure, a burglary has occurred. Furthermore, the structure need not be the house itself for a burglary to take place. Illegal entry of a garage, shed, or any other structure also constitutes household burglary. If breaking and entering occurs in a hotel or vacation residence, it is still classified as a burglary for the household whose member or members were staying there at the time the entry occurred.

Caretaker relative or household member: A relative or household member who is also in a caretaker relationship to a child. Can include grandparents, aunts, uncles, paramours, etc., responsible for the care and supervision of the child.

Carjacking: A type of robbery that involves the theft or attempted theft of a motor vehicle by force or threat of force.

Central city: The largest city (or group of cities) in a Metropolitan Statistical Area.

Child: A person less than 18 years of age or considered to be a minor by state law.

Child-based report: A system of receiving and counting reports of child abuse and neglect that counts as a report each child who is alleged to be a victim of maltreatment. A child-based report does not include multiple victims.

Child care services: Services which provide care for minor children of active clients, including supervised activities.

Child day care provider: A person who has temporary caretaker responsibility for the child and who is not related to the child, such as a day care center staff member, family day care provider, or baby-sitter. Persons with legal custody or guardianship are not included.

Child maltreatment: An action or failure to act by a parent, caretaker, or other person as defined under state law, having caused or allowed to cause physical abuse, neglect, medical neglect, sexual abuse, or emotional abuse harm, or risk of harm to a child.

Constant dollars: Dollars that have been adjusted for fluctuations in value over time. Converting dollar values to constant dollars enables a researcher to compare the cost of things in 1995 with what they cost in 1952.

Correctional facility: Includes adult or juvenile correctional institutions, reentry and diversion facilities, and prisons.

Criminal justice: Activities which include enforcement, prosecution, and sentencing to apprehend, convict, and punish drug offenders. Although thought of primarily as having supply reduction goals, criminal sanctions also have demand reduction effects by discouraging drug use.

Custodial/domiciliary: Provision of food, shelter, and assistance in routine daily living on a long-term basis for persons with alcohol or other drug-related problems.

Crimes of violence: Murder, rape, robbery, and assault. The National Crime Victimization Survey only counts rape, robbery, and assault as crimes of violence since it is impossible to survey murder victims.

Criminal homicide: The FBI definition includes murder and nonnegligent manslaughter and manslaughter by negligence.

Custody: To have custody of a prisoner, a state must hold that person in one of its facilities. One state may have custody over a prisoner over whom another state maintains jurisdiction.

Delinquency: Acts or conduct in violation of criminal law, when such acts or conduct are committed by juveniles.

Delinquent act: An act committed by a juvenile for which an adult could be prosecuted in a criminal court, but when committed by a juvenile is within the jurisdiction of juvenile court. Delinquent acts include crimes against persons, crimes against property, drug offenses, and crimes against public order, when such acts are committed by juveniles.

Detention: The placement of a youth in a restrictive facility between referral to court intake and case disposition.

Disposition: Definite action taken or treatment plan decided upon or initiated regarding a particular case.

Family counseling/therapy services: Services which are provided during the same session to members of a family/collateral group.

Glossary

Family murder: The killing of one relative by another. Victims and offenders can be spouses, common-law spouses, children, step-children, grandchildren, parents, step-parents, grandparents, siblings, step-siblings, cousins, in-laws, and extended family members.

Fatality: A death caused by an accident, a drug overdose, etc.

Firearm: Any pistol, revolver, rifle, or shotgun using explosive powder to propel a projectile or projectiles.

Firearm mortality: The total number of suicides, homicides, and accidental deaths caused by a discharged gun.

Forcible entry: A form of burglary in which force is used to gain entry to a residence. Some examples include breaking a window or slashing a screen.

Gang or street gang: Police departments differ on the precise definition of what a "gang" is. However, most agree that a gang is an association of about ten or more individuals who exhibit the following characteristics in varying degrees: a gang name and recognizable symbols, which can include certain types of clothing, decorations, and graffiti; a geographic territory; a regular meeting pattern; and an organized, continuous course of criminality.

Good time: When correctional authorities deduct from a prison or jail sentence, often to reward or encourage good behavior, they give "good time." When the good time is applied to a specific action, such as working in a prison industry or performing a meritorious deed, it is called "earned."

Guns available for sale: The Bureau of Alcohol, Tobacco, and Firearms counts firearms that are available for sale in the United States. The figure is calculated by adding together domestic production and imports, then subtracting firearms exports. The total does not include guns stocked by U.S. armed forces. The figure also omits the following: guns destroyed or rendered unfit for use, souvenir guns brought into the country after conflicts involving U.S. armed forces, guns smuggled into or out of the U.S., and guns manufactured illegally.

Hispanic origin: A person of Hispanic origin may be of any race. A few states, however, treat the ethnic category as a racial one. Reports usually rely on respondents identifying themselves as someone descended from any Spanish culture or origin. Examples might include self-descriptions such as: Mexican-American, Mexican, Mexicano, Puerto Rican, Cuban, Central American, or South American.

Hospital, inpatient: An institution that provides 24-hour services for the diagnosis and treatment of patients through an organized medical or professional staff and permanent licensed medical/psychiatric facilities that include inpatient beds, medical, and nursing services. Patients residing in hospital settings should be receiving services primarily for alcoholism and/or other drugs of abuse.

Household crimes: Attempted and completed crimes that do not involve personal confrontation. Examples of household crimes include burglary, motor vehicle theft, and household larceny.

Household larceny: Theft or attempted theft of property or cash from a residence in the immediate vicinity of the residence. In order to occur within a house, a thief must have a legal right to be in the house (such as a maid, delivery person, or guest), as unlawful or forcible entry constitutes a burglary.

Incident: A specific criminal act involving one or more victims and offenders. For example, if two people are robbed at the same time and place, this is classified as two robbery victimizations but only one robbery incident.

Jurisdiction: A unit of government or the legal authority to exercise governmental power. According to the latter meaning, prisoners under a state's jurisdiction may be in the custody of local jails.

Justifiable homicide: The FBI restricts this definition to the killing of a felon by a law enforcement officer in the line of duty and the killing of a felon by a private citizen during the commission of a felony, based on initial police investigation. Excludes excusable homicides and any criminal homicides ultimately ruled as noncriminal.

Juvenile: Youth at or below the upper age of juvenile court jurisdiction.

Juvenile court: Any court that has jurisdiction over matters involving juveniles.

Larceny: Theft or attempted theft of property or cash without involving force or illegal entry. This category is subdivided into personal larceny and household larceny.

Larceny-theft (except motor vehicle theft): The FBI definition encompasses the unlawful taking, carrying, leading, or riding away of property from the possession

Glossary

or constructive possession of another. Examples are thefts of bicycles or automobile accessories, shoplifting, pocket-picking, or the stealing of any property or article which is not taken by force and violence or by fraud. Attempted larcenies are included. Embezzlement, "con" games, forgery, worthless checks, etc., are excluded.

Local government funds: Provided by local government (city, county, etc.) to provide drug abuse or alcoholism treatment services.

Lock up: This term refers to individuals who have been arrested and locked up in a jail awaiting further legal procedures. A person who has been locked up may subsequently be released without being charged with a crime, or released pending a trial on crimes they are accused of committing. Consequently, because a person has been locked up does not mean he or she is guilty of the crime for which they are being held.

Maltreatment type: A particular form of child maltreatment that is determined by investigation to be substantiated or indicated under state law as physical abuse, neglect, or deprivation of necessities, medical neglect, sexual abuse, psychological or emotional maltreatment, and other forms specified by state law.

Manslaughter by negligence: The killing of another person through gross negligence, excluding traffic fatalities. The FBI's crime index does not include manslaughter by negligence.

Maximum sentence lengths: Some jurisdictions sentence prisoners to a range of years; the larger number in that range is the most that a prisoner may serve on the sentence. Often, good time is subtracted from the maximum sentence.

Mean: A single number that broadly describes an entire set of numbers. A mean (commonly called an "average") is calculated by adding the values of all the cases and dividing by the total number of cases. For the set of values [2, 3, 3, 5, 6, 6, 10] the mean is 7.

Median: The quantity or value of the case within a series of cases where one-half of all cases have values greater than the case itself and the other one-half of the cases have values less than the case itself. For the set of values [2, 3, 3, 5, 6, 6, 10] the median is 5.

Medical neglect: The harm by a caretaker to a child's health due to failure to provide for appropriate health care of the child, although financially able to do so, or offered financial or other means to do so. May include perinatal exposure to drugs.

Metropolitan Statistical Area (MSA): The Office of Management and Budget defines this as a population nucleus of 50,000 or more, generally consisting of a city and its immediate suburbs, along with adjacent communities having a high degree of economic and social integration with the nucleus. MSAs are designated by counties, the smallest geographical unit for which a wide range of statistical data can be obtained, except in New England where they are designated by cities and towns.

Mode: The most frequently occurring member of a set of numbers. For the set of values [2, 3, 3, 5, 6, 6, 10] there are two modes, 3 and 6, since both values occur most often.

Motor vehicle: An automobile, truck, motorcycle, or any motorized vehicle legally allowed on public roads.

Motor vehicle theft: The stealing or unauthorized taking, including attempted theft, of a self-propelled vehicle that runs on the surface and not on rails. Specifically excluded from this category are motorboats, construction equipment, airplanes, and farming equipment.

Movement: In corrections, the term refers to the admission to or release from a status—prisoner, parolee, or probationer. A transfer between facilities typically does not count as a movement.

Murder and nonnegligent manslaughter: The FBI defines this term as the willful (nonnegligent) killing of one human being by another. Deaths caused by negligence, attempts to kill, suicides, accidental deaths, and justifiable homicides are excluded.

Neglect or deprivation of necessities: A type of maltreatment that refers to the failure to provide needed, age-appropriate care, although financially able to do so, or offered other financial or other means to do so.

Nonstranger: A classification of a crime victim's relationship to the offender. An offender who is related to, well known to or casually acquainted with the victim is a nonstranger. For crimes with more than one offender, if any of the offenders are nonstrangers, then the whole group of offenders is classified as nonstranger. This category only applies to crimes which involve contact between the victim and the offender. The distinction is not made for personal larceny without contact since victims of this offense rarely see the offenders.

Glossary

Offender: The perpetrator of a crime; this term usually applies to crimes involving contact between the victim and the offender.

Offense: A crime. When referring to personal crimes, the term can be used to refer to both victimizations and incidents.

Offenses against the family and children: Nonsupport, neglect, desertion, or abuse of family and children.

Other offenses against persons: This category includes kidnapping, violent sex acts other than forcible rape (e.g., incest, sodomy), custody interference, unlawful restraint, false imprisonment, reckless endangerment, harassment, etc., and any attempts to commit such acts.

Personal crimes: Rape, personal robbery, assault, personal larceny with contact, or personal larceny without contact. This category includes both attempted and completed crimes.

Personal crimes of theft: Personal larceny. The theft or attempted theft of property or cash by stealth, either with contact (but without force or threat of force) or without direct contact between the victim and the offender.

Personal crimes of violence: Rape, personal robbery, or assault. This category includes both attempted and completed crimes, and the crime always involves contact between the victim and the offender.

Personal larceny: Equivalent to the personal crimes of theft. Personal larceny is divided into two subgroups depending on whether or not the crime involved personal contact between the victim and the offender.

Personal larceny with contact: Theft or attempted theft of property or cash directly from the victim by stealth, not force or threat of force. Includes both purse snatching and pocket picking.

Personal larceny without contact: Theft or attempted theft of property or cash from any place other than the victim's home or its immediate vicinity, without direct contact between the victim and the offender. This crime differs from household larceny only in the location in which the theft occurs. Examples of personal larceny without contact include theft of an umbrella in a restaurant, a radio from the beach, or cash from an automobile parked in a parking lot. Occasionally, the victim may see the offender commit the crime.

Physical abuse: A type of maltreatment that refers to physical acts that caused or could have caused physical injury to the victim.

Physical fight: A violent confrontation between two or more individuals who intend to injure each other.

Physical injury: The National Crime Victimization Survey measures physical injury in cases of rape, personal robbery, and assault. Completed or attempted robberies that result in injury are classified as involving "serious" or "minor" injuries. Examples of injuries from serious assault include broken bones, loss of teeth, internal injuries, loss of consciousness, and undetermined injuries requiring two or more days of hospitalization. Injuries from minor assault include bruises, black eyes, cuts, scratches, swelling, or undetermined injuries requiring less than two days of hospitalization. Assaults without a deadly weapon are classified as aggravated if the victim's injuries fit the description given for serious assault. All completed rapes are defined as having resulted in physical injury. Attempted rapes are classified as having resulted in injury if the victim reported having suffered some form of physical injury.

Psychological or emotional maltreatment: A type of maltreatment that refers to acts or omissions, other than physical or sexual abuse, that caused, or could have caused, conduct, cognitive, affective or other mental disorders, such as emotional neglect, psychological abuse, mental injury, etc.

Race: Classification by race often depends on the reporting program within the state. Some states may report only two categories: white and nonwhite. A few others may categorize Hispanics as belonging to "other race."

The term "white" generally refers to persons with ancestral origins in any of the indigenous peoples of Europe, North Africa, or the Middle East. The term "black" is used to signify persons with origins in any of the black racial groups of Africa. "Other" refers to persons having origins with any of the original peoples of North America, the Far East, Southeast Asia, the Indian Subcontinent, or the Pacific Islands.

Random sample: A sampling from some population where each entry has an equal chance of being drawn. Random sampling is used to obtain significant statistics about groups too large to sample individually.

Rape: The National Crime Victimization Survey defines this crime as carnal knowledge of a female or male through the use of force, including attempts. Statutory rape (without force) is excluded. Includes both heterosexual and homosexual rape.

Rape, forcible: FBI Uniform Crime Reports definition: Carnal knowledge of a female forcibly and against her will. Includes rapes by force and attempts or assaults to

Glossary

rape. Statutory offenses (no force used—victim under age of consent) are not included.

Some states have enacted gender-neutral rape or sexual assault statutes that prohibit forced sexual penetration of either sex. Data reported by such states do not distinguish between forcible rape of females as defined above and other sexual assaults.

Recidivist: A current prisoner with a previous adult criminal record of sentences to probation or prison.

Relationship of perpetrator: Refers to the primary role of the offender with the victim.

Representative sample: A sample so large and average in composition that it can be said to accurately represent the larger group from which it was drawn.

Robbery: Completed or attempted theft, directly from a person, of property or cash by force or threat of force, with or without a weapon.

Robbery with injury: Completed theft or attempted theft from a person, accompanied by an attack, whether with or without a weapon, resulting in injury. An injury is classified as resulting from a serious assault, irrespective of the extent of injury, if a weapon was used in committing the crime, or, if not, when the extent of the injury was either serious (e.g., broken bones, loss of teeth, internal injuries, or loss of consciousness) or undetermined but required two days of hospitalization. An injury is classified as resulting from a minor assault when the extent of the injury was small (e.g., bruises, black eyes, scratches, or swelling) or undetermined but required less than two days of hospitalization.

Robbery without injury: Theft or attempted theft from a person, accompanied by force or the threat of force, either with or without a weapon, but not resulting in injury.

Rural: A county or group of counties not located inside a metropolitan statistical area. The category includes a variety of localities, including smaller cities with populations less than 50,000. However, the term primary refers to sparsely populated areas.

School, open: A school in which students are permitted to leave the school grounds during lunch.

Schools, inside areas: Inside areas include hallways, stairs, cafeterias, restrooms, and any other areas inside of the school buildings.

Schools, outside areas: Outside areas include entrances into the school, parking lots, and any other areas on school grounds.

Sexual abuse: A type of maltreatment that refers to the involvement of a child in sexual activity to provide sexual gratification or financial benefit to the perpetrator. Includes contacts for sexual purposes, prostitution, pornography, exposure, or other sexually exploitive activities.

Simple assault: Attack without a weapon resulting either in minor injury (e.g., bruises, black eyes, cuts, scratches, or swelling) or in an undetermined injury requiring less than two days of hospitalization. Also includes attempted assault without a weapon.

Stranger: A classification of the victim's relationship to the offender for crimes involving direct contact between the two. Incidents are classified as involving strangers if the victim identified the offender as a stranger, did not see or recognize the offender, or knew the offender only by sight. Crimes involving multiple offenders are classified as involving nonstrangers if any of the offenders was a nonstranger. Since victims of personal larceny without contact rarely see the offender, no distinction is made between strangers and nonstrangers for this crime.

Suburban areas: A county or counties containing a central city, plus any contiguous counties that are linked socially and economically to the central city. Suburban areas are categorized as those portions of metropolitan areas situated "outside central cities."

Teen suicide prevention services: Services for youth, family members, and peers designed to educate, prevent, or intervene in teen suicidal behavior.

Truth-in-sentencing: In corrections, truth-in-sentencing describes a close correspondence between the sentence imposed upon those sent to prison and the time actually served prior to prison release.

Unlawful entry: A form of burglary committed by someone having no legal right to be on the premises, even though no force is used.

Upper age of jurisdiction: The oldest age at which a juvenile court has original jurisdiction over an individual for law-violating behavior. This age varies from 15–18 years of age depending on the state's statute, but most states have set the upper age of jurisdiction at 17 years of age. Within most states there are exceptions to the age criteria that place or permit youth at or below the state's upper age of jurisdiction to be under the original jurisdiction of the adult criminal court. For example, in most states if a youth of a certain age is charged with one of a defined list of what are commonly labeled "excluded offenses," the case must originate in the adult

Glossary

criminal court. Therefore, while the upper age of jurisdiction is commonly recognized in all states, there are numerous exceptions to this age criterion.

Victim: The recipient of a criminal act, usually used in relation to personal crimes, but also applicable to households.

Victimization: A crime as it affects one individual or household. For personal crimes, the number of victimizations is equal to the number of victims involved. The number of victimizations may be greater than the number of incidents because more than one person may be victimized during an incident. Each crime against a household is assumed to involve a single victim, the affected household.

Victimize: To commit a crime against a person or household.

Violence between intimates: Those murders, rapes, robberies, or assaults committed by spouses, ex-spouses, boyfriends, or girlfriends. Intimates are distinguished from other relatives, acquaintances, and strangers.

Weapons offenses and violations: Unlawful sale, distribution, manufacture, alteration, transportation, possession, or use of a deadly weapon, or accessory, or any attempt to commit any of these acts.

Weighted data: Statistics that are adjusted by scaling so that the weighted counts and proportions match the analyzed population. Weighting factors typically are used when researchers know that some aspect of the sample will not accurately represent that of the whole population.

White, not of hispanic origin. A Caucasian person having origins in any of the people of Europe (includes Portugal), North Africa, or the Middle East.

Workplace assault: A violent nonfatal attack where the victim was either at his/her place of employment or on duty at the time of the incident.

Workplace homicide: A murder where the victim was either at his/her place of employment or on duty at the time of the incident.

Youth population at risk: For delinquency and status offense matters, this is the number of children from age 10 through the upper age of jurisdiction. For dependency matters, this is the number of children at or below the upper age of court jurisdiction. All states define by statute the upper age of jurisdiction. In most states, individuals are considered adults when they reach their 18th birthday. Therefore, for these states, the delinquency and status offense youth population at risk would equal the number of children 10 through 17 years of age living within the geographical area serviced by the court.

Youthful offender status: State legislators create this status through statutes that provide for special sentencing, commitment, or record sealing procedures for young adult offenders adjudicated in a criminal court (as opposed to a juvenile court). Such offenders may be above the statutory age limit for juveniles but below a specified upper age limit.

Index

A

Accidental death
   by age 56
   by firearms 52, 54
   by type of firearm 58
   firearms used in 46
Accidents
   compared to other events 78
   firearms xvii, 46, 52
Accuracy, definition 205
Aggravated assault *see* Assault
Aggression xiii
Agriculture, murder in the workplace 192
AIDS, definition 205
Alabama
   assaults 24, 142
   assaults per population 142
   campus violence 176
   high school fights 172
   murders 50, 126
   murders per population 126
   rapes reported 128
   robberies 20, 134
   robberies per population 134
Alaska
   assaults 24, 143
   assaults per population 142
   campus violence 176
   murders 50, 126
   murders per population 126
   rapes reported 128
   robberies 20, 135
   robberies per population 134
Alcohol use, murder and 150
Allegation of child maltreatment, definition 205
American Indian/Alaskan Native, definition 205
American Samoa, high school fights 172
Arguments
   murder during 48
   murder during, by relationship to offender 122

Arizona
   assaults 24, 142
   assaults per population 142
   campus violence 176
   murders 50, 126
   murders per population 126
   rapes reported 128
   robberies 20, 134
   robberies per population 134
Arkansas
   assaults 24, 142
   assaults per population 142
   campus violence 176
   high school fights 172
   murders 50, 126
   murders per population 126
   rapes reported 128
   robberies 20, 134
   robberies per population 134
Armed robbery *see* Robbery
Arrests
   for assault 86
   for murder 86
   for rape 86
   for robbery 86
   violent crime 84, 86
   weapons violations 26
Arson
   definition 205
   murder during 48
Aryan Nation *see* Gangs
Asphyxiation, used in murder 44
Assault
   arrests for 86
   at school 166
   attempted vs. completed 108
   by characteristic of victim 140
   by juvenile delinquents 184
   by state 24
   compared to other events 78
   definition 205
   economic loss 112

Index

firearm involvement 38, 42
in families 146
in the workplace 194
injury during 108
number in prison for 80
per population 74, 104, 142
percent of inmates sentenced for 82
reported to police 100, 106, 142, 144
trends 76
victim's loss of work time 198
victims per incident 110
weapon used in 22, 32, 144
Assault weapon, definition 205
Assault weapons *see* Firearms, Rifles
Attempted forcible entry, definition 205
Auto theft *see* Motor vehicle theft
Automatic weapons, owned by juveniles 62

B

Baby-sitter *see* Child-care provider
Biting, injuries in the workplace 200
Black, not of hispanic origin
    definition 205
Bloods *see* Gangs
Blunt object
    used in assault 32
    used in rape 32
    used in robbery 32
Blunt objects
    used in assault 22
    used in murder 44, 48
Boston, MA
    high school fights 172
Boyfriend, murder of 154
Brady Bill xii
Brawls
    murder during 48
    murder during, by relationship to offender 122
Bureau of Justice Statistics xx
Bureau of Labor Statistics xiv
Burglary
    definition 205
    firearm involvement 38
    murder during 48
    murder during, by relationship to offender 122
Business disputes
    murder due to 190

C

California
    assault 24
    assaults 142
    assaults per population 142
    campus violence 176
    high school fights 172
    murders 50, 126
    murders per population 126
    rapes reported 128
    robberies 134
    robberies per population 134
    robberies 20
Cancer death
    compared to violent crime 78
Car theft *see* Motor vehicle theft
Caretaker relative or household member
    definition 206
Carjacking
    compared to other events 78
Carnegie Foundation xv
Causes of violent behavior xii
Census of Fatal Occupational Injuries xix
Centers for Disease Control xiv
Centers for Disease Control and Prevention xxi
Central city
    definition 206
Chicago, IL
    high school fights 172
    murders in the workplace 188
Child, definition 206
Child abuse
    by age of victim 162
    by child care providers 164
    by facility staff 164
    by foster parents 164
    by parents 164
    by relatives 164
    by reporting source 158
    emotional 160
    medical 160
    neglect 160
    physical 160
    relationship between victim and offender 164
    reported anonymously 158
    reported by family member 158
    reported by friend 158

Index

reported by perpetrator 158
reported by professional 158
sexual 160
trends in reporting 156
Child care provider
    as child abuser 164
    murder by 48
Child care services, definition 206
Child maltreatment
    definition 206
    See also Child abuse
Child, as violent crime offender 146
Child-based report, definition 206
Colorado
    assaults 24, 142
    assaults per population 142
    campus violence 176
    murders 50, 126
    murders per population 126
    rapes reported 128
    robberies 20, 134
    robberies per population 134
Connecticut
    assaults 24, 142
    assaults per population 142
    campus violence 176
    murders 50, 126
    murders per population 126
    rapes reported 128
    robberies 20, 134
    robberies per population 134
Constant dollars, definition 206
Constitution, U.S. xii
Construction, murder in the workplace 192
Correctional facility, definition 206
Correctional Populations in the U.S. xix
Crime
    at school 166
    fatal handgun 34
    gun firing during 38
    handgun injuries during 34
    weapons used 32
    See also Assault, Murder, Rape, Robbery,
        Violent crime
Crime index 72
    trends 74, 76
Crime rates xvii
Crime victims
    armed robbery 10

assault 140
by characteristic 98, 116, 140
economic loss 112, 114
handgun crime 35
in cities 99
in rural areas 99
in suburbs 99
in the workplace 196
injuries 108
loss of work time 198
number per incident 110
of murder, by age 120
offender is family member 146
police reports 144
rape 130, 132
robbery 136
self-protection measures 14
sources of assistance 118
violent and total 72, 102
Crime, property, trends 72
Crime, violent 72
Crimes of violence, definition 206
Criminal behavior, trends in xiv
Criminal homicide, definition 206
Criminal justice, definition 206
Criminals, handgun use in crime 40
Crips see Gangs
Current Mortality Sample xix
Custody, definition 206

D

Dallas, TX, high school fights 173
DC see District of Columbia
Death, accidental 52, 54
Deaths, by firearms 54, 56, 58
Deaths from disease, compared to violent crime 78
Delaware
    assaults 24, 143
    assaults per population 142
    high school fights 172
    murders 50, 126
    murders per population 126
    rapes reported 128
    robberies 20, 134
    robberies per population 134
Delinquency
    definition 206

Statistics on Weapons & Violence

Index

juvenile 184
Delinquent act, definition 206
Derringer *see* Handgun
Detention, definition 206
Detroit, MI, murders in the workplace 188
Disposition, definition 206
District of Columbia
    assaults 24, 142
    assaults per population 142
    high school fights 172
    murders 50, 126
    murders per population 126
    rapes reported 128
    robberies 20, 134
    robberies per population 134
Drowning, used in murder 44
Drug offenses, firearm involvement 38
Drug trafficking, gangs and 180
Drug use, murder during 48

E

Educationally deprived youths xviii
Eighth graders
    crime victims at school 168
    See also Students
Eleventh grade students
    crime victims at school 168
    fights at school 170
    who carried a weapon 60
    See also Students
Emergency room, crime victims getting help at 118
Employees, as murder victims 186
Explosives, used in murder 44

F

Family counseling/therapy services, definition 206
Family murder, definition 207
Family violence xiii
Fatalities *see* Death
Fatality, definition 207
FBI *see* Federal Bureau of Investigation
Federal Bureau of Investigation (FBI) xx
Feet *see* Personal weapons
Female crime victims 36
Fights
    at high school 170

at high school, by race 170
at high school, by state 172
Finance industry, violence and 202
Fire, used in murder 44
Firearm mortality, definition 207
Firearms
    accidents xvii, 52, 54, 58
    carried by students 60
    definition 207
    for sale, trends 2, 4
    owned by juveniles 62
    private citizens and xi
    purchase of xviii
    registration of 7
    sales by licensed dealers 5
    theft of 28
    use by first-time offenders 40
    use by repeat offenders 40
    use in assault 22, 24, 42
    use in federal offenses 30
    use in justifiable homicide 12
    use in murder 42, 44, 46, 48, 50
    use in rape 32
    use in robbery 18, 20, 32, 42
    use in self-defense 16
    use in suicide 46
    why juveniles own 66
    why students own 66
Fists *see* Personal weapons
Florida
    assaults 24, 142
    assaults per population 142
    campus violence 176
    high school fights 172
    murders 50, 126
    murders per population 126
    rapes reported 128
    robberies 20, 134
    robberies per population 134
Forcible entry, definition 207

G

Gambling, murder during 48, 122
Gangs
    African-American 180
    Asian 180
    at school 178

based in Los Angeles 180
crimes committed, by gender 182
definition 207
drug trafficking and 180
female 182
Hispanic 180
killings 48, 122
male 182
motorcycle 180
street, definition 207
violence xviii
violent crime and 90, 180
Gasoline stations, murder in the workplace 192
Georgia
assaults 24, 142
assaults per population 142
campus violence 176
high school fights 172
murders 50, 126
rapes reported 128
robberies 20, 134
robberies per population 134
Girlfriend, murder of 154
Good time, definition 207
Government, murder in the workplace 192
Grocery stores
murder in the workplace 192
violence and 202
Gun control, advocates xii
Gun owners
by age 6
by occupation 6
by race 6
by region of U.S. 6
by sex 6

H

Handgun crime
fatalities 34
injuries 34
Handguns
accidental deaths 58
crime 34
fatalities from 34
for sale, trends 2, 4
for sale, trends 2
injuries from 34

owned by juveniles 62, 64, 66
owned by students 64, 66
used in crime 40
used in justifiable homicide 12
used in murder xvi, 34, 44, 50
Hands *see* Personal weapons
Hawaii
assaults 24, 143
assaults per population 143
high school fights 172
murders 50, 126
murders per population 126
rapes reported 128
robberies 20, 134
robberies per population 134
Heart disease death, compared to violent crime 78
High school students
who carry a gun xviii
use of weapons xvii
Hispanic origin, definition 207
Homelessness, murder and 150
Homicide *see* Murder
Homicide rate xv
Homicide, justifiable 12
Hospitals
crime victims getting help at 118
inpatient, definition 207
violence and 202
Household crimes, definition 207
Household larceny, definition 207
Houston, TX, murders in the workplace 188
Hunting rifles
accidental deaths 58
See also Firearms, Rifles, Shotguns
Husband, murder of 154

I

Idaho
assaults 24, 143
assaults per population 142
high school fights 172
murders 50, 126
murders per population 126
rapes reported 128
robberies 20, 135
robberies per population 135

Index

Illinois
    assaults 24, 142
    assaults per population 142
    high school fights 172
    murders 50, 126
    murders per population 126
    rapes reported 128
    robberies 20, 134
    robberies per population 134
Incarceration *see* Prison sentences
Incident, definition 207
Index crimes xiv
Indiana
    assaults 24, 142
    assaults per population 142
    campus violence 176
    murders 50, 126
    murders per population 126
    rapes reported 128
    robberies 20, 134
    robberies per population 134
Industry, murder in the workplace 192
Inmates
    firearm usage in crime 40
    juvenile 62
    See also Prison sentences
Iowa
    assaults 24, 142
    assaults per population 142
    campus violence 176
    murders 50, 126
    murders per population 126
    rapes reported 128
    robberies 134
    robberies per population 135

J

Jersey City, NJ
    high school fights 172
Jurisdiction
    definition 207
Justifiable homicide
    definition 207
    use of weapons in xvii
    See also Murder

Juvenile court
    definition 207
    statistics xx
Juveniles
    definition 207
    firearm ownership, reasons 66
    handgun sources for 64
    violent crime xii

K

Kansas
    assaults 24, 142
    assaults per population 142
    murders 50, 126
    murders per population 126
    rapes reported 128
    robberies 134
    robberies per population 134
Kentucky
    assaults 24, 142
    assaults per population 142
    campus violence 176
    high school fights 172
    murders 50, 126
    murders per population 126
    rapes reported 128
    robberies 134
    robberies per population 134
Kidnapping, prison sentence for 88
Knives
    murders by 50
    used in assault 22, 32
    used in assault by state 24
    used in justifiable homicide 12
    used in murder 44, 48
    used in rape 32
    used in robbery 18, 32
    used in robbery by state 20
Ku Klux Klan *see* Gangs

L

Larceny
    definition 207
    firearm involvement 38
    murder during 48, 122
Larceny-theft, definition 207

Index

Los Angeles, CA, murders in the workplace 188
Louisiana
    assaults 24, 142
    assaults 142
    assaults per population 142
    campus violence 176
    high school fights 172
    murders 50
    murders per population 126
    rapes reported 128
    robberies 20, 134
    robberies per population 134

M

Maine
    assaults 24, 143
    assaults per population 143
    campus violence 176
    high school fights 172
    murders 50, 126
    murders per population 126
    rapes reported 128
    robberies 20, 135
    robberies per population 135
Male crime victims
    by age 36
    by race 36
Maltreatment type
    definition 208
Manslaughter
    by weapon 8
    definition 208
    number in prison for, trends 80, 82
Manufacturing
    murder in the workplace 192
    violence and 202
Maryland
    assaults 24, 142
    assaults per population 142
    campus violence 176
    murders 50, 126
    murders per population 126
    rapes reported 128
    robberies 20, 134
    robberies per population 134
Massachusetts
    assaults 24, 142
    assaults per population 142
    campus violence 176
    high school fights 172
    murders 50, 126
    murders per population 126
    rapes reported 128
    robberies 20, 134
    robberies per population 134
Mean, definition 208
Median, definition 208
Medical neglect, definition 208
Men
    as murder defendants 148
    as murder victims 148
    assault victims 140
    crime victims 36, 98
    murder victims at work 186
    violent crime victims 152
Mental illness, murder and 150
Miami, FL
    high school fights 172
    murders in the workplace 188
Michigan
    assaults 24, 142
    assaults per population 142
    murders 50, 126
    murders per population 126
    rapes reported 128
    robberies 20, 134
    robberies per population 134
Minnesota
    assaults 24, 142
    assaults per population 143
    murders 50, 126
    murders per population 126
    rapes reported 128
    robberies 20, 134
    robberies per population 134
Mississippi
    assaults 24, 142
    assaults per population 142
    campus violence 176
    high school fights 172
    murders 50, 126
    murders per population 126
    rapes reported 128
    robberies 20, 134
    robberies per population 134
Missouri 126

Index

assaults 24, 142
assaults per population 142
campus violence 176
murders 50, 126
murders per population 126
rapes reported 128
robberies 20, 134
robberies per population 134
Mode, definition 208
Montana
  assaults 24, 143
  assaults per population 143
  campus violence 176
  high school fights 172
  murders 50, 126
  murders per population 126
  rapes reported 128
  robberies 20, 135
  robberies per population 135
Motor vehicle, definition 208
Motor vehicle theft
  definition 208
  firearm involvement 38
  murder during 48, 122
Mott Foundation xv
Movement, definition 208
Murder 54
  alcohol use and 150
  arrests for 86
  by juvenile delinquent 184
  compared to other events 78
  definition 208
  during arson 122
  during burglary 122
  during business disputes 190
  during gambling 122
  during larceny 122
  during motor vehicle theft 122
  during personal disputes at work 190
  during prostitution and commercialized vice 122
  during rape 122
  during robbery 122
  during robbery at work 190
  firearm involvement 38, 42
  gang-related 182
  homelessness and 150
  mental illness and 150
  per population 70, 74, 126
  percent annual change 76

prison sentence for 80, 82, 88
reasons for 48, 122, 124, 190
unemployment and 150
weapon used in 44
Murder, by location
  by state 50, 126
  in agriculture industry 192
  in communications industry 192
  in construction industry 192
  in manufacturing industry 192
  in public utilities industry 192
  in the workplace 186
  in the workplace in cities 188
  in the workplace, by industry 192
  in the workplace, reasons for 190
  in transportation industry 192
Murder, by relationship between victim and offender
  by a stranger 122
  by acquaintance 122
  by age of murderer 120
  by age of victim 120
  by boyfriend or girlfriend 122
  by family member 122
  by friend 122
  by neighbor 122
  in families 148, 150
  of boyfriend 154
  of girlfriend 154
  of husband or ex-husband 154
  of wife or ex-wife 154
Murder, by weapon type
  by blunt object 8
  by firearm 8, 42, 54
  by knife 8
  by personal weapon 8

N

Narcotics, used in murder 44
National Center on Child Abuse and Neglect xiv, xx
National Child Abuse and Neglect Data System xx
National Crime Victimization Survey xx
National Institute of Justice xiv, xv
National Rifle Association (NRA) xii
Nebraska
  assaults 24, 142
  assaults per population 142

Index

campus violence 176
high school fights 172
murders 50, 126
murders per population 126
rapes reported 128
robberies 20, 135
robberies per population 135
Neglect or deprivation of necessities, definition 208
Nevada
    assaults 24, 142
    assaults per population 142
    campus violence 176
    high school fights 172
    murders 50, 126
    murders per population 126
    rapes reported 128
    robberies 20, 134
    robberies per population 134
New Hampshire
    assaults 24, 143
    assaults per population 143
    campus violence 176
    high school fights 172
    murders 50, 126
    murders per population 126
    rapes reported 128
    robberies 20, 135
    robberies per population 135
New Jersey
    assaults 24, 142
    assaults per population 142
    campus violence 176
    high school fights 172
    murders 50, 126
    murders per population 126
    rapes reported 128
    robberies 20, 134
    robberies per population 134
New Mexico
    assaults 24, 142
    assaults per population 142
    campus violence 176
    high school fights 172
    murders 50, 126
    murders per population 126
    rapes reported 128
    robberies 20, 134
    robberies per population 134
New Orleans, LA, high school fights 172

New York
    assaults 24, 142
    assaults per population 142
    campus violence 176
    high school fights 172
    murders 50, 126
    murders per population 126
    rapes reported 128
    robberies 20, 134
    robberies per population 134
New York City, NY
    high school fights 172
    murders in the workplace 188
Ninth grade students
    crime victims at school 168
    fights at school 170
    who carried a weapon 60
    See also Students
Nonstranger, definition 208
North Carolina
    assaults 24, 142
    assaults per population 142
    campus violence 176
    high school fights 172
    murders 50, 126
    murders per population 126
    rapes reported 128
    robberies 20, 134
    robberies per population 134
North Dakota
    assaults 24, 143
    assaults per population 143
    campus violence 176
    murders 50, 126
    murders per population 126
    rapes reported 128
    robberies 20, 135
    robberies per population 135
NRA *see* National Rifle Association
Nursing homes, violence and 202

O

Offender, definition 209
Offense, definition 209
Offenses against the family and children, definition 209

Index

Office of Juvenile Justice and Delinquency Prevention xiv, xx
Ohio
    assaults 24, 142
    assaults per population 142
    campus violence 176
    high school fights 172
    murders 50, 126
    murders per population 126
    rapes reported 128
    robberies 20, 134
    robberies per population 134
Oklahoma
    assaults 24, 142
    assaults per population 142
    campus violence 176
    murders 50, 126
    murders per population 126
    rapes reported 128
    robberies 20, 134
    robberies per population 134
Oregon
    assaults 25, 142
    assaults per population 142
    high school fights 172
    murders 50, 126
    murders per population 126
    rapes reported 128
    robberies 21, 134
    robberies per population 134
Other offenses against persons, definition 209
Ownership of handguns xi

P

Parent, as violent crime offender 146, 164
Parents, as child abusers 164
Pennsylvania
    assaults 25, 142
    assaults per population 143
    campus violence 176
    high school fights 172
    murders 50, 126
    murders per population 126
    rapes reported 129
    robberies 21, 134
    robberies per population 134
Personal crimes, definition 209

Personal larceny
    definition 209
    with contact, definition 209
Personal weapons (hands, feet, fists)
    injuries in the workplace 200
    used in assault 22–25
    used in justifiable homicide 12
    used in murder 44, 48, 50
    used in robbery 18–21
Philadelphia, PA
    high school fights 172
    murders in the workplace 188
Physical abuse, definition 209
Physical fight, definition 209
Physical injury, definition 209
Playground, violent crime at 94
Poison, used in murder 44
Police reports
    by state 134
    trends 106
    violent crime 84, 100, 137
Prison sentences 30, 86
    average time served 92
    length 88
Property crime
    firearm involvement 38
    trends 72
    See also Robbery
Prostitution, murder during 48, 122
Psychological or emotional maltreatment, definition 209
Public transportation, violent crime on 94
Public utilities
    murder in the workplace 192
    violence and 202
Puerto Rico
    assaults 142
    assaults per population 143
    murders 126
    murders per population 126
    rapes reported 129
    robberies 134
    robberies per population 134

R

Race, definition 209
Random sample, definition 209

Index

Rape
    arrests for 86
    at school 166
    attempted vs. completed 108
    by a stranger 132
    by acquaintance or friend 132
    by family member 132
    by juvenile delinquents 184
    by state 128
    definition 209
    firearm involvement 38
    in families 146
    in the workplace 194
    murder during 48, 122
    per population 74, 104, 128
    prison sentence for 80, 82, 88
    reported to police 100, 106, 130
    trends 76
    victim of 110, 196, 198
    weapons used in xvi, 32
Rape, forcible, definition 209
Recidivist, definition 210
Relationship of perpetrator, definition 210
Relatives, as child abusers 164
Representative sample xv
    definition 210
Restaurants
    murder in the workplace 192
    violence and 94, 202
Revolver *see* Firearm, Handgun
Rhode Island
    assaults 25, 143
    assaults per population 142
    campus violence 176
    murders 50, 127
    murders per population 127
    rapes reported 129
    robberies 21, 134
    robberies per population 134
Rifles
    for sale, trends 2, 4
    owned by juveniles 62
    used in justifiable homicide 12
    used in murder 44
    See also Firearms, Shotguns
Robbery
    arrests for 86
    by juvenile delinquents 184
    compared to other events 78
    definition 210
    economic loss 112, 198
    firearm involvement 38, 42
    in families 146
    injury during 108, 136
    murder during 48
    per population 74, 104, 134
    prison sentence for 80, 82, 88
    reported to police 100, 106, 134, 136
    trends 76
    victim of 110, 196, 198
    weapons used in xvi, 18, 32
    with injury, definition 210
    without injury, definition 210
Robbery, by location
    at a bank 138
    at a convenience store 138
    at a residence 138
    at commercial establishment 138
    at gas station 138
    at school 166
    by site 138
    by state 20
    in the workplace 194
    on street or highway 138
Rural, definition 210

S

San Diego, CA, high school fights 172
San Francisco, CA,
    high school fights 172
    murders in the workplace 188
Schools, violent crime at 94
Seattle, WA, high school fights 173
Second Amendment xii
Security guard, murder of, at work 190
Self-protection
    crime victims 14
    in armed robbery 10
    measures used by victims 14
Seventh graders
    crime victims at school 168
    See also Students
Sex offenses
    murder during 48
    prison sentence for 88

Index

Sexual abuse, definition 210
Shootings
    accidental 52, 56
    at work 191, 200
Shotguns
    accidental deaths 58
    for sale by type, trends 4
    owned by juveniles 62
    used in justifiable homicide 12
    used in murder 44
    See also Firearms, Rifles
Sixth graders
    crime victims at school 168
    See also Students
Skinheads *see* Gangs
Sniper attack
    murder by 48
    relationship between victim and offender 122
Sourcebook of Criminal Justice Statistics xiv
South Carolina
    assaults 25, 142
    assaults per population 142
    campus violence 176
    high school fights 173
    murders 51, 127
    murders per population 127
    rapes reported 129
    robberies 21, 134
    robberies per population 134
South Dakota
    assaults 25, 143
    assaults per population 143
    campus violence 176
    high school fights 173
    murders 51, 127
    murders per population 127
    rapes reported 129
    robberies 21, 135
    robberies per population 135
Spouse, as violent crime offender 146
Stabbing, injuries in the workplace 200
Statistics
    interpretation of xiv
    limitations of xiv
    presentation of xv
Stores, murder in the workplace 192
Stranger, definition 210
Strangulation, used in murder 44
Strong-arm methods *see* Personal weapons

Students
    crime victims at school 166, 168
    fear of violence 178
    firearm ownership, reasons 66
    handgun sources for 64
    high school, 60
    in fights at school 174
    who carry weapons to school 174
    who feel unsafe at school 174
Suburban areas, definition 210
Suicide, 54
    compared to other events 78
    firearms used in 46, 54
    rates, 20th century 70

T

Teen suicide prevention services, definition 210
Tennessee
    assaults 25, 142
    assaults per population 142
    campus violence 176
    high school fights 173
    murders 51, 127
    murders per population 127
    rapes reported 129
    robberies 21, 134
    robberies per population 134
Tenth grade students
    crime victims at school 168
    fights at school 170
    who carried a weapon 60
    See also Students
Texas
    assaults 25, 142
    assaults per population 142
    campus violence 176
    high school fights 173
    murders 51, 127
    murders per population 127
    rapes reported 129
    robberies 21, 134
    robberies per population 134
Transportation
    murder in the workplace 192
    violence and 202
Twelfth grade students
    crime victims at school 168

fights at school 170
who carried a weapon 60
See also Students

U

U.S. Constitution xii
Unemployment, murder and 150
Uniform Crime Report xiv
Unintentional injury *see* Accidental death
Unlawful entry, definition 210
Upper age of jurisdiction, definition 210
Use of firearms in violent crimes xi
Utah
    assault 25
    assaults 143
    assaults per population 143
    campus violence 176
    high school fights 173
    murders 51, 127
    murders per population 127
    rapes reported 129
    robberies 21, 134
    robberies per population 134

V

Vermont 176
    assaults 25, 143
    assaults 143
    assaults per population 143
    campus violence 176
    high school fights 173
    murders 51, 127
    murders per population 127
    rapes reported 129
    robberies 21, 135
    robberies per population 135
Victim, definition 211
Victimization, definition 211
Victimize, definition 211
Victims *see* Crime victims
Violence
    at school 174
    gangs and 178
    in the workplace 200, 202
    on campus 176
    See also Violent crime

Violence between intimates, definition 211
Violent crime
    arrests 84
    assistance for victims 118
    at school 166, 168
    attempted vs. completed 108
    by own child 146
    by parent 146
    by spouse or ex-spouse 146
    compared to other events 78
    deaths caused by 70
    economic loss 112
    firearms and 18, 20, 22, 24, 32, 42, 50,
    gangs and 90, 180
    in families xviii, 146
    in the workplace 186, 194, 196, 200
    juvenile delinquency and 184
    location of 94
    number in prison for, trends 80
    on campus 176
    per population 74, 104
    percent of all crime 102
    percent of inmates sentenced for, trends 82
    prison sentence for xvii, 88
    proposed solutions xviii
    reported to police 84, 100, 106
    trends xvii, 72
    use of handgun xvii, 32, 40, 44, 50
    victims of xvii, xviii, 96, 110, 116, 152, 198
    weapons used 32
    while commuting to work 194
Violent crime index 72
    trends 74, 76
Virgin Islands, high school fights 173
Virginia
    assaults 25, 142
    assaults per population 143
    campus violence 177
    murders 51, 127
    murders per population 127
    rapes reported 129
    robberies 21, 134
    robberies per population 134

W

Washington
    assaults 25, 142

Index

assaults per population 142
campus violence 177
high school fights 173
murders 51, 127
murders per population 127
rapes reported 129
robberies 21, 134
robberies per population 134
Washington, DC
   murders in the workplace 188
   See also District of Columbia
Weapons
   offenses and violation, definition 211
   used in murder 8
   used in violent crime 32
   violations, by age 26
   See also Blunt objects, Knives, Firearms, Handguns, Personal weapons
Weighted data, definition 211
West Virginia
   assaults 25, 143
   assaults per population 143
   campus violence 177
   high school fights 173
   murders 51, 127
   murders per population 127
   rapes reported 129
   robberies 21, 135
   robberies per population 135
Wife, murder of 154
Wisconsin
   assaults 25, 142
   assaults per population 143

campus violence 177
high school fights 173
murders 51, 127
murders per population 127
rapes reported 129
robberies 21, 134
robberies per population 134
Women
   assault victims 140
   crime victims 36, 98, 140, 148, 152, 186
   murder defendants 148
   murder victims 148, 186
   violent crime victims 140, 152
Workers, as murder victims 186
Workplace assault, definition 211
Workplace homicide, definition 211
Workplace violence xviii
Wyoming
   assaults 25, 143
   assaults per population 142
   campus violence 177
   high school fights 173
   murders 51, 127
   murders per population 127
   rapes reported 129
   robberies 21, 135
   robberies per population 135

Y

Youth population at risk, definition 211
Youth Risk Behavior Surveillance System xxi
Youthful offender status, definition 211

ELIHU BURRITT LIBRARY
C.C.S.U.
NEW BRITAIN, CONNECTICUT

REFERENCE